*Liberal Learning as a Quest
for Purpose*

Liberal Learning
as a Quest
for Purpose

WILLIAM M. SULLIVAN

OXFORD
UNIVERSITY PRESS

OXFORD
UNIVERSITY PRESS

Oxford University Press is a department of the University of Oxford. It furthers
the University's objective of excellence in research, scholarship, and education
by publishing worldwide. Oxford is a registered trade mark of Oxford University
Press in the UK and certain other countries.

Published in the United States of America by Oxford University Press
198 Madison Avenue, New York, NY 10016, United States of America.

© Oxford University Press 2016

Library of congress Cataloging-in-Publication Data
Names: Sullivan, William M., author.
Title: Liberal learning as a quest for purpose / William M. Sullivan.
Description: New York, NY : Oxford University Press, 2016. |
Includes bibliographical references and index.
Identifiers: LCCN 2015044617 (print) | LCCN 2016006463 (ebook) |
ISBN 9780190499242 (cloth : alk. paper) | ISBN 9780190499259 (updf) |
ISBN 9780190499266 (epub)
Subjects: LCSH: Education, Humanistic. | Transformative learning.
Classification: LCC LC1011 .S85 2016 (print) | LCC LC1011 (ebook) | DDC 370.11/2—dc23
LC record available at http://lccn.loc.gov/2015044617

1 3 5 7 9 8 6 4 2
Printed by Sheridan Books, Inc., United States of America

*For today's student generation, who by learning to care for it,
can renew the world.*

Contents

Acknowledgments

THANKS ARE DUE to the many persons who inspired, supported, and contributed to this book. It is a pleasure to thank my former colleagues at the Carnegie Foundation for the Advancement of Teaching. Under the leadership of president Lee S. Shulman, that warm intellectual community greatly enriched my understanding of the workings of higher education. It was there that I conceived the ideas that have guided this project. I am especially grateful to Anne Colby, Thomas Ehrlich, and Charles Foster who provided early direction and critical response. It was at Carnegie that I began working with Molly Sutphen, who was essential to translating the initial idea into actual research. Molly was an excellent colleague during the research and early writing phases. I am deeply grateful to all of them.

The research was vetted and significantly improved by a number of interlocutors who were gracious enough to correct my understanding of the Lilly Endowment's Program for the Theological Exploration of Vocation and also expanded my understanding of contemporary undergraduate life. I want to thank Dorothy Bass, Charles Blaich, Larry Braskamp, Tim Clydesdale, Kim Maphis Early, Mark Edwards, Douglas Jacobsen, Rhonda Jacobsen, Gary Phillips, and Shirley Roels. They gave me timely advice and, later, feedback on early drafts of the manuscript. My thinking was also enriched by conversations with a number of colleagues, including Robert N. Bellah, Kathleen Cahalan, Cathy George, Don Harward, John Lewis, Richard Madsen, Karen McTigue Musil, Donald Ottenhoff, Carol Geary Schneider, Douglas Schuurman, Margot Soven, Martha Stortz, Ann Swidler, and Steven Tipton. I also want to thank Dennis McGrath, educational researcher, long-time intellectual partner, and friend. He provided not only sound criticism but support and indispensable wit.

I am greatly indebted to the Lilly Endowment, which supported the research, and especially to the program staff of the Religion Division. Craig Dykstra, then vice president for Religion, was enthusiastic about this project from the start of our conversations. Chris Coble, who succeeded Craig in his position, gave his insight as well as counsel as the project matured. Gayle Doucey provided me with access to the reports and other key documents from the archives of the Endowment.

I owe another large debt of gratitude to the campuses I visited. At each location, our research team was courteously received and supported by project leaders and staff who went beyond what might have been expected to provide insight, including critical perspectives, on how the project had unfolded in their campus community.

This book finally came to completion thanks to the talents and devoted work of two remarkable colleagues who served as editorial assistants in the drafting of the manuscript. Molly Breen helped me to improve the early drafts. Kristen Garabedian saw the book through to completion. Both improved the writing with tact and admirable good spirit.

Thanks, finally, to Cynthia Read, executive editor at Oxford University Press, whose encouragement I much appreciate; and to Glenn Ramirez, editorial assistant. They guided me through the submission process and in a highly professional manner.

*Liberal Learning as a Quest
for Purpose*

Introduction

"WHAT SHOULD I BE DOING WITH MY LIFE?"

STUDENTS PREPARING FOR the first semester of college might reasonably assume two things: graduating will provide them a credential crucial to their professional success, and they will make a lot of friends and future connections. Both assumptions are correct. The physical campus where they attend classes doubles as a formative psychic environment where students can forge new identities for themselves through social experience. Yet, important as these purposes are, higher education makes a larger contribution to the lives of its students than as a site for career preparation and development of personal identity. Like invisible magnetic fields, universities and colleges shape those who attend them. The experience exerts a powerful influence not only over the sort of life a graduate will live, but also the kind of person she will become. At its best, higher education fosters wonder and curiosity, enabling students to make sense of the world, what has traditionally been known as liberal education. But that quest becomes personally significant when students begin to explore their own potential place in the world they are coming to understand. Exploring purpose enables students to discover concrete ways in which they might contribute to bettering the world as well as themselves.

It is their ambition to address this full range of higher education's mission that makes the achievements of a group of colleges and universities remarkable. Over the first decade of the century, a group of 88 private colleges and universities worked together in one of the largest such undertakings in the history of American higher education to think anew about how they could better fulfill this mission for their students. The focus of their efforts was the idea of making the exploration of purpose a way to re-center the undergraduate experience around the development of the whole student. The immediate catalyst for this effort was a major funding initiative from a large philanthropic organization, the Lilly Endowment. But the content and specific direction of their efforts came from the various campuses who shared a heritage that made them open to the idea of vocational exploration as an aim of undergraduate learning. Some were actively, others only historically church-related. But all discovered that an emphasis upon vocational exploration gave new energy and significance to their mission to educate today's students.

Over a decade of experimentation and reform, many of the institutions that participated in the vocation project developed effective means of fostering the development of purpose among their students. The common feature was use of the term "vocation" to designate an understanding of life purpose that involved both self-development and service to others. For many of the campuses, the language of vocation proved a way to reimagine their educational mission that energized students to become more engaged with their learning. For their faculty, the effect was a significant intensification of professional commitment as educators. In some cases, the projects fomented a reinvention of liberal education around engaging students in conversations that explored the relationships between learning and the meaning of their lives. But perhaps just as notably, these efforts often swept up administrators and staff in the enterprise, forging or renewing a sense of common purpose around the educational mission of the institution.

As a result, many of the colleges and universities involved in the vocation initiative became more vital centers of learning for both students and faculty as well as more actively connected to the society beyond their campuses. This is a significant story. It points to new directions for the nation's many colleges and universities whose religious affiliation makes the notion of vocational exploration congenial. But these developments also hold valuable potential more broadly by showing that a focus on purpose can engage the energies of both students and faculty in ways that are highly productive for the core mission of higher education. The aim of this book is to examine this potential by both providing insight into how these campuses developed the educational potential of vocational exploration and by exploring what might be learned that could help colleges and universities in today's difficult environment to make undergraduate education more effective and valuable for all students.

The Context: The Narrowing Focus of Higher Education and the Recovery of Purpose

The achievements of these campuses are especially important when viewed within the context of today's larger debate over the ends of higher education. The past decade has seen growing public discontent. There are worries about the economic value of a college degree relative to its rising cost. These anxieties are reasonable. Yet, the current narrowing of educational perspectives risks the eclipse of higher education's deeper value for students and its importance for revitalizing American democracy. Too often, national opinion leaders, and many leaders in higher education as well, describe college as only an investment in future earning power, an experience made enticing by a rich array of leisure activities and social networking. This portrayal ignores or downplays the deep potential of undergraduate experience for students in search of a way to enter adult life competently equipped and guided by significant purposes. Left unchecked, these trends threaten to further weaken today's students' ability to navigate a confusing and shifting environment.

On the other hand, modern understandings of how learning happens and how motivation works to promote learning are opening up new possibilities. These new insights offer ways to refocus higher education on its core mission of enabling students to make something of themselves while also becoming persons who can contribute actively to the life of their times.

For optimal use of the scarce resources of highly trained personnel and instructional technology, educational environments must both challenge and support participants in mastering the knowledge and skills of higher learning. It is now clear that these "generic skills" of higher order thinking—especially analytical ability, critical and synthetic thinking, logical reasoning, and cogent speaking and writing—are the most important factors for career success in all fields. It turns out that when learning is at issue, the whole really is greater than a mere sum of its parts.

Recent research has also made clearer how the contexts and relationships within which instruction occurs play a crucial role in enabling learning to take place. Thinking develops only when learners are actively engaged with a subject matter or task. Further, this crucial factor of engagement is itself heavily dependent upon the social and cultural environment in which it takes place. Motivation to learn is at its core a matter of the quality of human relationship, especially relations between teacher and student and among peers. And so the coherence of content, teaching methods, and educational aims is essential to making education effective (including cost-effective). These findings place new importance on the alignment of various parts of the enterprise of higher education to support students in undertaking the strenuous journey toward maturity in its various dimensions.

This broadening of the contemporary understanding of learning is helping to support new perspectives on what has traditionally been called liberal education. The new developments feature stronger connections among academic learning and student development in its social, moral, and civic dimensions. These initiatives seek both to provide undergraduates with concrete knowledge and skills useful in the workplace, a broad understanding of the world in which they find themselves, and the capacity to discover direction and meaning for their own learning and future lives. By renewing concern with students' developing sense of direction while also honoring the integrity of rational inquiry in its many forms, this renewal of liberal learning offers a public resource for adapting inherited values to the uncertainties of the global era. The trajectory of today's students' personal lives and careers has become increasingly uncertain. This has caused rising levels of anxiety. For these students, elevating the exploration of a life worth living into a major focus of their undergraduate education is a great benefit. This new direction offers a path toward recovery of morale and sense of mission for institutions of higher learning as well. It is as an experiment in this direction that the vocation project finds its significance.

Background: The Vocation Project

The beginnings of the vocation project, which will be the focus in the chapters that follow, lie with the Lilly Endowment, a major national philanthropy. What became the PTEV, or Program for the Theological Exploration of Vocation, was an initiative of the philanthropy's religion division that began in 1999–2000. The new initiative was conceived and carried out primarily by the then vice president for religion, Craig Dykstra, and program officer Christopher Coble. While this was not the Endowment's first foray into higher education, the scope of the vocation initiative was broader than any of its previous studies or programs and its scale was unprecedented. In the program design, the Endowment asked campuses to respond to key issues: how they might employ their distinctive theological heritage to foster students' exploration of the notion of vocation in a broad sense of purpose, and how they could make faculty and staff mentorship of students more effective.

The response was strong among church-related institutions to which the invitation was addressed. From around 400 applicants, the Endowment selected 88 campuses to receive planning grants followed by full program grants of about $2,000,000 each over 10 years. The intent was to spark innovation and creativity. Accordingly, the campuses had considerable latitude to develop approaches to the exploration of vocation that fit their particular campuses and drew on the college or university's distinctive religious tradition. These ranged across the Christian spectrum, from Mainline Protestant to Evangelical Protestant, and included both Eastern Orthodox and Roman Catholic campuses, as well as institutions whose affiliation with a church was largely historical. While Lilly provided technical support and required regular reports, the variation among programs was intentional in order to provide considerable variation among experiments.

The intellectual premises of the PTEV were explicit in the request for proposals. Lilly drew upon contemporary philosophical and psychological understandings of human development as well as theology. The core premise was that individuals develop their capacities, their identities, and ultimately their purposes by participating in various ways of living, trying out social roles and perspectives of thought. By experimenting and then reflecting on these experiences, persons gradually establish a sense of self-identity. Key to this process is the individual coming to accept responsibility for attitudes, actions, and relationships. For this way of thinking, education of the whole student had obvious resonance. It was a gesture toward this kind of holistic conception of vocational exploration as a journey toward responsible adulthood.[1]

The value of religious traditions for higher education found a novel expression in the way the Endowment formulated its approach. Religious faith and life were conceived as providing valuable cultural templates with cognitive, affective, and behavioral dimensions. Very importantly for the initiative, these cultural templates were understood primarily as scripts for plausible ways of living that can attract interest and invite exploration because of the values they embody. Around the exploration of such cultural templates, the initiative's authors imagined, communities gather. They called these "communities of conviction." Religious congregations were obvious models of this type but groups of many kinds also fit the definition. Such communities were understood as essential to personal development because it is within them that individuals learn to take part in key social practices that carry meanings.

It would be within and against these shared practices, the project's initiators argued, that students would be best able to experiment in developing their own purposes and identities. Within this perspective, then, "religion" was understood less as a set of dogmatic beliefs than as a way of living, like a culture or a language within which individuals weave their distinctive patterns of thought and action. The value added by bringing religious understandings of vocation explicitly to students' attention, in this view, was that because religious languages and practices embody a stance toward reality as a whole, they make it possible to conceive a meaning for life as a whole. Furthermore, these traditions are all themselves the result of long efforts within communities of faith to argue out ways to meet and balance the tensions of living, tensions between individual and group, desire and obligation, meaning and despair. In putting forward the vocation initiative, Lilly was making a bet that, so understood, conversation about purpose framed by religious traditions would prove a valuable resource for students struggling to navigate the highly pluralistic, conflicted, and often incoherent waters of contemporary life.

Outcomes and Effects

Such were the starting assumptions and aspirations of the project. Over the 10-plus years of its life, the PTEV represented one of the largest single investments in enhancing academic and co-curricular life in the history of American higher education. What, then, did it accomplish? Was it enough to justify further study of its lessons and how they might be carried further into higher education as a whole?

The answers to these questions are, overall, yes and yes. On the basis of a careful study of the project's results, sociologist Tim Clydesdale was able to demonstrate that the vocation programs produced improved rates of degree completion, an issue that is central to concerns about the costs of college. He also discovered that the programs measurably improved students' abilities to engage with the world in ways that furthered their advancement, including academic learning, co-curricular involvement, and discernment of career and life goals. Surveys and interviews with recent graduates also revealed substantially higher levels of life satisfaction and persistence toward goals in the face of setbacks: the factor of "grit" that the programs were able to enhance through providing students with perspectives on themselves and their possible role in the world that sustained realistic ideals. As Clydesdale points out, this last effect amounts to an educational "home run" in that it approximates the long-term goals that college administrators often seek but all too rarely find.[2]

Having started his research as a self-confessed skeptic, Clydesdale describes how he became convinced of the efficacy of the programs in fostering greater student engagement with academic learning, and especially students' ability to connect their formal study with entry into career paths. He noted that on surveys, large majorities of participants in the programs expressed appreciation for the experience. In part, he argues, this was due to students' genuine gratitude for having found in their studies some larger narratives about life that allowed them to imagine a base for constructively engaging their circumstances. But he also argues that the programs were of value to today's students because they found that the "exploration of purpose or vocation lessens the stress that surrounds student decisions." This is important, Clydesdale insists, because of the considerable evidence of rising levels of stress-related mental health issues among a millennial generation who must confront high-stakes choices about their futures that are at the same time less certain.[3]

To capture his findings, Clydesdale employs a striking analogy from the world of baseball. He imagines the 88 participating campuses as 88 aspiring baseball players chosen from 400 applicants to attend a summer baseball camp. (Clydesdale notes there was more variation among the 88 institutions than between the Lilly participants as a group and the rest of higher education.) Some players have years of experience, some none, with the majority falling in-between. They are supported and given some coaching by more experienced players but mostly urged to keep returning to their goals and work out better ways to achieve them. After more than a decade taking part in this summer camp, 66 of the original group have become varsity collegiate baseball players. Fewer than one-third of the programs seemed simply ordinary, not having produced such dramatic effects.

By comparing a significant number of randomly selected graduates from the PTEV programs with their demographic peers in academically comparable settings, Clydesdale was able to show sizable positive developmental effects that distinguished the PTEV students from those whose college experiences lacked a coordinated focus on purpose. In some cases, the comparison groups included students on the same campuses; in others the study compared students from similar campuses that were not part of the initiative. The programs largely reversed the commonly reported trends toward student disengagement from learning and avoidance of adult responsibility. Everywhere in the PTEV, Clydesdale noted, students and faculty became "engaged and intrigued" by taking part in vocational exploration within a campus context that intentionally connected academic learning with personal self-awareness, community participation, and occupational investigation.

Although an examination of the institutional data Clydesdale analyzed is beyond the scope of this book, his report is essential reading for anyone interested in the future of higher education. As he sums up his conclusions: " . . . theological exploration of vocation provides a mechanism for life examination and that it appeals to a wider swath of students than traditional liberal arts curricula do and that when combined with regular involvement in a congregational community (or surrogate), it fosters connections to others that sustain lives worth living in spite of setbacks."[4] The chapters that follow will try to show through a range of examples why this was so.

To achieve these extraordinary outcomes, the PTEV campuses embraced a wide range of initiatives in the area of teaching and learning. Applying the insights of the learning sciences, the programs employed first-year seminars that brought students and faculty together in small groups around themes of meaning, identity, and purpose. They created new courses in a variety of disciplines with themes exploring self, world, and theological ideals of vocation. They engaged students in courses that interwove social service beyond the campus with social and ethical reflection, including courses of active study abroad. They developed new partnerships with community organizations and religious organizations, and enriched campus affiliations that had previously been nominal. These relationships turned out to be particularly important in spurring an upsurge of interest among undergraduates in careers in the clergy and religious service organizations. And, very importantly, the PTEV programs pioneered a variety of new forms of campus community life around themes of calling and purpose that drew in both faculty and staff, even including alumni and senior administration.

The PTEV wove connections among parts of the campus—the faculty, the student services and counseling staff, the religious life and career planning offices—that previously had maintained little contact. By treating all these areas as integral to the educational mission of their institutions, the PTEV programs revitalized their campuses and helped to produce the strong educational outcomes noted by Clydesdale. On most of the campuses involved, they have remained an enduring legacy of the PTEV.

The PTEV also enhanced the integrative nature of education at these institutions, helping to make concrete the ideal of educating the "whole student." By bringing faculty and students together in innovative programs that explored weighty contemporary issues such as poverty and injustice, pollution and climate change, and the use of new technologies, the programs revived liberal education's traditional concern with integrating critical investigation, knowledge, and practical concerns. This has been another enduring legacy of the programs to their campuses.

How They Did It: Learning and the Metaphor of Apprenticeship

One of the important developments of modern learning science is the reinvigoration of the metaphor of apprenticeship as a way to describe learning. A great deal of research has shifted the understanding of how learning happens toward an emphasis upon participation in structured practices as the social mechanism that underlies learning in areas ranging from physical skills such as writing to the manipulation of abstract concepts. The shift to a participatory understanding of learning highlights both the social contexts of learning, such as the classroom or field experience, and, importantly, also the changing social position and personal stance of the learner as the learner moves across an arc from beginner toward competence and expertise.

The chance to imitate and then to receive feedback to improve performance is critical to improving at anything. But so is the learner's active, personal engagement with the activity and the others taking part in the activity. Like apprentices in traditional trades, or like apprentice artists, learners in all fields do not simply "acquire" knowledge and skill. They develop toward competence in particular activities, a process that depends on cooperation between the learner and the expert, both acting within a larger context of shared practices and aims. This is why the metaphor of apprenticeship has proven so useful as a way of conceiving the complex processes of education.

The metaphor of apprenticeship seems an especially illuminating way to frame an interpretation of the vocation project. Framing learning as apprenticeship immediately highlights an important feature of today's undergraduate experience. Considered as an apprenticeship for adulthood and engagement with the world, the context that college students encounter when they enter a campus is as much a challenge as a help. The reality of campus life, for most students, is far from the idealized "ivory tower" of legend and imagination. Undergraduate experience is typically not a unified apprenticeship to the life of the mind but a set of parallel, rarely interacting experiences. Taken as a whole, it is fragmented and often self-contradictory.

One kind of apprenticeship to which all students are subject is academic. This is the world of the curriculum, the classroom, and the laboratory, presided over by the faculty. It is this academic apprenticeship that is usually conjured up in public discussions of undergraduate performance and aims. However, the academic apprenticeship is only one among several contexts of learning in which students engage. Its ways of operating, the expectations about student performance, and what is valued and so appropriate for higher education do not dominate most students' college experience.

Rather, a second, quite different set of values and expectations prevail in the sphere of the second, or social, apprenticeship. The college personnel who preside in this sphere are rarely faculty members but student affairs professionals, chaplains and religious life personnel, and athletic coaches. The priorities of life in the residence halls and in extracurricular activities emphasize different expectations from those in the academic curriculum. For many undergraduates, this is where the "real" college experience lies. But as concerns about student mental health and serious behavioral problems have risen, it has become increasingly apparent that a wide gap often separates the social apprenticeship from the academic.

Far from a coherent learning environment, then, the reality students confront makes finding direction and moving toward adulthood an even more difficult transition than it might otherwise be. In particular, it is the relative rarity and weakness of this important dimension of undergraduate learning that the vocation project has called attention to. To emphasize its importance for enabling students to divine a path toward their future and to develop strong, mature identities, this dimension can be seen as a third apprenticeship, no less important than the other two but often too little attended to. This book will call it the apprenticeship of meaning and purpose. It was particularly toward this sphere that the efforts of the vocation programs directed their efforts, and it was in integrating the concerns of the third apprenticeship with the academic and social spheres of college life that the vocation programs were so strong, especially when compared with the neglect of these issues on many campuses.

Socratic Questions and Purposeful Exploration: The Vocational Pattern

The vocational projects used self-discovery as a motive for student engagement. This emphasis upon giving students ways to grasp their own interests and abilities proved attractive to many students. Enabling students to understand their interests and abilities have become goals of a number of recent campus efforts, not just the vocation programs. Often, these efforts are concerned to enable students to be better prepared for entry into further professional study or to distinguish themselves as competitors in the job market. These are valid and important functions of undergraduate education today. Particularly in this time when many students and their parents are highly anxious about future job prospects, it is natural that courses and programs that enable students to present themselves, their abilities, and their accomplishments in college to advantage, especially to prospective employers, would be popular and valued. These trends mirror the larger society's growing emphasis on the need to be able to grasp opportunities and present oneself to advance in life.

The vocation programs, however, all attempted something more ambitious. The chapters that follow will illustrate this in a variety of cases. While they spoke with particular vocabularies and inflections derived from their individual campus cultures, the programs articulated a common grammar. They reaffirmed the importance of self-discovery and enhanced self-awareness as long-standing values in liberal education. These values are a continuing inheritance from the tradition of humanistic learning grounded in the philosopher Socrates's teaching that "the unexamined life is not worth living." Especially when it speaks publicly about its mission, higher education has continued to affirm the Socratic injunction to "Know Thyself," in theory if not always in practice. But it was the seriousness with which the vocation projects took the Socratic injunction as a prime impetus for student development that made them distinctive. That, and their awareness that the examined life, as Socrates practiced it, goes beyond discovering one's competitive advantages and how to maximize these. Socratic self-knowledge leads directly into the question of what might be worth doing with one's capacities. It raises the issue of what is worth living for, or in other words, the question of purpose.

It is in this connection that the tradition of humanistic, Socratic education resonates with the contemporary understanding of learning as participation in meaningful practices. If, as the modern theorists of learning argue, to learn means assimilating new ways of perceiving and thinking and gradually working toward competence in them, then Socratic inquiry involves students in questions about their situation in the world and their hopes for the future. The vocation project supports students' expanding awareness in concrete ways. Once engaged in self-discovery, which often attracted students to the vocation programs in the first place, students found themselves drawn into questions about the nature of the self and the world. They began to explore different answers to the question of what is a fulfilling or good life. Growing self-awareness provoked their realization that they were already connected to a number of communities, from family of origin to their immediate peers on campus as well as linked to a much wider world.

Students in the vocation programs were discovering these connections not as isolated individuals but as participants in an organized group. Because of this social context, the students also found themselves recognized as persons whose learning mattered and also as persons whose attitudes and actions had consequences for others. They discovered that developing themselves entailed an awareness of how they affected others. Empathic understanding of others therefore mattered. Self-direction (and so self-knowledge) mattered. "Character," so understood, mattered. They realized, perhaps more than before, that they shared responsibility for the quality of the learning experience of other members of their group. They discovered that there were things at stake in their growing knowledge of self and others and that there was already a seriousness to their lives, a gravity the vocation programs sought to help students understand and, finally, accept and embrace. They were already engaged in the discovery of purpose.

The framing of these programs as exploration of vocation provided students with important perspective on their lives. The vocational framing helped students distinguish between immediate goals such as graduation and career and longer-term aims of becoming a certain sort of person or contributing to certain values through their work and relationships. The idea of vocation functioned to keep students focused on discovering what psychologist William Damon calls life purposes. By this Damon means discovering or developing a deep motivation to achieve values that orient the particular decisions of life and give shape to a life's work. Such purposes represent desires that "accomplish something that is at the same time meaningful to the self and consequential for the world beyond the self." The literature on emerging adulthood has established a strong, causal relationship between developing such a sense of purpose and resilience in the face of life's challenges.[5]

This vocational framing of the quest for purpose was a major unifying theme of the programs. It also set the PTEV off from other efforts in a Socratic vein to help undergraduates gain direction as emerging adults by better understanding themselves and making better decisions, and some of these other projects will be featured in later chapters.[6] The notion that life is a vocational journey toward finding purpose and thereby fulfilling oneself by contributing to the world turned out to be a powerful metaphor for giving coherence to students' curricular and co-curricular experiences. In cultural origin, the metaphor is an ecumenically Christian description of life. In its theological form it is an expression of a faith that human well-being lies in cooperating with a divine mission to bring fuller life to the world. It turned out that articulations of this metaphor of vocational journey, despite or perhaps because of their rootedness in specific traditions of reflection on life, were perceived by students as more generative of new possibilities than narrow or exclusionary. The relative definiteness of the vocational perspective, as compared for instance to a more generic "spirituality" of growth, seemed to be an important asset of the PTEV.[7] In addition, the programs often showed a spontaneous community-building reflex, a tendency to make vocational exploration a significantly social activity that fostered lasting bonds and interaction among different groups on campus. That also seems to have drawn upon long-established habits of religious affiliation but expanded them.

The Key Features of the Successful Vocation Programs

The PTEV evolved a set of powerful pedagogical practices, curricular and co-curricular, which made the exploration of responsible purpose both a plausible and attractive perspective. Explicit affirmation of the vocational conversation as a core feature of undergraduate education provided a broad platform on which students could analyze, challenge, debate, and try out possible ways of answering the overriding question posed by the initiative: "What should I be doing with my life?" Whatever answer students gave—and they often changed their answers in the course of their explorations—the programs demonstrated the great educational value of insistently raising the question. While not all PTEV programs achieved these goals as well as others, with as we have noted, about two-thirds in the high-performing category, the key features were clear in most and visible in all of them.

In broad summary, as a distinctive family of programs giving an overall shape to undergraduate experience, the common features were the following. The first, Socratic dimension has already been noted. The stress on self-knowledge helped tie intellectual exploration in the tradition of liberal education with both personal experimentation and career planning. It was important, however, that personal abilities were reframed within the vocational narrative. From being individual assets they came to be talked about as "gifts" for which the individual should be grateful but about which the right question was how might these gifts be developed and employed. That opened up the question of the relationship between careers and longer-term purposes that could employ personal capacities and interests for the advancement of the larger community. These concerns gave the programs a civic dimension. Students were repeatedly asked to think about how they might best use their unique capacities and energy to engage with the world's tasks, local as well as large-scale. These questions were often made concrete by being tied to students' experiences of civic engagement beyond a specific campus.

The PTEV's conversations were often explicitly structured to expand students' imaginations. To do this, as later chapters will show in detail, some programs employed the intellectual disciplines to illuminate world problems or personal possibilities. Most programs also emphasized opportunities to sustain contact with people caught up in today's biggest problems, such as poverty and economic development, the struggles of immigration, education, or environmental degradation. They sought to foster students' ability to empathize with others in different and usually less fortunate situations than themselves, to cultivate a civic imagination that extended out into the world as a whole.

These developmental processes of expanding awareness and reflection were also made more concrete in and out of the classroom by giving students access to many examples of lives committed to purpose. The historical and social horizons involved were wide. For example, contemporary and past exemplars of different vocations provided specific life scripts, and students were asked to examine the decisions that shaped these lives, and explore and debate the outcomes of their vocational journeys, as lived out in different organizational and national settings. These cases became exemplary not only for their successes but because they often included mistakes, major failure, and suffering. Learning to cope with the adversities likely to befall any life committed to a serious purpose was an essential part of these conversations. The aim was to ground the students' idealism in a realistic but hopeful set of theoretical perspectives and concrete relationships.

By making the metaphor of life as a vocational journey vivid in a variety of educational experiences, the PTEV expanded students' sense of what could matter in their own lives. It also extended the undergraduate time horizon, teaching participants to think of their college experience as a resource for shaping their growing identities and commitments well into adult life. To a striking degree, the general rubric of exploring vocation proved cohesive and yet flexible enough to sustain considerable diversity of approach among the PTEV programs. Sometimes directly through linked sets of academic courses or capstone experiences, at other times by programs that provided experience or placements off-campus, these programs gave continuity and a center of reference to individual students' experiments with developing a meaningful stance in the world.

The Essential Components: Vocational Journey, Learning Communities, and Reflection

One. As we have seen, the metaphor of life as a vocational journey provided the PTEV initiative with its overarching perspective and suggested much of the direction of the pedagogical dynamics at work in the programs. This was the first essential component.

Two. The effectiveness of the vocational framing was grounded in the ability of campuses to form and sustain communities of learning focused on these goals. These learning communities made up the second essential element. By connecting students with groups of people in other communities or with projects that addressed significant problems beyond the campus, the PTEV programs stimulated deepened engagement in learning. They also enhanced students' quest for self-knowledge, while they aroused a sometimes-urgent curiosity in a variety of areas. It seems that the sense of community the programs engendered also significantly eased students' anxieties, allowing them to expand the range within which they explored possibilities.

Three. In all these learning communities, practices of group and individual reflection played an essential role. These practices included Socratic efforts at self-understanding, as well as probing the assumptions underlying varying (and sometimes conflicting) views of the good life. Such reflection made it possible for students to gradually construct an understanding of life as a whole and make connections between their interests, immediate goals, and longer life trajectories. Reflection was practiced in multiple settings and in a variety of ways, both within and outside the formal curriculum. Reflective activities helped students integrate academic learning and practical experience with important dimensions of meaning in their lives. That made it more likely that they would maintain a sense of direction through the sometimes difficult and disturbing undergraduate years. Organized reflection also laid a basis for continuing use of these practices beyond graduation.

In sum, the exploration of purpose that took place within a community of shared interest and support organized around the theme of vocation shifted the framing of higher education for many students and faculty. The three elements of the PTEV programs—vocational narrative as basic structure, the grounding of this narrative in learning communities, and the cultivation of reflective practices—invited students to conceive their college experience as a serious enterprise with lifelong consequences. In this way, these programs have revealed that it is possible to recover the formative power of liberal education, even at a time when a narrow fixation upon only the instrumental value of college threatens to overwhelm the deeper and more public ends of higher education.

The Research

The research on which this book is based began in the fall of 2010, when the evaluation study had already begun to show the vocation project's generally positive outcomes for students. The author approached the Lilly Endowment with a proposal to examine further how the campus vocation programs' introduction of various methods of reflecting on purpose had reshaped practices of teaching and learning. The author's approach was an adaptation of methods developed in studies of higher education at the Carnegie Foundation for the Advancement of Teaching, in one of which Lilly had been a funding partner.[8] The research project was centered on field observation and continued through 2013. It focused on a group of campus programs that achieved strikingly positive results. It is worth noting that the Endowment made no stipulations regarding either the findings or their publication. As a result, the argument and conclusions of this book are entirely the author's own, acknowledging the value of the evaluation study in arriving at these judgments.

The study documented and analyzed how "vocational discernment" was embodied in practices of teaching and learning in both curricular and co-curricular programs, as well as how the programs were organized and staffed at the campus level. Throughout, the study aimed to capture the ways in which the "theological" dimension of the "exploration of vocation" played out in the programs, looking especially at the ways in which distinctive theological traditions contributed toward shaping and articulating particular educational practices for students and faculty.

The fundamental method employed was a qualitative approach employing interview and participant-observation techniques.[9] After an extensive literature review, consultations with Lilly Endowment project staff, and meetings with scholars of higher education with expertise on the initiative, the two-person research team began a series of visits to campuses during the academic years 2010 to 2011 and 2011 to 2012, concluding in the fall of 2012. For these site visits, the team selected a group of 8 campuses, supplemented by interviews with PTEV participants at three additional campuses, providing a total sample of 11 institutions.

The choice of sites was based on two criteria. First, the PTEV programs had to have focused in a significant way on the academic life of their institution, in contrast to being concerned primarily with co-curricular or other aspects of campus life. The intent was to investigate whether and to what degree the programs were able to connect with and affect the academic culture of the campus. The second criterion concerned sampling the range of religious diversity among Christian denominations represented in the 88 campuses selected by Lilly, including campuses with Mainline Protestant, Roman Catholic, Lutheran, Evangelical Protestant, and Anabaptist affiliation. Given the limited resources in time and personnel available for the study, some denominational traditions, such as Eastern Orthodoxy, were unfortunately left out.

Augsburg College is Lutheran. Earlham College affiliates itself with the Society of Friends or Quakers. Gordon College describes itself as providing a liberal arts education in the Evangelical Protestant tradition. Our Lady of the Lake University is Roman Catholic in affiliation. Santa Clara University is a Roman Catholic, Jesuit institution. Interviews were also conducted at Wake Forest University and at Baylor University, both Christian universities in the Baptist tradition, and at Messiah College, which is rooted in the Brethren in Christ tradition. Researchers conducted interviews by telephone at Marquette University, a Roman Catholic and Jesuit campus. To better gauge the impact of the PTEV in connecting religious with secular educational viewpoints, the sample included Butler University and Macalester College. Butler, which cut its ties with the Christian Church in 1957, has for over a decade operated the Center for Faith and Vocation, to "serve as a model for how non-church-related universities, private and even public, can support the study and practice of religion and spirituality, how they can be pluralistic and not simply secular."[10] Macalester College, though formally affiliated with the Presbyterian Church USA, describes its campus culture as nonreligious.

Each campus visit lasted for two or three days. After reviewing materials sent by the campus PTEV program, as well as the publicly available websites, the research team conducted interviews and observed classes or co-curricular activities connected to the PTEV. All interviews were audio recorded, and some were transcribed. These provided the basis for the cases presented in each of this book's subsequent chapters.

On each campus, the researchers interviewed faculty members, including those who taught in PTEV-related courses and some who did not, as well as nonacademic staff, especially those responsible for service learning, residential life, and educational experiences outside the classroom. There were also interviews with administrators, including presidents, provosts, and deans where relevant and possible, and chaplains or religious life personnel. All visits included focus groups with students, both those participating in the PTEV and some who had not.

The interviews were designed to capture as much of the PTEV experience as possible in the words of the participants themselves. They included questions about how the programs worked, who was involved, and the campus home of the program and personnel. The interviewers made a particular effort to probe connections between the campus PTEV and its academic program and faculties, including collecting and reviewing course descriptions and descriptions of other pedagogical practices. Throughout the visits, the research team gave special importance to collecting and documenting the practices through which the programs attempted to teach and support student reflection. The interviews became more focused as the study proceeded and common themes emerged, themes that have become the basis for the analysis in the chapters that follow.

This Book: An Overview

The book covers an arc that begins by introducing some examples of the PTEV experience as hopeful responses to a misalignment between the expanded aims of higher education and its actual organization of learning. Three key elements of the programs then receive illustration and analysis: (1) the theme of vocation and its integration of curricular and co-curricular learning to address the "whole student"; (2) the educative power of building learning communities of students, faculty, and staff; (3) examples of the powerful practices of reflection drawn from different religious traditions and how their adaptation by the vocation programs promoted in students a proactive and self-aware stance toward learning and life. These achievements are then compared with efforts outside the initiative to rethink liberal education in a holistic way, identifying common themes. The book culminates in the argument that humanistic education as practiced in the PTEV provides common ground for dialogue and enrichment among religious and secular approaches in higher education, converging toward the development of an effective approach to educating students for the 21st century.

Chapter 1 introduces an example of the PTEV experience at Santa Clara University, where the elements of vocational narrative, reflective practice, and participation in a learning community reanimated classic aspects of liberal education for a new context. Higher education currently faces challenges to its goal of educating the "whole student," and these features of the PTEV enabled it successfully to address those challenges, as well as the particular stresses affecting the current generation of undergraduates.

In Chapter 2, the PTEV's response to the contemporary misalignment of higher education is explored through the development of the metaphor, drawn from recent research on cognition, of learning as apprenticeship. The chapter analyzes undergraduate experience into three, often only loosely connected "apprenticeships": an academic apprenticeship, a social apprenticeship, and—the strength of the programs—an integrating apprenticeship of identity and purpose. Augsburg College's Senior Keystone for the Business major provides an illustration of how this integrative strategy works, comparing it to other recent efforts to realign academic, social, and career learning.

Chapters 3 and 4 focus on the curricular and pedagogical implications of the PTEV's language of "calling," particularly as compared to the familiar image of students as individually "driven." In contrast to the self-focused implication of the language of "drive," the metaphor of calling or vocation stresses an openness to engagement with others and the larger world, allowing learning to become a quest to understand, guide, and intensify these connections among self, others, and world through the finding and cultivation of purpose.

Chapter 3 shows this approach at work in PTEV initiatives at Butler University and Macalester College, campuses marked by a largely secular approach to education. In these cases, themes of personal exploration, social service, and interreligious dialogue proved attractive ways to engage questions of purpose and practical wisdom. These experiments suggest ways to bring secular and religiously inflected aims into mutually fruitful dialogue. Chapter 4, by contrast, examines the way in which two programs, at Earlham College and Santa Clara University, were able to draw on their respective religious traditions to develop practices of reflection that led students to assume a proactive stance toward their learning and thinking about their future lives.

Chapter 5 presents three very different examples of a key strength of the PTEV: its ability to foster communities of learning around vocational themes. Our Lady of the Lake University's largely first-generation college students were drawn into deeper engagement with their own quest for purpose and a meaningful future by entering into service learning among communities of recent immigrants. At Marquette University, the PTEV was able to creatively adapt the Jesuit tradition of spirituality to form learning communities among faculty and staff that in turn deepened the commitment of the participants to their educational mission. This effort converged with the program at Messiah College, where, drawing upon very different Protestant traditions, faculty and staff developed a learning community that began to recast professional identities around the discovery of their common calling as educators.

Chapter 6 examines a set of efforts outside the PTEV to revitalize liberal learning by integrating the academic and social apprenticeships around themes of purpose, service, and community. The chapter examines programs at Harvard University, Wagner College, and Wake Forest University, as well as the Bringing Theory to Practice program of the Association of American Colleges and Universities. (The Wake Forest program is part of NetVUE, a successor movement to the PTEV that now involves a larger group of institutions than the original Lilly effort.) The chapter argues that these developments take on fuller significance when they are recognized as forms of humanistic education aiming at the cultivation of practical wisdom. This requires consciously cultivating a bifocal vision, valuing the achievements of detached, analytical thinking while also recognizing its roots in appreciation for and engagement with the world. It has been the mission of liberal learning, especially the study of the classics of East and West, to provide training in both these points of view, while recognizing that intelligent problem solving ultimately needs to serve the purposes and responsibilities embodied in human culture. These capacities, more than any specialized skills, are likely to prove key resources for confronting the challenges of the 21st century.

Chapter 7 returns to the opening themes of the book, probing the meaning of the "theological exploration of vocation" for humanistic educational practice. These issues are illustrated through the example of Gordon College's efforts to educate students in both "Jerusalem" and "Athens" for the sake of leading lives of intelligence and integrity. The chapter asks how the themes of humanistic understanding might supply common ground for mutual learning among those concerned with providing an integrated undergraduate experience able to foster purposive learning.

The Conclusion provides a summary of the argument and its illustrations. It proposes a question that is also a challenge. Given the effectiveness of the vocation programs as a strategy for integrating undergraduate education, what might be learned from this experiment to enable U.S. higher education as a whole to better promote student growth in academic learning, social development, and the formation of identities sustained by purpose? The book ends by placing the efforts analyzed in the intervening chapters back into the larger context of the situation confronting higher education, students, and American democracy, arguing that they provide resources for renewal.

I

Personal Meaning, Public Purpose

ON A SUNNY California afternoon on the Santa Clara University campus in the city of Santa Clara, students sat huddled in groups poring over primary works by Shakespeare, Michelangelo, and Teresa of Avila. These sophomores and juniors, themselves on the cusp of major choices regarding personal and professional identity, were discussing how each of these Renaissance figures had enacted his or her sense of calling. Entitled "Vocation: Your Personal Renaissance," and taught by Professor Diane Dreher, a scholar of Renaissance literature who has also done research on the psychological value of vocation, the course is designed to provide students midway through their college careers with the opportunity to consider the question of calling in an engaged and sophisticated way. "As you become more aware of your calling," writes Dreher, "it weaves like a bright thread through the daily fabric of your life, and as you move through life's seasons, into new roles ... every stage in your life invites you to discover your calling on another level."[1]

Taught each year at Santa Clara, a midsize, selective institution in the Catholic, Jesuit tradition, "Vocation: Your Personal Renaissance," is part of a sequence known as the Vocation Pathway, the newest strand of Santa Clara's required Pathways core curriculum and a direct outgrowth of the Lilly Endowment's program at Santa Clara. The Pathways are sequences of three or four courses in a variety of disciplines that articulate a common, interdisciplinary theme. Themes include Sustainability; Democracy; Leading People; Justice and the Arts; Design; and now, thanks to the Lilly Endowment's Program for the Theological Exploration of Vocation (PTEV), Vocation. Students taking Pathway courses develop samples of their work, creating a portfolio of academic achievement to be revisited in a final reflective essay during their senior year. This "double helix" curriculum is intended to help students connect learning in their major and minor fields with a wide range of other intellectual disciplines so as to deepen their understanding of the world and enhance their ability to engage meaningfully with it.

"Vocation: Your Personal Renaissance" sets out to fulfill three sets of learning goals mandated for courses in the Pathways core curriculum. It promotes "critical thinking," as Santa Clara defines it, by "examining and analyzing the concept of vocation in the context of history, culture, faith, and identity." It aims to improve students' ability to handle what Santa Clara calls intellectual "complexity" through requiring demonstration of the capacity to "reflect, compare, and integrate approaches to vocation from religion, literature, art, and contemporary psychology." Third, it directly stimulates "religious reflection" by using "comparative analysis, ongoing contemplative practice, reflection, and your own vocational narrative" to "clarify and express your beliefs about your own vocation."[2]

The idea of vocation as personal renaissance draws together Dreher's expertise in comparative literature of the European Renaissance and developmental psychology with an exploration of the religious dimension of life. According to Dreher, the new emphasis by religious leaders of the Reformation on "a sense of calling" proved empowering to men and women of the Renaissance, such that "their identities were informed by a sense of personal destiny, their faith in a meaningful universe and their place in it." Because of this religious understanding, Dreher continues, such figures were accustomed to "seeing themselves as creative agents, not passive victims of fate."[3]

These ideas form the nucleus of Dreher's course. Its fundamental strategy involves both imagination and analytic rigor. Each student must choose one life to explore in depth from a group of 28 Renaissance figures. They undertake this exploration from both inside and outside perspectives, reading works authored by their chosen subjects and researching their activities and context. These Renaissance lives then function as distant mirrors for the students as they explore their own lives in similar terms.

The motivating questions of the course are, finally, how should I live? Who might I become? What is my public purpose? Understanding how exemplary men and women in the Renaissance answered these questions by finding their vocations is intended to provide "insights for your life today." In addition to practicing skills for gaining intellectual perspective, including intensive reading, writing several argumentative papers, and discussion, this process of seeking insight is complemented by a spiritual practice of group meditation intended to keep the personal questions vivid and immediate.

The actual classes are dynamic events during which students take part in a rhythm of varying activities. The course includes tools for self-exploration such as the "Signature Strengths" survey developed by psychologist Martin Seligman and colleagues. Significantly, classes begin with a few minutes of formal meditation, based on a "passage meditation" technique developed by Easwaran Eknath. The practice encourages participants to repeat silently the words of a spiritual text (for example, the well-known Prayer of St. Francis of Assisi, "Lord, make me an instrument of your peace"). The instructor coaches and monitors this practice by requiring students to hand in short informal essays relating their experience of meditation to their thinking about vocation.

Throughout the course, students read and discuss a series of primary documents, such as Giorgio Vasari's *Lives of the Artists* and works by Shakespeare and Milton, as well as secondary literature. They then respond to formal presentations by the instructor that model the application of religious, literary, historical, and psychological concepts to the subject matter. For example, the instructor might present an overview of how the notion of vocation developed from medieval theology through Luther to Calvin, asking what was at stake and what were the conflicts that marked this development.

The Renaissance figures are grouped according to vocation, including Artists, Philosophers, Religious Leaders, Humanists, and Political Leaders. The students then join small groups corresponding to the vocation of the figure they have chosen to study. Following the instructor's major presentation, students meet for 20 minutes per class in these groups, where they seek to understand how the lives of the historical figures appear in light of that day's theme: Did all artists think of their callings in the same way? Can they be grouped according to the different theological understandings of vocation of their time? What about statesmen and philosophers? For whom were specific concepts of vocation most salient and influential? Do these ideas resonate today?

The course is tied together by several major written requirements. It is in these that the underlying pedagogical purpose becomes clearest. They combine academic rigor with an imaginative extension of the concepts of the course toward making sense of the students' own experience. The first half of the course culminates in a paper in which each student presents and analyzes the "vocational narrative" of the Renaissance figure under study. In the second paper, toward the end of the course, students repeat this exercise, only now focusing on their own "personal vocational narrative."

Both narratives are structured by a set of five themes or "stages": The first is Discovery, the person's realization that she possesses certain gifts. The second is Detachment, the person's need to detach herself from older habits or patterns of life. The third theme is Discernment: when did the person discern core values and a calling, and did this occur in response to a crisis; did it involve a mentor, or was it a solitary, reflective experience? The fourth theme is Direction, meaning how the person developed her sense of possibility into a realized vocation, including successes but also detours, confusion, and failures. Finally, there is the theme of Lessons, the application to the student's own life of insights gained by studying another person's vocational quest.

As an educational experience, "Vocation: Your Personal Renaissance" is organized around the vocational narrative of self-discovery. Finding a vocation is presented to students as a live option that admits of various religious interpretations as well as secular ones. Vocational decision making is examined from the "inside" point of view of those involved as well as analytically from "without," as historical phenomena. Students gain insight into the content and assumptions of a number of academic approaches. They must show analytical skill and synthetic capacity in relating these approaches to the course themes. But students in this course are also being explicitly taught how to *make use of* that learning to inform their judgment about their education and their lives. For the students excitedly discussing Teresa of Avila that sunny afternoon on campus, the educational significance of following the "bright thread" of vocational narratives was clear.

Vocational Narrative as Formation of Purpose

Through learning experiences that center on a vocational narrative, such as "Your Personal Renaissance," campuses involved in the initiative have been experimenting with ways to re-engage students in some of the big questions that have typically marked liberal arts education. By taking students' own arc of development as their starting point, the vocation programs have made students aware that their own concerns are being taken seriously. But the programs have not stopped there. Through the idea of vocational narrative they have proposed to students a way of thinking about life that illuminates the value of developing a sense of purpose.

Developmental psychologist William Damon has shown the importance of forming what he calls "life purposes." By this term, Damon aims to distinguish particular, often-shifting career goals from longer-term dispositions to "accomplish something that is at the same time meaningful to the self and consequential for the world beyond the self."[4] As an educational objective, this means enabling students to make sense of themselves, their relationships, and context, but it also focuses attention on their connection to the larger world in its various dimensions.

Historically, such focus has been a great strength of the liberal arts tradition. Today, in the face of widespread student disengagement with academic learning, the traditional approaches need broadening. Educators are being called upon to help students learn to take responsibility for understanding and addressing the significant challenges of occupational and civic life. For contemporary psychologists such as Martin Seligman, the key lies not only in discovering adequate understandings of self and world, but in the development of a virtue he calls "grit," meaning perseverance toward goals even in the face of obstacles and setbacks.[5] Research makes clear that achieving such resolution turns on the formation of the kind of purpose Damon describes. By orienting the individual toward significant values, purpose provides motivation to learn, pulling young people out of themselves toward concern for others and the fate of the larger world.[6]

Seen in this light, the initiative proposes an incipient educational agenda that helps students connect the needs of career preparation with the needs of self and world.

The Program for the Theological Exploration of Vocation acknowledges preparation for job and career as an important, but not all-controlling, goal. It is a practical means through which students can mediate their own developing sense of purpose with the complex needs of a global society. It is the students' continuing aim at vocational purpose that promotes resilience in the face of adversity, enabling these emerging adults to recover direction in uncertain situations—an especially useful capacity in a time of unstable personal prospects. Such an educational agenda foregrounds the development of purpose as a motivation for learning and as the basis for resilience in coping with challenges. It encourages hope for the enterprise of higher education at a time when it is in real danger of losing its own sense of purpose.

The Problem with College Today: The Narrowing of Educational Vision

Education is the institution through which societies shape and renew themselves. Educational institutions provide models of human development. They embody images of how the world is thought to be. They also set standards for how it ought to be. The organization and functioning of educational institutions are therefore important clues to how a society understands itself and its future. For modern nations, educational systems provide comprehensive visions of what is important to teach the young, how best to learn, and what learning is for.

Because educational systems are more than instruments for achieving certain outcomes, their form and content differ, reflecting and intensifying the values held by various societies. Among nations noted for high-performing systems of public education, there is no consensus on how best to organize schooling. South Korea, for example, emphasizes intensive drill, competition, and frequent, high-stakes testing, while Finland, which scores equally high on performance measures, does little testing. Instead, Finland emphasizes cooperative learning complemented by individualized instruction and assessment. Both South Korea and Finland employ a highly selective and professionalized teaching corps. Both produce impressive results, but they differ profoundly on the question of what education is about and how it is best conducted.[7]

In the case of higher education, the landmark models likewise reflect different understandings of situation, needs, and possibilities. In the early 19th century, Wilhelm von Humboldt's new model university in Berlin stressed the formative power of deep immersion in classical sources in order to fit independent citizens for a new age. In the mid-19th-century United States, the state land-grant universities were publicly chartered to spread knowledge and practical skills among the citizenry to build the nation. After World War II, James Bryant Conant's new model of general education at Harvard was intended to shape free and responsible citizens with a world perspective. More recently, the Spellings Commission has sought to promote a vision of U.S. higher education organized to upgrade the workforce.

Today, there is little question that the conception of higher education embodied in both the Spellings Commission's work and in many American curricular developments is instrumental in character and private in focus. In this understanding, college is a resource for enhancing individuals' capacities in an increasingly competitive global marketplace for skills and talent. This narrowed educational regime is touted as more democratic than the allegedly elite educational culture of the past. Yet, as higher education has come to be seen more and more as a private good, funding for public higher education has declined, increasing the burden on families and individuals whose health insurance, retirement, and very living situations have become less secure.[8]

These trends have affected college entrants of all ages, but they have had the most marked effects on traditional college-age students and their families. And these developments at the level of higher education policy and funding have done nothing to reassure a public increasingly suspicious that higher education is failing to make the welfare of America's youth its main priority.[9] If present trends continue, the likely trajectory is a growing divergence between an "elite" sector focused on a broad education for those academically ambitious and able to pay, and a "mass" sector providing some skills training for midlevel jobs along with modest amounts of general knowledge. Such an outcome would be a reversal of the entire thrust of American educational effort since World War II: to enhance equal opportunity within a general commitment to national inclusion and well-being.

Students Caught in a Narrowing Pass

As the major economic changes that have taken place since the 1980s have become better understood, their interrelation to other challenges facing young Americans becomes more visible. The steadily increasing shift of economic resources toward the very top of the socioeconomic scale has resulted from the capture of virtually all technology-driven gains in productivity by the owners of investment capital. The result has been stagnation in wages for most jobs, encouraging more family members to attempt to join the workforce even as employment has grown more precarious for much of the working population. For large numbers at the lower end of the socioeconomic scale, the result has been poverty even in the midst of hard work.[10] Over the same period, there is strong evidence that Americans, especially younger ones, have come to trust less not only in institutions but in their neighbors and fellow citizens.[11]

These economic and social trends point to a big shift in the macroenvironment facing today's students. They make more intelligible the widely noted rise of anxiety and uncertainty on the part of students and their parents about the viability of traditional middle-class career paths—not to mention the exploratory attitude toward learning that was often extolled as a valuable facet of gaining a college education. As the costs of higher education have risen and the burden of financing tuitions has fallen more heavily on individuals and families, the instrumental stance toward undergraduate education has come to be seen as a necessity rather than a choice.

Some college entrants respond to these conditions by choosing educational pathways that lead most directly to secure employment, while others seem disengaged from academic learning entirely, in spite of its potential instrumental value.[12] The American public as a whole seems reluctant to reduce the four years of college to a simple instrument for improving access to jobs. There remains widespread support among Americans for many of the traditional values of liberal education. However, the evidence indicates mostly vagueness about what higher education should be for and who should gain entrance, as well as who should pay for it.[13] The present national dialogue lacks a compelling public purpose that could connect the instrumental need to prepare for careers with the value of a deep exploration of world and self that college traditionally has offered.

This narrow instrumental conception of the purpose of higher education has made it an arena of competitive striving for relatively fewer rewards. In this, higher education follows several larger national trends. Over the past three decades, economic opportunity for women and people of color has improved significantly due to greater inclusion for previously underrepresented groups in higher education. Yet, over the past thirty years, despite technological advances and overall economic growth, these improvements have been mitigated by the growth of markedly Darwinian features in American life as a whole. Economic opportunities in particular have become less widely available than in the postwar decades and, as the Great Recession showed so brutally, far less stable. Gaps in opportunity for students based on their parents' socioeconomic status are far greater than in past decades. Whereas fifty years ago the United States led the developed world in rates of social mobility, it now falls squarely in the middle of the pack.

Compared to the lives of previous American generations, for example, even children of the already college educated, the most affluent and secure segment of the American population, now live with intense anxiety about their futures. The importance of these developments is only now becoming apparent. Epidemiological studies have found correlations between growth in income inequality and rising rates of anxiety and depression, drug and alcohol addiction, obesity, and diabetes. These ominous trends have been far more marked in the United States than in Europe or Japan, both of which suffer significantly lower rates of these psychosocial pathologies as well as significantly less socioeconomic inequality.[14]

In this constricting social context, the emotional defense of the self, with its relentless efforts to raise "self-esteem," becomes a more consuming task for everyone, but especially for adolescents. The macroenvironment, in other words, is making finding a job, let alone stable career possibilities—the essential platforms for other life involvements and commitments—significantly harder to come by. These trends long antedate the onset of the Great Recession, but they have been seriously exacerbated by it. The consistent finding of growing mental health issues among college-age young adults fits with these larger trends.[15]

For many of the already college educated, life has been restructured around gaining entrance for their children into the "right" college, often at high cost to the family, not least in the form of crushing financial debt. Achieving this goal requires early cultivation of a competitive achievement ethic in these future students, often including an expensive series of investments to ensure academic success.[16] Once entered into higher education, a similar logic dictates that such students, at the encouragement of their ambitious parents, must focus on accumulating the credentials and experiences that provide entry into occupations of high income and status.[17] At the same time, for many first-generation college students, including students of ethnic and racial minority backgrounds, the achievement of credentials is paramount for the ever more difficult achievement of gaining entry into the middle class.

These trends have been noted for some time, leading researchers to talk of "ambitious but directionless" young Americans.[18] For some, then, there emerges a kind of hyperactivity with no larger end than winning. But for many other students, the same conditions prompt a disengagement from the academic status race in favor of immersion in other forms of young adult life. For teachers and others invested in the academic enterprise, this often appears as a kind of sullenness.[19] These students think of college as less of an investment in future earnings than the purchase of a lifestyle. While concerned about acquiring the credentials needed for a desirable job, these students are disengaged from academic learning. Instead, they focus heavily on a "college experience" of social activity among their peers, postponing as long as possible decisions about future directions and adult responsibilities.[20] This divergence among highly competitive and academically adrift students eerily echoes the radical divergence in family economic well-being between the very rich and the middle class.

For few students of any background, however, do learning for self-understanding, expansion of intellectual horizons, or engagement with larger social purposes, bulk large. Students seem rarely to encounter, among their peers or the adults on campus, compelling examples of the life of the mind integrated with meaningful purpose and social contribution.[21] Despite much hand-wringing over students' preoccupation with self-image and marketing of self, colleges and universities devote little attention to the cultivation of students' capacities for reflection or deeper engagement with the life of their times—a contradiction explored in greater depth in chapter 2. Once major concerns of college freshmen, the goals of developing a meaningful philosophy of life and a commitment to contributing to social well-being declined in importance among students' stated aims over a number of decades.[22]

Fortunately, of course, this is not the whole story. A trend toward greater attention to questions of meaning and social well-being appears to be on the rise.[23] Research also shows that college-age students are not exclusively concerned with the economic benefits of their education, but also, at least to some degree, with how they can make sense of their lives and live them well.[24] National studies also make it clear that today's students have concerns about religion and spirituality when they enter college. According to these same studies, however, students often report that their educational experiences provide what they consider inadequate opportunity for spiritual or religious reflection.[25]

In the larger picture, these are countertrends to the dominant flow. Despite significant amounts of volunteering and expressed concerns about a swiftly changing roster of causes by today's students, what mostly seems to matter is acquiring tools and connections useful in the competition for income and status, and enjoying a life of social connections and relative leisure—or at least of avoiding a fall into poverty.[26]

The New Significance of "Educating the Whole Student"

These seem to be hard times for the liberal arts tradition of educating the whole student, even as current social and economic realities make

that aim more important than ever. There exists an urgent need to provide young adults with a coherent educational experience designed to help
them understand themselves and their relationships better, to develop the
intellectual capacities to make sense of the world, and to begin to imagine
and experiment with possible futures.

It is striking that on most contemporary campuses, these aims are the
province of a variety of separate groups and functional divisions of the
organization. While the faculty controls the formal curriculum, much of
student life, not least students' psychosocial well-being, remains invisible to teachers. The powerful educative influences of activities, clubs,
and organizations operate in the very different domain of student affairs.
On many campuses the majority of undergraduates hold paying jobs, and
work experiences also shape knowledge, skills, and dispositions toward
life. To the influences of paid work and student affairs must be added the
staff members who organize other important educative contexts: offices
of religious life, athletics, community service and internships, and career
planning. All these aspects of campus life, however, should gain significance from their contribution to the larger educational aim of educating
the whole student. Too rarely is this apparent in the day-to-day activities
of students, and too little do faculty, staff, and institutional leaders consciously work together in pursuit of common educational objectives—
even as the coherent educational platform students need demands just
such an effective sense of shared purpose.[27]

While this instrumental conception of educational purpose does not go
entirely unchallenged in academia, most often the challengers are cham-
pions of "critical thinking" who believe college should instill in students
the distanced intellectual stance typical of the sciences and other analytical disciplines. They advance the cultivation of critical detachment as a
higher goal than the utilitarian aim of workforce training, and sometimes
connect training in critical thinking with the development of reflective
citizens. These higher aims are presented, justifiably, as genuine benefits
to both individuals and the larger society.

The instrumental and critical thinking positions often contend, and
sometimes intersect, within national debates about the point and value
of higher education. The notion that higher education's purpose could be
genuinely practical without being simply instrumental, and intellectual
without being only detached, is heard less often. Yet, one of the defining
commitments of the tradition of liberal education has been just such a
purpose: one that is practical in that it aims to enable students to engage

with their lives, motivated by a response to values that transcend the individual, while remaining open to critical exploration. This is the idea of liberal education as preparation for a life of significance and responsibility. At the center of such an education lies practical wisdom, the art of discernment. This is a trained capacity to recognize the worth of things and to respond appropriately in shaping a meaningful life. Discernment provides a synthetic aim that can do justice to the claims of both utility and critical thinking while giving them a larger significance.

The Core Challenge: A Threefold Misalignment of Ends and Means

Before exploring in detail the achievements of the PTEV programs, it is important to recognize a further obstacle the programs faced in their goal of educating the whole student. This obstacle takes the form of a major misalignment of educational means with the end of educating the whole student. This misalignment has three aspects. One concerns student life and learning. Another is bound up with the disparate way in which faculty and staff roles have developed in modern higher education. The third misalignment involves academic leadership and institutional priorities.

First, students: analysts of American education have for decades noted that students' expectations about their own capacities as well as the demands of learning are often poorly aligned with the demands of modern work and life.[28] The chief manifestation of this phenomenon is the disengagement of students from academic learning. The measures of this disengagement are several, but perhaps most striking is the small amount of time that students in four-year colleges spend studying. Compared to students in the 1960s, today's students spend about half as much time involved with class work. On average, this amounts to about 12 hours per week. In other words, academic learning is often not much more than a part-time activity for supposedly full-time students.[29] Combined with the instrumental stance most students take toward their academic pursuits, this means that, rather than participating in the activity of academic learning, as they might with athletic skills or musical arts, students approach their learning as consumers attempting to get the most valuable credential for the least outlay of time, money, and energy.[30]

This, of course, is bad news for the development of intellectual curiosity and imagination. But it is also counterproductive for enhancing the general cognitive capacities that faculty and the general public expect higher education to provide. Through use of the Collegiate Learning Assessment (CLA), an instrument designed to measure capacities to perform complex thinking tasks and apply cognitive skills to real-world problems, a recent national study discovered disconcerting evidence of the consequences of such disengagement. The study's authors found that many students, especially those from less-educated families and racial and ethnic minority groups, fail to develop significantly their ability to solve complex problems during their first several years in college, when students are enrolled in the most liberal arts courses. This suggests that, far from remediating existing social and economic inequality, college preserves or even enhances it, since students at more selective institutions and those from more educated families made greater gains in complex thinking, allowing greater access to advanced training in the more prestigious and rewarding occupations.[31]

Second, faculty and staff: as higher education has grown more comprehensive and complex, faculty and staff roles have diverged and grown increasingly specialized. For faculty, the chief development has been the ratcheting up of demands for scholarship or scientific research, not only at research-intensive universities but at institutions once considered primarily focused on undergraduate teaching. This trend has been driven in part by the expansion of doctoral programs, forcing a ballooning number of PhDs to distinguish themselves through research in order to obtain a permanent teaching position and tenure. Nonteaching demands on faculty are only intensified by the fierce competition among campuses for status in relation to peer institutions.

Liberal arts courses resemble scaled-down versions of specialized graduate-level courses in ever-narrower research fields. This narrowed focus is poorly matched with the kinds of thinking and communication skills that lend themselves to unstructured problems of actual experience. Faculty members often find themselves torn not only between research demands and teaching, but also between teaching the specialized knowledge their fields increasingly emphasize, on the one hand, and guiding students through the nuanced understandings that traditionally define liberal education, on the other.[32] Of course this tension makes discussions of curricula and pedagogy more difficult, and often acrimonious.

With the attention of faculty diverted from undergraduate teaching to research, the burden of student advising, counseling, and support has been taken over by a wholly different set of campus professionals. Some work in the areas of student affairs, some in psychological counseling, some in religious life or chaplaincy, and others in career planning and placement. These fields, too, have become more specialized, or "professionalized," and self-enclosed, with their own associations, publications, career trajectories, and hierarchies of status. Such staff serves at the pleasure of college and university administration and lacks tenure. On many campuses, it is uncommon for faculty and staff to work cooperatively or even to meet around issues of student welfare.

Finally, misalignment of purposes is widespread in academic leadership. Here, too, the long-term trend has been to pull academic leadership—deans, provosts, presidents and the boards of trustees who appoint them—away from other members of the campus. Academic leaders have adopted a way of thinking and style of acting more akin to that of modern corporations than colleges and universities. Like most sectors of American society in this era of slow growth and rising inequality, the higher education "industry," as it is often described, is a much tougher environment than previously. Competition for students and tuition income, the drive to increase or maintain position in national rankings, and often enough simply the need to keep the ship afloat in the face of rising costs, all impose heavy pressures on administrative leaders. In these conditions, it has proven hard for campuses to keep educational mission and quality from being overwhelmed by the immediate pressures of economic survival.

These pressures reinforce short-term, bottom-line thinking, just as the competitive environment, rather than encouraging experimentation, tends toward homogenization. As noted earlier, these tendencies in academic administration encourage students to approach their learning as consumers attempting to get the most bang for the buck. As a result, academic leaders often find little incentive to engage with questions of educational mission beyond the issues of degree completion, demographic data, and financial outcomes. Because today's trends in higher education do not favor placing the formation of student identity and purpose high on the institutional agenda, it takes conscious leadership to bring this topic to practical focus. Administrators, like faculty and students, need to cultivate ways of bridging the gap between their values and beliefs and the often harsh realities of their situation.

Toward Realignment: Plotting a Change of Direction

To correct this threefold misalignment of means with educational ends demands imagining anew the coherent formation of "the whole student" as an informed, responsible, and engaged participant in the larger world. To do so requires in turn real shifts in campus life for academic leaders, faculty and staff, and students. The positive news is that abundant evidence shows the organization of educational institutions, especially their everyday operating norms and expectations, to have great formative power. In particular, it is the quality of relationships between students and faculty that count, along with expectations shared among peers that learning is seriously important. Students' motivation is very strongly influenced by a sense that faculty care about their learning and growth.[33] "Ultimately," one researcher has argued concerning the expectations that shape student learning, "it is about the culture."[34] But that culture must be nurtured intentionally. It must be focused on institutionalizing as everyday practice the fostering of student learning and the formation of purpose. Such cultural revitalization—a reimagining of institutional purpose—needs to become the key task of academic leadership.

Available evidence suggests that faculty and staff can be most effective in fostering the development of the whole student when they function as communities of learning. But such communities are hard to achieve on today's fragmented campuses, where each institutional sector seems to pursue its own goals. Faculty roles need to be consciously examined in relation to the institution's educative mission. The same is true of staff in today's highly specialized, mobile campus world. It is probable that these two processes would have to be more than parallel play. They would have to be interconnected around the common purpose of student formation.

Students, for their part, would need to enter more effectively into the core processes of learning and personal development. The instrumentalist, consumer orientation frequently promoted by today's institutions is itself a major deforming influence. It would need to be replaced, or at least leavened, by a serious effort to combine academic rigor with emotional, social, and practical relevance. Students deserve a coherent undergraduate experience that allows them to grow in understanding of themselves as well as of the complexities of the world they must engage.

The PTEV: Catalyst to Invention

It is from within this perspective that the achievements of the 88 PTEV institutions command attention. As we have seen in the previous chapter, even against the background of the educationally entropic pressures just described, the PTEV campuses succeeded in offering students a chance for sustained participation in meaningful forms of intellectual, social, and moral life. Indeed, in his recent study of the PTEV, sociologist Tim Clydesdale documents the surprising success of most of the programs at substantially increasing two key educational goods for participating students: they enlarged opportunities for self-knowledge, and they increased motivation for learning.[35] Clydesdale's analysis is the more striking in that it began with a good deal of skepticism and ended with an endorsement of the programs' claims to have achieved meaningful educational improvement. As already noted, Clydesdale's research provides a significant point of reference for the arguments of the present book.

How the PTEV's use of the metaphor of life as a vocational journey worked as an integrating platform for student development is the theme of the chapters that follow. However, it also has significance for higher education as a whole. Far from its common (and commonly pejorative) association with vocational training, "vocation" as understood by the PTEV programs proved to be a specific cultural theme with which many students and faculty were able to identify, with significant positive effects on their lives.

Realigning around Vocation: The PTEV Culture

The PTEV picked up a foundational thread of American higher education that has recently been obscured by the rush to streamline and recast the appeal of college as simply a means toward a better economic future. Of course, it has always been that, especially for students who were the first generation of their families to attend a college or university. However, the primary aims of higher education in the American vision of democracy were from the beginning conceived as benefiting the public by providing skilled and responsible leaders and professionals.[36] This was the shared assumption of those like Thomas Jefferson, who hoped that a secular University of Virginia would spread enlightenment, as well as the leaders of the religious colleges in which Christian clergy played the central roles.

The need for leadership that would embody and exercise a strong sense of public responsibility was especially important in a new nation constantly forming and reforming communities and institutions. In that context, intellectual training took on a distinctly practical cast: such leaders were to be knowledgeable in the arts and sciences, but able as generalists to take up roles with a strongly practical, even activist side.

What came to be called "liberal arts" education was conceived in the United States as a curriculum to shape civic leaders as practical intellectuals with dispositions toward responsibility and public service. As an educational ideal it was intended to provide a moderating influence on the other American tendency to go for the main chance regardless of consequences.[37] The United States remains unique in requiring a collegiate liberal arts education, along with a specialized, "major" curriculum of study, as a universal preparation for careers. To observers educated outside the United States, such as British scholar Alan Ryan, the distinctive aspect of liberal arts education is its embodiment of a core tension in modern culture. On the one hand, it seeks to develop students' capacities for the kind of skeptical, empirical inquiry that risks a loss of meaning and nihilism, while, on the other, it employs reason to recover a sense of moral purpose by enabling students to locate themselves in the larger human drama. Ryan sees this characteristic emphasis upon connecting individual cultivation with a sense of participation in a larger order of reality as a distinctly religious—though not sectarian—impulse shared by educational leaders as otherwise diverse as John Henry Newman and John Dewey. Ryan argues that this "dilutedly religious quality" is what continues to give American liberal education much of its force and appeal.[38] It is particularly striking that this quality has survived in an era when religion on campus has become more private and pluralized and, some would say, marginalized.[39]

A Distinctive Framing of Educating the Whole Student

The PTEV explicitly built upon those American cultural foundations. The previous chapter (Introduction) explained how the vocation programs were encouraged by the granting philanthropy to reach into their distinctive religious traditions for language in which to engage students in conversations about life purpose. The common terminology was the theme of vocation. As the following chapters will explore in detail, the success of these efforts is especially striking given the religious diversity of faculty, staff, and students at many of the participating campuses. Almost as striking was the tendency of most PTEV programs to provide students with opportunities to explore vocations across several sectors of campus life. The PTEV programs took place in traditional classrooms—the academic heartland of the institutions—while also operating in religious or student life offices; in advising and career counseling; in projects of service and travel in the United States and abroad; in residential living arrangements with a vocational theme; and, sometimes, in campus-wide programs linking several of these areas through conversation about vocation and purpose. These activities increased overall student engagement with education, connecting academic learning, students' social development, and their exploration of future possibilities in mutually reinforcing ways.[40]

For faculty, the programs provided opportunities to explore with colleagues from many disciplines the challenges of shifting faculty roles and identities. On many campuses, faculty conversations grew to include staff, promoting a new sense of common purpose with professionals in student affairs, religious life, and career and counseling. For administrators, too, the institutionalized discussion of vocation opened possibilities for thinking in new ways. Sometimes this was quite personal, as in programs the Lilly Endowment organized for college presidents and administrators during the PTEV years that focused on reexamination of careers.[41] But administrators also began to rethink campus leadership and campus relationships with other institutions, their sponsoring religious bodies, and the larger society. For some campuses, the PTEV has meant strengthening and expanding a preexisting emphasis on tying together academic and student life programming. For others, it opened up new directions and strategies for engaging students and faculty. But for most of the participating institutions it resulted in a renewal of educational aims, as suggested by the fact that most of the participating campuses chose to continue at least some aspects of the vocation programs beyond the funded period, even at significant additional cost to themselves.[42]

Overall, the PTEV programs disrupted the drift toward misalignment and provided conditions for an intentional reshaping of institutional life—all with the aim of recovering the "vocation" of undergraduate liberal education itself.

Core Features of the PTEV and the Renewal
of Liberal Education

The campus programs experimented with a number of ways of putting the educational focus on vocation. But in all of them, three salient features can be identified: (1) the use of the language of vocation to frame the undergraduate experience, (2) the formation of learning communities of faculty and students engaged with questions of vocation, and (3) the explicit teaching of practices of individual and group reflection.

"Vocation: Your Personal Renaissance," the course profiled at the beginning of this chapter, exemplifies these three core features at work on the Santa Clara University campus. The language of vocation is explicit even in the title of the course, which asks students to consider such questions of life purpose as "How should I live?" and "Who might I become?" while using methods of literary, religious, historical, and psychological analysis to explore vocation in the lives of Renaissance figures. The search for personal meaning becomes the horizon within which tools of various academic disciplines are learned and applied.

The course cultivates the formation of community, both within and beyond the classroom walls. The students' insights are not intended to be solitary discoveries. Students spend time in groups with others who are researching figures with similar lives, engaging in lively disagreements as well as mutual learning as they come to grips with the complexities of the struggle to find purpose. This classroom learning community operates within Santa Clara's larger efforts to support its students' search for meaning through a variety of campus contexts, including the curriculum in which Pathway courses such as "Your Personal Renaissance" hold an important place, but also civic learning projects and "immersion" service trips to other countries. In these ways, the course represents a powerful, innovative approach to revitalizing intellectual inquiry as a means toward the larger end of finding oneself in the world, a traditional goal of all liberal education.

Reflection is also a key theme of the course, embodied in an in-class meditation practice and explored through informal and analytic essays. In the midterm paper, students are asked to present their Renaissance figure's life as a vocational quest, asking how their figure was able to accomplish something personally meaningful and yet consequential for the world beyond the self. In the culminating assignment, they are asked to become explicitly self-reflective, imagining how the "insights for your life today" gained through historical analysis might actually be applied in the major field and in future career possibilities.

While the most successful PTEV campus programs, like Santa Clara's, became explicit and intentional about fostering these three core elements— vocational language, the formation of learning communities, and the teaching of reflective practices—all campuses shared them to varying degrees, with an overall effect of enriching the campus culture of learning. The language of vocation, drawn from each campus's religious tradition, pointed toward holistic student development. The PTEV employed the search for purpose as a kind of master narrative around which to focus and inspire academic learning as well as personal and career development. In addition, students' ability to interpret their present learning and social experiences in relation to the theme of finding purpose was greatly strengthened through the explicit development of practices of reflection. These reflective practices enabled students, and often faculty and staff as well, to connect the liberal arts disciplines, experiential and civic learning, and career preparation in ongoing ways. Throughout, the exploration of vocational purpose was rooted in campus learning communities, which supported students in their developmental path.

The chapters that follow will trace some of the ways in which the vocation programs wove the theme of vocation through campus life, including curriculum, faculty experience, administrative leadership, and institutional identity. Through examining specific examples of teaching and learning in campus programs, the following chapters are intended to present the PTEV as an incipient educational agenda, an alternative to today's apparently exclusive choice between narrow instrumentalism and detached critical thinking. The purpose of this investigation is to describe resources useful for addressing issues central to the improvement of undergraduate education. The next chapter will advance that effort by locating the PTEV's distinctive innovations within the larger story of today's struggles to realign and reinvigorate undergraduate learning.

2

Grounding Liberal Education

DEVELOPMENT OF THE student as a whole person has been a key theme of liberal education throughout its history. Despite its many, quite different historical embodiments, liberal learning has always addressed the relationship between learning and the positive growth of students as persons. Proponents of liberal learning have sought to provide students with the ability to make sense of the world and their place in it, equipping them for responsible engagement with the life of their times.[1] This formative purpose has motivated an educational experience intended to affect the outlook and abilities of the learner. The student has been expected to grow in understanding, purposes, and presence in the world. That aim requires the student to deliberately cultivate an increasingly self-aware and proactive stance toward both learning and the shaping of her life. Liberal learning, then, means genuine change—greater sophistication in knowledge, greater mastery of skill, and greater maturity.

Formative education of this kind demands active engagement on the part of both student and educator. The process resembles the way in which crafts have long been imparted through apprenticeship. The key point of the analogy is that genuine learning of a formative kind is, like apprenticeship, the initiation of a beginner into a domain of knowledge, skill, and comportment. It is a gradual, step-by-step process that requires the learner to immerse herself in new challenges to stimulate growth into recognized competence within a community of others who share that competence. Effective learning requires that educators, for their part, make visible to the learner the features and purpose of the competence she is trying to master. They must furnish opportunities for the learner to practice the new capacity and receive feedback on performance, while providing her with guidance and support in the effort. Through it all, educators must strive to engage the attention and goodwill of their students by emphasizing the value and significance of what is being learned for both the learners and for the larger world.

The apprenticeship approach has received substantial support from the findings of contemporary learning theory. The learning sciences have emphasized features of apprenticeship as essential for coherent, continuing growth in knowledge and skill.[2] The important implication for higher education is that, like the immersion in craft typical of traditional apprenticeship, learning requires educational experiences that are integrated and coherent in process and purpose. Seen from this perspective, the vicissitudes of liberal education, often described as a decline from a presumed better time, look rather different.

The Academic Revolution and After

The present situation of poorly integrated and weakly formative learning is also a side effect of the academy's half-century of vast expansion, funded by historically unprecedented national spending on scientific research, as well as expansion of the college-going population through legislation such as the G.I. Bill. Even further back, the story of the modern university has been marked by great, though unassimilated and uncoordinated growth of knowledge in specialized disciplines, along with a simultaneous ramification of more specialized cognitive skills within these, all supported and loosely coordinated by an ever more complex administrative organization. Driven forward by these developments, the university has emerged as a major research engine, whose social importance has been massively enhanced by the applicability of that knowledge to technological advance and economic value. For the educational mission of higher education, however, this growth has been more problematic.

Within the context of university research and scholarship, future educators follow the lodestar of specialized expertise, which has defined professorial striving across much of higher education. A half-century ago, Christopher Jencks and David Reisman famously declared an "academic revolution" had taken place in the way higher education was organized and universities governed; they argued that at leading universities the faculty was emerging as the key actor in setting the pattern for higher education. Jencks and Reisman also noted that, propelled by the increasing specialization of academic research, differentiation seemed likely to prove a continuing challenge to the traditional aims of liberal education unless countered by specific efforts at integration.[3] As predicted, these developments have narrowed the purview of faculty and students to particular areas and withdrawn attention from the larger educational mission.

This movement toward specialization in research proved particularly disorienting to the educational mission of colleges and universities that had not been primarily research-focused. In attempting to model themselves after the pace-setting institutions, they lost track of what had been the defining characteristics of their undergraduate education. This disorientation was compounded as a different population of students entered college in the 1980s. These students came from less affluent backgrounds than traditional college students, were less academically focused, and included far more women and students of color. These trends marked the beginning of a pattern in higher education that would only intensify in the 21st century.

These challenges have made administrative oversight of academic affairs both more necessary and more difficult. The economic pressures affecting both students and institutions discussed in the previous chapter, the changing needs of students, and the continuing conflicts over social and political values—the so-called culture wars—have reduced the space in which academic leaders can maneuver. Given these trends, little wonder that schools struggle to develop coherent, formative undergraduate programs that can speak to a wide range of students.

Fragmented Apprenticeships: Academics, Social Skills, Identity, and Purpose

The scattered nature of undergraduate learning on most campuses has given rise to a good deal of discontent on the part of both faculty and students. Most often, undergraduates experience their education as divided into three dimensions of learning, disjoined and often discordant. Imagine these as three different kinds of apprenticeship supervised by different groups of college personnel. The apprenticeships attempt initiation into three disparate domains—the divergent goals of which students are expected to somehow put together.

The first apprenticeship is cognitive or academic. It is structured by the modern disciplines of the natural sciences, the social sciences, and the humanities, which define the "content" of college learning. The competitive context in which this learning takes place tacitly emphasizes to students the importance of standing out from other learners. While such differentiation is a genuine value, spurring intellectual development and supporting the student's growth as an individual, it can also devolve into a simple contest for relative advantage in which achievement becomes a goal without content. The risks of an education based exclusively in the first apprenticeship are twofold: for competitive, academically oriented students, it can encourage striving without a greater understanding of self or social context, while in less academically driven students it can fail to connect with their motivations and concerns.

The second apprenticeship, by contrast, involves the development of personal capacities and social or "life skills" that traditional-age students need to acquire in their transition to adulthood. As Tim Clydesdale has summarized and much research confirms, "navigating relationships and managing gratifications are the primary foci of culturally mainstream American teens."[4] In college, even the more mature students often need to expand their personal skills in order to negotiate the complexities of managing study, adult relationships, and career. In this social apprenticeship the emphasis is typically on students' individuation, focused around individual or group differentiation, though less concerned with academic achievement and more with peer relationships and with entry into society beyond higher education.

The third apprenticeship ideally functions as the connective tissue often missing or weak between the first two apprenticeships. It consists in the teaching and learning of identity and purpose: the shaping of an orientation toward important values. This is the educational area in which moral, civic, and spiritual concerns can become objects of direct examination and reflection. Much more than in the first two apprenticeships, the third apprenticeship provides students access to larger worlds of ideas, as well as cooperative relationships centered on common values. While arguably as important for the long-term development of students as the other two, universities have often treated this third apprenticeship as a stepchild, an afterthought in the design of undergraduate programs. As the rest of this book will show, the Lilly emphasis on vocation has made it possible to reintegrate the three apprenticeships.

The apprenticeship model can help clarify both the challenges facing undergraduate education today and the efforts to address those challenges. Reform typically begins from the perspective of one of the three apprenticeships. That is, some efforts at reform have understood the problem as essentially the need to upgrade the cognitive apprenticeship, with an emphasis on providing more effective intellectual growth and, some-times, more coherence. Others have focused on systematically enriching a whole range of students' personal capacities, addressing concerns of the social apprenticeship such as personal skills, psychological well-being, career preparation, and motivation.

By contrast, the PTEV has been among a smaller number of reform efforts to embrace the third apprenticeship of identity and purpose. It has sought to reground both liberal learning and career preparation through a reflective engagement with larger life aims, especially engagement with civic and ethical purposes.[5] The significance of the PTEV for today's acad-emy lies in its demonstration of a liberal education in which intellectual growth and personal capacities are systematically connected on a trajec-tory shaped by a sense of purpose. To gain perspective on the distinctive-ness of the PTEV approach, the rest of this chapter will focus on strategies for reform originating in each of the apprenticeships, including their philosophical and historical basis, as well as examples of how these efforts take shape in particular courses on campus.

Strategy One: Strengthening the Academic Apprenticeship

"Academics," as it is revealingly called in campus slang, forms the first apprenticeship. It defines the most distinctive feature of college life: initia-tion into the cognitive dimension of personal development. This is mostly an apprenticeship to the systematic modes of thinking practiced in the disciplines of the arts and sciences. Through this apprenticeship, a faculty organized by academic discipline provides a great range of knowledge in programs leading to a bachelor's degree. The primary stance inculcated by such learning is critical distance and detachment. And indeed, these disciplines and their faculties continue to define central values of the acad-emy: analytical rigor, critical probing, and systematic explanation.

These values establish a hierarchy of prestige among the disciplines, giving pride of place to tested, systematic, and abstract forms of knowl-edge, such as those exemplified by the natural sciences, and placing less value on involvement with personal or social contexts. Growth in the aca-demic apprenticeship is typically displayed as specialized expertise within a discipline. In today's academy, this initiation is often unconnected to the contexts of students' daily experience. In addition, the arts, with their attention to developing the disciplined imagination, have long been seen as ancillary to the core project of teaching analytic rigor. These tendencies have become ever more marked over the past half-century.[6]

Today, however, most students experience the most important parts of first apprenticeship not in the natural sciences, the humanities, or the social sciences, but in technical and professional fields such as business, engineering, education, and other forms of "applied" knowledge. In contrast to the more theoretically oriented disciplines of the arts and sciences, the professional disciplines employ general, theoretical thinking in various ways to address problems in their areas of competence.[7]

At the same time, the professional fields also carry an important educational value often missing from the arts and sciences. The professional fields must prepare their students to enter the contexts of practice in which they will need to deploy their academic knowledge for the benefit of their clients and in order to serve society. Undergraduate students in engineering, nursing, teaching, business, and other professions need to master the theoretical knowledge that undergirds their fields. But professional programs must also teach their students to couple theoretical knowledge with practical skills in pursuit of the field's defining purposes by making sound judgments in particular situations. Besides theoretical abstraction, they must learn another set of cognitive skills: those involved in practical reasoning. For example, engineers must be concerned with the safety as well as the efficiency of their designs. Nurses must know how to adjust the field's routines of practice to particular patients in particular settings, as must teachers. These decisions demand an engaged and participatory stance toward clients and situations.[8] To accomplish this kind of learning, professional programs have developed a variety of pedagogical vehicles such as case studies, simulated practice, and formally organized apprenticeships in the form of guided responsibility in actual practice.

Like these professional programs, liberal education also has a practical purpose: to prepare young adults with both the critical and moral capacities to contribute to society. Developing the whole student in the first apprenticeship means challenging students to acquire facility in both the distanced, analytical stance typical of disciplinary knowledge and the engaged, participatory posture essential to bringing such cognitive perspective into play in the actual contexts of human affairs.[9]

Unfortunately, neither the professional and career-oriented fields nor the liberal arts and sciences are doing well in developing such bifocal vision in their graduates. Even as professional and career preparation has come to dominate most of students' attention in higher education, there are indicators that all is not well with these efforts. There is evidence that students in these applied or professional majors, outside engineering, tend to remain weaker in cognitive skills than majors in the arts and sciences.[10] Paradoxically, perhaps, students who major in professional fields, including engineers, also show less interest in relating their developing knowledge to public issues and concerns.[11]

Efforts to "leaven" professional training by "exposure" to the liberal arts have produced limited effects. Liberal education, for almost all undergraduates, continues to mean a set of required courses, often chosen from a list, "distributed" across disciplines such as mathematics and science, social science, humanities, writing, and so forth. As the pedagogical weaknesses of this familiar pattern have become more obvious, institutions of all stripes have experimented with curricular alternatives designed to enhance both thinking skills and intellectual range and coherence. For example, several institutions have tried to improve students' scientific literacy by using small-group learning practices, experiential learning, peer teaching, and other forms of student–faculty collaboration.[12] Other approaches include varied instructional modes, where students make site visits or Internet searches, including research on sociocultural situations and in diverse communities.[13]

Today's academy provides many examples of such efforts. Some aim at cognitive upgrade, typically within disciplines, such as major revisions in teaching of mathematics and natural science. Other experiments attempt to combine cognitive enhancement with coherent intellectual expansion: freshman-year seminars, senior capstone courses, interdisciplinary programs in the natural sciences and engineering, joint humanities and professional programs, honors programs and honors colleges, and more.

These reforms of undergraduate education centered on the first apprenticeship, especially those aimed at broad, coherent learning, largely remain on the edges of the standard, discipline-based curriculum. It has often proved difficult to persuade established faculty members to teach experimental or integrative courses. And, with the exception of a very few outlier colleges, nowhere have these programs dislodged the discipline-centered "major" as the core of every student's first apprenticeship. To some degree this is simply a manifestation of the sheer inertia of the academy's long-established organization into disciplinary departments to which faculty are appointed and which control faculty advancement and tenure. Yet also at play is the fact that today, tenured or tenure-track faculty have become a minority. Most teaching is done by contingent, often part-time teachers who, nonetheless, function within the disciplinary system. Such faculty members are less likely to be part of an academic community where interdisciplinary teaching might develop.

Two Big Truths, Not One: Arguments Over College Curriculum

Liberal education, as noted earlier, has never spoken with a single voice. On the contrary, like all vital traditions, it has been marked by contention over some of its most basic and important values. These debates have ranged across a historical arc that stretches from the 19th-century American college, in which the curriculum prescribed a common course of study taught by a faculty that shared responsibility for student development, through the "elective revolution" of the late 19th century in which the disciplines of the research university came to organize instruction, all the way to the current situation in which specialized expertise in the disciplines has largely eclipsed all other understandings of cognitive development.

The contemporary controversy over reforms of the first apprenticeship generates heat precisely because it taps into long-standing tensions within the modern academy. Movements toward cognitive upgrading can usually work fairly easily within existing disciplinary structures. On the other hand, efforts at intellectual integration in the curricular and institutional levels, particularly when deliberately linked to student engagement with larger social values (and therefore political values), call out resistance from defenders of the existing dominance of the disciplines.

Scholars have usefully mapped the genealogy of this divergence. Bruce Kimball has described two major tendencies. One emphasizes "liberal" as the intellectual freedom to pursue truth, the cardinal value of what Kimball calls the "liberal-free ideal." It has powerfully shaped the modern sciences and the disciplinary culture of the university. The contrasting impulse connects intellectual development with the idea of a public sphere, seeking to link intellectual cultivation with moral and civic concerns. Kimball traces this tendency to the Roman and medieval "*artes liberales* ideal" and to the "republic of letters" of the Renaissance humanists. As European education since the Renaissance has developed forms of humanistic learning, increasing contact with non-Western cultures has revealed mutual resonances among various humanistic traditions, suggesting ways to reimagine the formation of citizens for the current century. This subject will be explored in greater depth in chapter 6.

Each side of this debate has a reasonable claim to the truth about how knowledge and intellect ought to figure in education and cultural development. The problem for modern higher education has been to devise forms of pedagogy and organizational structures that can "do justice" to the truths of each contending side. The big truth behind the liberal-free ideal is the value of knowledge as a good in itself. The distanced stance cultivated in the first apprenticeship is both valuable and necessary for comprehending modern life and culture. This is not only true because the liberal-free posture provides the indispensable basis for scientific analysis and technical ingenuity, but also because analytical distance is needed to gain a mature understanding of oneself and the context in which one lives. On the other hand, the *artes liberales* ideal also contains an indispensable truth: knowledge makes moral demands on the individual, and the fulfillment of those demands requires responsible participation in the human community and the natural environment.

The paramount educational problem is how to nurture development of students' analytical capacities while also providing opportunities for them to learn to employ those capacities thoughtfully. Recent curricular innovations in "experiential education" and "authentic learning" take a leaf from pedagogies used in educating professionals. Through the opportunity to apply their academic knowledge directly in real-world contexts, students learn to take responsibility for how that knowledge impacts the lives of others. At their best, the innovative programs fostered by the initiative tried—and to a considerable degree succeeded—in guiding students to just this awareness, as will become clearer later on.

Before looking at how the programs managed to nurture development of students' analytical capacities while also providing opportunities for them to learn to employ those capacities responsibly, it will be helpful to understand the historical basis of their separation and some insight into earlier efforts to overcome that separation.

The two tendencies Kimball identifies have never been simply matters of "academic" disagreement. They are deeply entwined with some of the most fundamental conflicts roiling modern culture itself. In the late 19th century, as he transformed Harvard from a prestigious but provincial college into a prototype of the cosmopolitan research university, Charles Eliot replaced a prescribed, classical curriculum with what has come to be known as the "elective system." President Eliot's thinking was informed by the new understanding of Darwinian evolution fashionable in educated circles at the time. As W. B. Carnochan notes, "in the environment of free election, the fittest would survive best: the fittest students would succeed, the fittest teachers and the fittest courses would attract the best students, the fittest subjects would dominate the intellectual scene," making the university a training ground for a life of self-reliance.[14] One might add that the university most successful in attracting the best students and faculty would ultimately prove "fittest" in competing for prestige and endowment funds.

These developments in Cambridge stirred James McCosh of Princeton to counter with a compromise. This was the origin of the "distribution" requirement familiar to most undergraduates today. Critically, it operates within a curriculum structured by a major and the elective system. McCosh aimed to develop a sense of intellectual community around common study of great models of thought. His pedagogical disagreement with Eliot was deeply enmeshed in clashing social and moral visions. Eliot's curriculum was designed to foster progress through competitive differentiation in the struggle of ideas. Here was Kimball's "liberal-free ideal" actualized. McCosh's "liberal arts" curriculum, on the other hand, aimed to provide an integrated common culture within which students could also grow in specialized knowledge relevant to the needs of the age. The issues were sharply drawn: could, and should, modern society develop the perspectives of its future professionals and leaders on the basis of competitive differentiation alone, or was it also necessary to consciously seek ways to integrate the advancing provinces of knowledge within a set of shared, if necessarily argumentative, commitments?

Bertrand Russell and John Dewey: Freedom, Education, and Progress

In the 20th century, this battle erupted in a new idiom with more explicitly political overtones involving some of the leading intellectual figures of the time. Two philosophical giants, Bertrand Russell and John Dewey, embodied the clash over the practice and significance of liberal education. As Alan Ryan notes, Russell and Dewey were exemplars of cultural and political liberalism. That is, they both espoused a distinctly modern trust in the good of universal intellectual freedom to foster a "society of free spirits" emancipated by critical reason from unexamined beliefs and inherited involvements. Thus for both the purpose of education was inherently "liberal." It meant the formation of modern individuals able and willing to join in "cheerfully and intelligently cooperating in creating a lively and high-spirited experiment in political and social self-government."

Both figures were at once academics and prolific public intellectuals who spoke to large general audiences all over the world. However, Russell prized and pursued mathematics and science for their capacity to purify thought, enabling the educated person to "stand outside the concerns of his fellow-citizens," by adopting a distanced and critical perspective on affairs. Dewey, on the other hand, understood philosophy as a call to "embrace those [fellow-citizens'] concerns in a properly self-conscious way."[15] This divergence encapsulated an enduring struggle over which tendency should hold primacy in modern intellectual and cultural development. Without the drive toward differentiation embodied in distanced skepticism and critical analysis, intellectual progress would remain stalled. Absent integrative efforts grounded in concern for mutual understanding and forging common purposes, the prospect for progress would be equally bleak.

Russell, as leading philosopher and mathematician, considered higher education a valuable means of transcending the messiness of human affairs into a realm of disinterested truth. His liberal educational philosophy placed great emphasis on learning to distance the critical mind from its inherited involvements. Greater individual and social differentiation, including more intellectual specialization, was the important thing. Dewey's philosophical direction, despite sharing Russell's concerns with intellectual and social freedom, tended quite otherwise. He veered toward an emphasis on participation and connection. Perhaps most importantly, Dewey saw intelligence itself as arising from humanity's social nature and finding its purpose in the elevation and cultivation of social progress. Liberal learning for Dewey, then, meant honing intelligence, including specialized pursuit of truth in the sciences, within a moral and aesthetic aim of constructing cultural wholeness, contributing thereby to the evolving ideal of shared living he called "democracy."

A "Pragmatic" Basis for Integrative Learning

Dewey called his approach Pragmatism. It was intended to supersede the oppositions and dualisms that characterized the received understanding of education and culture. The Pragmatist standpoint could overcome these oppositions between mind and world, theory and practice, science and art, because it recognized the distanced perspective of scientific analysis and critical skepticism as reliant upon a deeper, practical stance toward the world grounded not in rational self-evidence but in various kinds of social interaction. Dewey distinguished between "intelligence" and the narrower term "rationality." Intelligence was a way of designating humanity's progressive and evolutionary ability to consciously learn and improve its situation. Rationality designated an emergent ideal for guiding human thinking. It employed critical analysis and was embodied in scientific pursuits. But it was also shaped by imagination and tested out by action and experience, in what he called the experimental method. Traditionally philosophers have searched for principles that would ground knowledge in self-evidence, much the way the principles of geometry certify the theorems deduced from them. To the contrary, Dewey argued knowledge needed no such antecedent foundation.

Like the hermeneutical and phenomenological philosophies developing in Europe, Dewey's Pragmatism provided a critique of the alleged self-evidence of the detached viewpoint. That view imagines objects are naturally encountered as neutral "stuff." Value and significance are imagined as being added subsequently by human projection. It follows that truth is found by sloughing off the "subjective" and measuring the remaining, "objective" aspects of experience. On the contrary, in Pragmatism human cognition arises from a pre-rational sense of the significance things have for us as embedded in forms of physical and social interaction. Knowing is founded in acting, hence the term Pragmatism. Value and meaning are not then added; they are already essential aspects of experience lived within contexts of engagement. They provide the basis for human cognition and are therefore even more basic to human functioning than detached observation. The latter idea represents a change in stance, a deliberate detachment from qualitative engagement in order to take an "outside" point of view. It finds its point in solving problems confronting human action in the world of lived experience.

This philosophical approach has important educational implications and, as will be discussed more fully later in the book, proves vitally important to understanding the success of the PTEV programs. When disconnected from its role in improving lived experience, critical reasoning easily degenerates into nihilistic skepticism and alienation (a common risk associated with intellectual awakening among undergraduates). Pragmatism as applied to undergraduate education also reverses the epistemological assumptions underlying the academic priority given to specialized knowledge over grasp of context, which is, after all, one of the primary goals of liberal education. That is why the success of the first apprenticeship depends ultimately upon students developing a sense of direction and purpose compatible with their academic focus.

For Pragmatism, the knower's perspective is rooted in a stance toward the world that is, in turn, cultivated within the participatory, value-laden contexts of particular communities. This is obviously the case with the arts and with cultural and religious perspectives, but it is also true of critical skepticism and scientific investigation. It is only through a process of historical development that modern culture has achieved, in specialized domains such as mathematics and science, the detached, critical perspective that has provided the valuable insights into how the world functions. Mind, even in the modes of critical and scientific inquiry, is always embodied, social mind.

Dewey hoped Pragmatism could produce more holistic understandings of the human place in nature, emphasizing human participation and responsibility within evolution. It was also the platform on which Dewey hoped, perhaps naively, to reconcile partisans of skeptical criticism with those of inherited meaning. Dewey was by temperament unsympathetic to the claims of tradition, including the claims of traditional Christianity. But he also recognized that many of the adherents of religious and cultural traditions in other realms were motivated by vital moral and spiritual ideals.

Dewey construed religion as a deep cultural strand, which grew from the currents of relatedness he found at the root of human experience. He thought such an interpretation of human experience could provide common ground for both adherents of religious traditions and advocates of modern, secular "intelligence" such as he. "The community of causes and consequences in which we, together with those not born, are enmeshed," he wrote, "is the widest and deepest symbol of the mysterious totality of being the imagination calls the universe." Imagination was necessary for science as well as religion because this experience of immersion in a community went deeper than intellectual distinctions. Such immersion was, Dewey declared, "the matrix within which our ideal aspirations are born and bred. It is the source of the values that the moral imagination projects as directive criteria and as shaping purposes."[16]

In today's academy, these are still very much live issues, reawakened by the extraordinary pluralism in culture and values that a more interconnected world has revealed. Some of these issues, especially those concerned with religion in education, will be explored in later chapters. Nonetheless, if meaning indeed derives from practical involvement in relations and connections, strengthening the first apprenticeship is unlikely to succeed if academics remains isolated from concerns about students' developing sense of self and purpose. This raises in a more precise way the question of how the academic apprenticeship should relate to the larger project of educating students as whole persons. Pursuing this line of thinking leads directly to the second apprenticeship and the question of its relation to the first. That inquiry cannot help, in the end, returning to the need for a serious engagement with the apprenticeship of identity and purpose.

Strategy Two: Enhancing Personal Skills through the Social Apprenticeship

Students' practical concerns are the subject of the second form of apprenticeship. In place of the cognitive rigor of the first, this social apprenticeship gives great importance to learning how to get on in the world and to express oneself authentically. It is concerned above all, one might say, with self-actualization, while also encouraging the development of moral and social awareness—echoing the concerns and tensions of Dewey's progressive school. While much of this apprenticeship is unsystematic and casual, colleges and universities also provide an extensive array of activities and physical facilities concerned with students' nonacademic lives.

A great deal of student learning in college concerns matters rarely addressed within the academic apprenticeship. It is in this social apprenticeship that students learn how to navigate the all-important subtleties of context and networks, discovering for themselves how the various spheres of life actually work. The range of the apprenticeship is considerable. It begins with the transition from high school and the attendant complexities of establishing a more independent identity, including the practicalities of time management and daily tasks and chores as well as negotiating social relationships with peers and adults. It continues through a variety of campus-based activities including fraternities and sororities, athletics, and clubs. At its upper end looms the transition to work and adult life after graduation.

On most campuses, the social apprenticeship is presided over by a dean of students. It involves large numbers of certified professionals, usually distinct from the academic professionals composing the faculty. They include residential counselors; a separate campus counseling staff; chaplains and religious affairs staff; the athletic department; offices of career planning and placement; and the essential agencies that handle finances, food services, health care, and so forth.

Particularly on campuses with large residential populations and concentrations of traditional-age students, this organized social apprenticeship is where students develop the skills needed for success in the social and occupational world. For all their formative impact, however, these skills are usually of only tangential concern for academic personnel. It is equally exceptional for the student affairs professionals to involve themselves in the first apprenticeship in any substantive way. Small wonder students often experience their undergraduate lives as divided into compartments with little mutual influence.

Enabling Students to Make Sense of Their Learning

To understand how the social apprenticeship can enhance the college learning of the first apprenticeship, consider an innovative new course at the University of Texas at Austin entitled "The Major in the Workplace." Although not a PTEV enterprise and not concerned with the full range of purposes embodied in the third apprenticeship, it links the first apprenticeship with the second within the clearly delineated objective of succeeding in the job market. Developed and taught by Dr. Katharine Brooks of the career services office, "Major in the Workplace" teaches senior liberal arts majors to "articulate the value of what they are studying" by training them to analyze their academic experience in ways "that apply to the workplace."[17]

Brooks asks students to develop a "major map" in which they enumerate the intellectual skills and concepts they have learned in their major field of concentration. For example, students learn to describe their academic experience with a focus on skills learned and capacities demonstrated. On résumés, for example, students are encouraged to write not just "majored in English literature," but "learned to read, analyze, and summarize complex written texts." Students also learn to translate their academic experience into job-related skills, such as the ability to do specific kinds of research; develop conceptual, written, and verbal skills; or acquire mastery of interactive skills through internships or volunteer experiences.

As Brooks notes, this is for many seniors, astonishingly, "the first time they've ever focused on their education—what they've learned and how their majors have influenced their mind-sets, perceptions, and ways of thinking." The class gives students instruction and then practice in making sense of their four years of academic experience. What have been the most memorable courses, teachers, books, or experiences? By asking students to think, discuss, and write about this kind of question, Brooks's course utilizes some of the counseling skills typical of the social apprenticeship. Yet, by having students analyze how they responded to specific challenges in their educational experience, Brooks also enables them to explore themselves: discovering and documenting personal traits and interests that could be of value in giving them a distinctive profile as job applicants.

What this unusual course does, then, is bend the cognitive abilities of senior liberal arts majors toward a consciously reflective task. Students are encouraged to retrieve and reframe the learning they have undertaken in their respective majors, with the goal of understanding their education not simply as a set of tasks accomplished or credits earned, but as a series of formative experiences. That is, students learn to interrogate their own experience, asking essentially formative questions: How has this course, or that project or experience, influenced the way I perceive the world? How have they affected my ability to make sense of similar situations or problems? What abilities have I developed through those experiences?

Students describe the fields in which they majored as having provided them with specific "mind-sets." For example, sociology and anthropology majors might reframe their learning as the acquisition of analytical lenses offering special insight into how ethnicity, race, and gender affect hiring, workplace evaluation, and networking—skills useful for human resources, consulting, and public service work. Math and science majors might present their skills with handling complex data analysis as valuable to technology jobs in a variety of public and private institutions.

Katharine Brooks is thus teaching students how to conduct a reflective exploration of their investment of time and attention in their academic majors. This social apprenticeship course, in other words, supports a salient feature of liberal learning: self-reflection. The course is shaping

the stance students adopt toward their learning, making them less passive and more proactive in relating their conceptual expertise to the future
context of their lives and careers.

It should be emphasized that the students' retrieval, or reexamination, of the formative dimension of their individual learning trajectories
is undertaken within the course's imperative to consider "how that education applies to the workplace." True to the social apprenticeship's emphasis on individual differentiation and self-fashioning, the salient feature of
this course is personal utility. Students undertake self-inquiry not in order
to achieve the Socratic ideal of the examined life, but as a prerequisite for
career success.

This limitation of perspective diminishes the larger value inherent
in reflecting critically upon one's own formation. The diverse goals of
the undergraduate major fields, and the students who enter them, are
reduced to the single aim of career utility—the competitive differentiation
of the student from other students and job seekers. There is no room in
the course for students to explore how their own formative experiences
might complement those of their peers, or how those experiences, shared
through engagement with larger, common purposes, might serve the
common good. In other words, the student's consideration of her acquisition of career-relevant skills—the story she tells about who she is and how
she got there—never develops into a full-fledged vocational narrative.

This is where the third apprenticeship—the apprenticeship of identity
and purpose—comes in. As will become clear in the next section, the
PTEV and other programs working from the third apprenticeship often
provide students with cognitive tools similar to those of "The Major in
the Workplace." Yet in addition to helping students gain more insight into
their formative educational experiences and possible future careers, these
programs frame the students' growing individuation against a much
larger horizon.

Strategy Three: Integrating through the Apprenticeship of Identity and Purpose

Educating the whole student takes more than simply adding the practi-
cality of the second apprenticeship to the cognitive growth of the first.
The tradition of liberal learning also demands that students be educated toward a sense of purpose. Education grounded in the third

apprenticeship incorporates and builds upon both academic learning and the enhancement of students' life skills. It treats personal—and ultimately professional—identity not as a given but as a hard-won achievement, one directly dependent on the student's development of life purpose or, in the language of the PTEV, sense of vocation. The best way to understand the impact of the third apprenticeship on liberal education is to examine how it played out in a particular course on a particular PTEV campus: the Senior Business Keystone course at Augsburg College in Minneapolis, Minnesota.

The Third Apprenticeship in Action: Augsburg College's Senior Business Keystone

Augsburg is located close to downtown Minneapolis, amid the city's large Somali immigrant community. Roughly half of its 4000 students are of traditional college age, enrolled in undergraduate day programs. Of the remaining 2000 students, half attend undergraduate courses during evenings and weekends, with the rest enrolled in graduate programs. Women make up half the "traditional" student body; one-fifth are students of color. A quarter of these students identify as Lutheran. Most of the evening and weekend undergraduate students are women somewhat older than traditional age; like the day programs, the evening programs include courses addressing the theme of vocation.[18]

Augsburg embraced the Lilly Endowment's Program for the Theological Exploration of Vocation by infusing the theme of vocation across a wide spectrum of campus activities: in the curriculum, in student life, in the college's involvements with the surrounding community of Minneapolis, and in the way it portrays itself to prospective students and to alumni. Augsburg's vocation program, "Embracing Our Gifts," builds on the work of Augsburg's former president, William Frame, as well as the current president, Paul C. Pribbenow. Thomas Morgan, a professor in the Religion Department who has worked with the program since the beginning, describes its key message to students as an admonition: "You need to recognize—and to nurture—your giftedness. And now you must do something with those gifts."

The prominence of the Embracing Our Gifts program ensures that all Augsburg undergraduates recognize what they sometimes call the "V-word," for vocation. Students take two courses in the Religion Department that explore the Lutheran heritage of the College while also learning about other religious traditions, including Islam as practiced by many of Augsburg's neighbors. Significantly, these courses also emphasize reflection on the students' own values, interests, and religious beliefs in relation to the Lutheran tradition of discerning personal vocation.

Along with Liberal Arts Foundations, a distribution requirement of courses in the humanities, arts, and social and natural sciences, students are required to take the "Augsburg Experience." This program offers students an opportunity to "apply their academic study to the broader community" through study abroad, community service-learning, research with a professor, or an off-campus immersion project. "Engaging Minneapolis," for example, is an experiential learning course on Minneapolis's diverse urban community in which students work with local organizations to address ongoing community needs and later reflect on their experiences using a number of intellectual disciplines. Finally, in the senior year, students take a Senior Keystone designed "to help students identify their professional skills, vocation, goals, and gifts in order to transition to their lives after college."[19]

Among these Senior Keystones, perhaps the most remarkable is that taken by business majors. As for so many other American institutions of higher education, the most popular field of study at Augsburg is business. What sets Augsburg apart is that business majors spend much of their final year enrolled in not one, but two courses designed to consolidate and integrate their learning. One is a "capstone" course, taught by faculty from the various business specialties of accounting, finance, management, and marketing. Like an increasing number of such courses nationwide, this capstone helps students bring together the various strands of their major field in one synthetic experience.

It is with the Senior Business Keystone, however, that Augsburg truly makes its mark. Entitled "Vocation and the Meaning of Success," the Senior Business Keystone is an intentionally interdisciplinary course taught by faculty from both the religion and business departments. It focuses not simply on consolidating students' knowledge of business as a discipline, but on fostering their ability to use that knowledge in pursuit of a life lived with social purpose. Martha Stortz, a religion professor who teaches in the Keystone, characterized it as "a summative course in the Augsburg experience"—an experience strongly inflected by the theme of vocation as interpreted through Augsburg's Lutheran heritage.

"Vocation and the Meaning of Success" is a direct outgrowth of the initiative and remains a pedagogical experiment under development.

Business majors evinced some initial skepticism about the course's goals; many of them felt overwhelmed by the sheer scale and complexity of the questions implied by the vocation theme. As Mark Tranvik, another veteran faculty leader in the Embracing Our Gifts program, put it, "The course asks three large questions of students: Who are you? What is your sense of mission? What are you going to do with your knowledge?" Participating faculty also note that first-generation college students elect business as their major in numbers well in excess of their proportion in the student body. These students approach college as a key step toward improving their circumstances in life. Because they, and often their parents, are focused on achieving economic success, they are naturally wary of questions that might fracture their attention from pursuit of this goal.

The response of the Business Keystone faculty has been to link the large and potentially threatening vocational questions with knowledge and skills of immediate practical value for the next step in the students' careers, especially the immediate need to search for post-college jobs. The seniors who enter the course have become accustomed to approaching business enterprises with a set of analytical questions. They have learned how to inquire into a business organization's purpose, its strengths and assets, and its debts. They also inquire into its potential areas of growth, and can strategize about how the organization might achieve this growth. The Keystone seeks to connect these habits of mind with larger questions of what it means to lead a purpose-driven life or a life of service to others.

Students in all sections of the course read passages from the Bible designed to establish a common frame of values derived from Augsburg Lutheran tradition. Within the context of this tradition, students take stock of the choices and challenges that face them at this "important point of transition in their lives as [they] prepare to move from college to the world of work and career."[20]

Throughout the course, students read a variety of texts presenting different ethical reflections on careers in business and the role of business in society, among them Jack Fortin's *A Centered Life*. An instructor in the Business Keystone and a member of the Augsburg Religion Department, Fortin argues that when one lives a centered or faithful life, one becomes "awake to God's presence; lives one's faith in all situations; contributes one's unique gifts to the world; and belongs to a community of faith that is nurturing and supportive"—a restatement of the central tenets of the Embracing Our Gifts program.

The Senior Business Keystone, like the other Senior Keystone courses, follows what Jacqueline de Vries, a professor of history who heads the vocational aspects of the general Keystone curriculum and teaches in the Senior History Keystone, describes as a clear narrative structure. Students are asked to look backward, analyzing and interpreting their college experience with an enriched understanding of their gifts and interests. Yet the course also leads to forward-looking reflections, including a statement of vocational purpose designed to promote thinking about "the meaning of success" in the context of a whole life. Most importantly, perhaps, the course translates the big questions about identity, purpose, and possible commitments into a series of more manageable steps, each with specific tasks to be accomplished.

For example, all sections of the Keystone require students to complete personal inventories of their strengths and interests, while reflecting on the occupational implications of those inventories. The dual nature of the exercise is a deliberate effort by the faculty to assure students of their strengths even as they are confronted by the challenges of mission and calling. Students are also required to develop electronic portfolios in which they list the courses they have taken and how they believe their major (business in this case) and particular professors or peers have affected their ways of seeing and responding to things. These portfolios provide a connecting thread through the semester, as students incorporate what they have learned about their own capacities and interests in their personal inventories. Exercises devoted to résumé writing and interviewing strategies maintain links between the larger themes of vocation and faith and the immediate needs of seniors facing decisions about work.

In the second half of the semester, the emphasis shifts from inventory of the past to contemplation of the future. Students read and work together on case studies, a proven pedagogy borrowed from the business curriculum. These cases involve the students in analyzing a series of contemporary business challenges with important ethical and public dimensions. Students must analyze how different stakeholders—a company's shareholders, workers and their families, communities in which the business functions, and governments—are likely to interpret and respond to a given scenario. They must then research various possible solutions to the challenges presented by the scenario, finally arguing for a course of action that maximizes benefit to all the stakeholders involved.

In this part of the course, students draw on readings about the personal meaning of success and the role of business in society in order to discuss the business professionals they admire, the values these figures embody, and, finally, the business people they aspire to become. Instructors assess each student's written analysis of the case studies as they would any other piece of academic writing, so as to promote what Mark Tanvik calls "academic rigor—while also involving the whole self, values and all." As an added benefit, students can later present the written analysis to prospective employers as evidence of their ability to handle complex and challenging problems in contemporary business from more than a purely technical perspective.

In some sections of the Senior Business Keystone, students are required to use the analytical tools they have developed in their business courses in order to "read" organizations from an ethical as well as strategic point of view. As Martha Stortz put it, this approach helps students prepare directly for "where they will be going occupationally ... it is a way of 'applying' conceptual tools vital for living an ethically aware life." Students subject every business they encounter, including prospective employers, to both strategic analysis and to questions concerning the business's code of ethics or statement of values, and how those values are exemplified—or not—by the firm's performance. A study of this kind naturally prompts the student to think about the "fit" between a particular employer or occupation and her own developing sense of identity and purpose. The exercise also ties the broad, humanistic questions of personal identity and mission directly to the challenges students face in the present and near future, providing a depth of perspective otherwise missing from this important "moment of transition."

In the Senior Business Keystone, vocation turns out to be a live issue that mediates this back-and-forth between the students' present concerns, on the one hand, and the "big questions" of the humanities, on the other. According to Mark Tranvik, "Vocation is a topic that creates a lot of energy. It builds community, even without agreement about matters of religious faith or meaning ... because the topic elicits the sharing of personal experience. People recognize one another as like themselves in seeking to live a life that matters."

If vocation at Augsburg generates educational energy among students, it also affects many participating faculty in the same way. Jacqueline de Vries notes how involvement in this kind of teaching has changed the way she relates to her students. "As a new PhD, when I first started teaching," she confides, "I now realize that I often tacitly saw students mainly as brains ... [I was] looking at classes as sources of future historians who could clearly write at the graduate level." While de Vries still looks for future historians in her classes, she says, "I can now see better the students' other gifts, for example their ability to organize groups or to see the value of historical concepts for actual situations with which they are struggling in the present. Maturity is the important emergent value that we see manifested by students in these courses." The Keystone is still in its early stages of development at Augsburg, but it appears to have already become for students and faculty alike an important educational experience grounded in the third apprenticeship of identity and purpose.

Making the Discovery of Purpose More Deliberate

The use of this apprenticeship of identity and purpose to pull together and give depth to the first two apprenticeships is the essence of the PTEV's strategy for revitalizing undergraduate education. The key focus of this strategy is teaching students to discern a vocation in life, a sense of meaning that encompasses occupation but extends more broadly into all the dimensions of a life worth living.

In his summary of the findings of recent research on young adults, William Damon describes a quality essential to their well-being: "a stable and generalized intention to accomplish something that is at the same time meaningful to the self and consequential for the world beyond the self."[21] This quality is very close to what the PTEV programs like that at Augsburg mean by the term "vocation." Research has shown that young people who develop this intention show markedly positive attitudes toward learning, a result of the exhilaration and satisfaction that a sense of purpose causes. Purpose animates academic life "by bringing people out of themselves" and helping students become "fascinated by the work or the problem at hand," thus opening the way toward "a life that combines forward movement with stability." These turn out to be the key traits underlying "resilience" in both youth and adults.[22]

Programs grounded in the third apprenticeship emphasize student involvement with projects and goals that point beyond the self. Life purposes are not understood to be "outlets" for preexisting energy or desires. Instead, purposes that incorporate yet transcend the individual develop and expand the sense of self by extending what is of value and concern to the person into the world around her. That is, while life purposes, habits, and relationships include and build upon preexisting personal traits and inclinations, these involvements come to enlarge and constitute new parts of the person's emerging identity. They are sources of genuine growth into new understanding, desires, and capacities. Through her involvement with goals consequential to others as well as herself, the individual achieves an identity impossible without commitment to those larger goals. Seen from this developmental perspective, the academic apprenticeship gains added importance: it provides the understanding and critical testing of the "world" within which particular purposes can make sense.

Purposes beyond the self also draw the individual into relationships and deeper cooperation with others. In order to develop purpose, an individual must recognize and develop trust in others who, because of their shared purpose, become significant to that individual. Achieving a new, expanded sense of self requires recognition from others that one is actually enacting the goals and aims one wishes to espouse. Interpersonal recognition thus plays a role like the feedback and support of deliberate learning processes. By becoming a responsible member of a community centered and connected through a shared purpose, the individual achieves a dignity attainable in no other way.

Enjoying the expanded sense of efficacy that growth into purpose makes possible is achieved through participation in organized practices, institutions, and social projects. As the example of Augsburg's Senior Business Keystone reveals, identity can develop in a variety of purposeful communities. Professional work and organizations, voluntary groups engaged in civic and public life, and communities committed to the cultivation of spiritual capacities and values all provide opportunities for vocational exploration. Achieving a meaningful identity typically involves exploration of some of these ways of living and finally literal apprenticeship in one or more educational experiences that connect undergraduate learning with the larger trajectory of career and life.

When they talked about how the process of vocational exploration unfolded in their lives, both faculty and students in the PTEV emphasized the importance of "reflection." By this they meant particular activities such as reading, seeking insight from others, or thinking over the challenges and outcomes of one's life experience in relation to valued models. But reflection is also a central value of liberal education. Katherine Brooks provided a form of reflection that students found useful in clarifying the significance of their own educational experiences for their occupational futures. Examples of courses like "The Major in the Workplace" and the Senior Business Keystone only begin to suggest the potential of the intentional cultivation of reflective practices for enhancing student learning in the context of vocational exploration. In the following chapter, we will examine some of the ways in which reflection figured in the PTEV and how the practice of reflection functioned when connected to discernment of vocational purpose—for both students and educators.

3

The Examined Life

REFLECTION AND PRACTICAL WISDOM

WHAT DIFFERENCE MIGHT it make, for learning about purpose, when educators speak of students as "driven," as contrasted with being "called?" Today's academy seems more comfortable speaking of how various things "drive" student motivation to produce learning outcomes than of students discerning and responding to their sense of being called to particular purposes. Yet, drive and calling are not just descriptions of the same thing. The two terms are actually metaphors that structure thinking more than they simply report an objective reality. Metaphors such as drive or calling at once reveal and highlight some aspects of experience while they conceal others.[1] They give rise to different postures toward learning and life.

The metaphor of drive structures thinking by highlighting those aspects of our experience in which we feel ourselves impelled to act in a certain way, virtually automatically. Our attention seems directed by forces deeper than our consciousness but within us. The drive metaphor draws attention toward both our "passions" and what they move us toward, including how most effectively to obtain these things. In this perspective, then, ideas are instruments, tools for attaining our desires. It is a metaphorical posture that promotes skepticism about the ideas, and especially the ideals, put forth by others, since they are judged as likely to be mere rationalizations of their originators' underlying drives or interests.

In contrast, call has a different metaphorical resonance. It focuses our attention outward, toward the larger world of relationships and connections. The metaphor of call highlights precisely what is neglected by the drive metaphor: our experience of living with others within a context characterized by values and relationships that attract us or to which we feel drawn to respond. This perspective also elicits reflection, but in a different posture. By inclining us to place ourselves imaginatively within a set of larger relationships, the metaphor of call prompts questions about the significance of the individual's desires as well as their value for a life within this larger environment.

From much repetition, these metaphorical ways of talking about student motivation may come to seem natural. In any case, they are rarely seen as metaphors. It is their apparent naturalness that enables such metaphors to play an important, if often unobserved, role in determining how educators come to think as well as how conceptions of educational development are shaped. So, while educators seem almost universally to endorse the promotion of student "reflection" as an important goal of college learning, the meaning of the term, and the nature of the practices through which reflection is taught, are likely to vary depending upon which metaphor is shaping a particular educational approach.

Reflection, as its etymology suggests, describes a "bending back" by the learner to notice that learning has taken place and take stock of what has been learned. Reflection adds a dimension of self-awareness to the learning activity taking place. Reflective learning, then, means that rather than just mastering the skill or subject matter, the learner can also monitor performance, making it possible to improve performance through incorporating feedback. Progress in reflection is marked by the learner's increasing self-awareness of the process itself, making further learning more efficient and effective. Like other habits of mind, reflection is a skill that can be modeled, taught, and consciously developed through a process that resembles developing expertise in any field. Like musicians or athletes, students can learn to notice the factors in their practice that make for more or less successful performances, shaping their habits to emphasize the more effective activities. As a process of learning, reflection means acquiring skills in discerning the import of situations and their demands, while using experience to hone more effective strategies for meeting them. A reflective posture lays the groundwork for expanding self-awareness toward directing one's own learning, a consistent goal of liberal education.[2]

Reflection can serve different ends. Here is where the structuring metaphors guiding the educational process become important. The drive metaphor is likely to lead toward the weaving of reflection into learning to think well strategically or instrumentally, suiting means efficiently to ends. Such reflection promotes self-awareness and suppleness in consolidating and organizing knowledge to achieve a goal. However, when the focus is on the underlying drive and its satisfaction, the purposes themselves are not likely to become objects of critical scrutiny. Such a reflective posture, however, can offer valuable protection against being taken in by illusory or deliberately misleading goals and ideals. This defensive posture has given rise to sophisticated intellectual techniques, a range of practices of unmasking or "debunking" that have been prominent in recent decades in the "postmodern" turn of humanistic scholarship.[3]

It is possible to grant the value of practicing reflection for self-protection and enhancing autonomy and yet recognize that these are not the only values that reflection can serve. The metaphor of call brings to attention the way in which practices of reflection can also promote self-awareness of living within a larger life. If the drive-language suggests forces that "push" from within and below, the call metaphor emphasizes "attraction" from without and above. It encourages enlisting reflection to open up the apparently automatic quality of our desires and aversions. By shifting the direction of attention, the metaphor of call highlights the peculiarity of human motives. Unlike simple reflexes, motives always contain an element of meaning, a reference to a shared world of significant interaction. Motives include, in other words, an element of openness beyond the given, an ideal. Understood this way, practices of reflection create a freedom from immediate compulsion that allows for conscious forming of habit and the development of purpose. For liberal education, this means that the cultivation of empathy becomes possible and important.[4] It is this openness to reflective awareness and empathy that the metaphor of call opens up.

While both metaphors highlight important features of human development, the logical relationship between the two metaphors is not reciprocal. The language of calling can include and draw upon those aspects of experience that are evoked by talk of drives. As we saw in the last chapter, Josiah Royce's idea of loyalty employed just this twofold structure of practical reasoning. Royce argued that finding a cause, or calling, must utilize and include the individual's inner passions. But these drives, however they arise, only become meaningful and contribute value to a life when they are interpreted, and therefore to some degree transformed, from the standpoint of engagement in a socially shared purpose. But the reverse is not true. This is because the contextual referents of the calling metaphor give it a logical priority over drive-language. Significance arises from context and interaction within a context. The metaphor of drive abstracts impulses from their context of significance. But as the practice of psychotherapy shows, drives can only be understood on analogy to judgments concerning the value to the self of particular objects, persons, contexts, and purposes. The metaphor of call serves as a reminder of this potentially open horizon within which we as individuals assert our desires and give direction to our interests.

The metaphor of call, unlike the self-contained language of drive and passion, implies that motives are not self-interpreting. Rather, understanding one's, or another's motives, requires serious reflection about our relationships and the world that we inhabit. Reflection therefore need not remain limited to the strategic aim of achieving preset goals. It can logically expand to include investigation of one's life situation, and indeed of the larger world, exactly the goals of liberal education. One value of speaking about purpose as finding a call is that the metaphor throws into relief the dependence of individual orientation upon networks of communication and the sharing of the perspectives of others. And indeed, for the tradition of liberal education, the metaphor of calling has been a preeminent way to understand what motivates human growth.

As Elaine Scarry has reminded us, for classical Greek thinkers, it was especially beauty that called human beings into self-reflection and ethical development.[5] Plato famously presented his philosophy in dramatic images of life as the quest for significant unity, patterns of living that could provide motivation and analogies for reflection on both individual and social living. The call of beauty is perhaps most eloquently described in Plato's fable of the charioteer in his dialogue, *Phaedrus*. There the growth of the human personality is analogized to the struggle of an aspiring chariot racer to blend into a cooperative team two initially opposed horses. One horse is pure drive, aiming only at its own immediate gratification. Its very different companion horse aspires toward something higher. It seeks to participate in the larger life of the race, finding fulfillment through succeeding in this participation.

In the dialogue, Plato has Socrates explain that although each aspiring charioteer wants to yoke these steeds into a winning team, this can only happen through an encounter with a divine example reflected in a person living an integrated life. Such encounters are mediated through specific human relationships, catalyzed by mutual intimations of the call of beauty. These relationships, when rightly ordered, propel the developing charioteer upward toward imitating the life of the gods, sharing the majestic vision of cosmic harmony. Such education brings the charioteer to a new self-awareness, open to examining life from a higher vantage point. The charioteer now recognizes beauty, the intimate attunement of each part with the social and cosmic whole, as the real fulfillment of desire but also discovers that this attunement with the whole must be sought anew in each new race, so to speak, as life unfolds.

The campus' vocation programs provided analogies to Plato's philosophical image of the quest for meaningful and integrated living. These images gathered communities in the various campus programs to reflect on the purpose of liberal learning, and also the purpose of living. Focused on the metaphor of call, and stimulated by the terms in which the Program for the Theological Exploration of Vocation was articulated, the participating institutions heightened, or rediscovered, ways their religious heritage had spoken about education's purpose as finding one's calling. While rooted in the specific religious traditions of the individual institutions, participants found that reflection on calling, once its larger significance was understood, could also become important for students and staff not part of those traditions.

The language of calling came easily to some of the programs in the initiative. For other institutions, it was a matter of new awareness of an almost forgotten language. And many were somewhere in-between. But by bringing vocation into their educational discourse in new or renewed ways, all the PTEV schools found themselves engaged in teaching their students reflection. They all came to realize that discovery of vocation is a work of engaged human investigation, a form of discernment. Such discernment is a cognitively complex, interpretive skill, a practice of reflection directed toward discovering and understanding one's calling. The various campus experiments with devising ways to teach this skill and to support students—as well as faculty and staff—in learning to practice it, constitute one of the PTEV's most important contributions to the renewal of liberal education. Providing systematic opportunities for reflection on the theme of calling has dramatically positive effects on students' engagement with their own learning.[6]

Among the PTEV schools visited, each style of reflective practice derived from the circumstances and resources of a particular campus and campus personnel. Not so much templates as context-specific examples, they provide illuminating cases of how the metaphor of calling was able to spark and sustain growth in reflective awareness. This chapter and the next will present a spectrum of the practices of reflection used by PTEV programs that allowed students to make sense of their lives through the language of calling. While the following chapter will focus on campuses that were able to build on practices of discernment found in their religious traditions, the two cases that follow, Butler University and Macalester College, are remarkable because they developed powerful forms of vocational reflection in contexts that lacked organized efforts to give educational prominence to reflection on calling.

Reflecting on Vocation through the Great Books
at Butler University

Speaking about the way he had undergone a dramatic shift in perspective while at Butler University, a student described his inauspicious freshman starting point. "I didn't like Butler," Quinn emphasized, "I didn't like Indianapolis. I was going to transfer. I was down in the dumps. It was February." He went on to say that "there were also other more substantial things going on. Important people in my life had died that semester. I was feeling kind of depressed. I really wanted to get out of here." Now a senior, he ascribed the beginning of his turnaround to his freshman honors seminar, "Faith, Doubt, and Reason." This was a two-semester course offered as part of the range of freshman seminars among which all beginning students must choose. For Quinn, the reason this course made a personal difference was the combination of challenging reading and writing assignments; interesting out-of-class experiences such as the ballet; and the motivating force of the instructor, Paul Valliere of the Philosophy and Religion Department.

During his year taking Faith, Doubt, and Reason, Quinn found Dostoyevsky's *Crime and Punishment* and the questions that the instructor posed about the text especially provocative. He found himself thinking more about how his reading and issues brought out in class discussions might apply to his own struggles. Later in the year, when he found himself moved by reading Hermann Hesse's *Siddhartha* on his own, he e-mailed Paul Valliere. The response was, "'Come on, let's go get tea or coffee and talk about it.' And we did." Quinn noted that his instructor "does that all the time." This openness on the part of faculty to student concerns seems a feature of the Butler campus, though one the PTEV has accentuated and developed. So, beyond this class, Quinn also found himself, like some of his classmates, visiting the Center for Faith and Vocation, the location of Butler's PTEV program. Here he encountered small "introverted groups," led by staff of the Center such as the director, Judith Cebula; and

Charles Allen, an Episcopal campus minister at Butler. In these groups, students could explore their doubts and questions about faith and purpose in an interfaith setting. "At that particular time, where I didn't want to be pushed or called or pulled," Quinn noted, an unpressured yet sympathetic space to gain some perspective on his situation was important for him. He stayed at Butler, where he underwent a subtle shift over several years, from feeling untethered to being able to articulate his values, faith, and vocation, using a semester abroad and a scholarship to study agricultural development in India, to solidify his decision to pursue, after service with the Peace Corps, graduate work in South Asian studies.

These opportunities for reflection were complemented by other activities of the Center for Faith and Vocation, such as service learning projects in which students were asked to think critically about the significance of their experiences working in the larger Indianapolis community. Kala, one of Quinn's fellow students, noted that these activities were not "like the typical service projects that I used to do at my church. Here, there's a self critique going on." In those situations, she had engaged in the work and then those around her talked about the work as "now we're all better people for doing it." In comparing such experiences with those that she had at the Center for Faith and Vocation, Kala drew on her reading of *Don Quixote* in Faith, Doubt, and Reason, to illustrate her realization that it was important to reflect critically even on one's good intentions.

It is noteworthy that other students also moved back and forth between their reflective experiences at the Center for Faith and Vocation and the more strictly "academic" practices in their courses. One sophomore Pharmacy major asserted that his involvement in the Center for Faith and Vocation and his participation in Valliere's freshman courses have led him to understand his learning in a deeper way than do most of his peers in the School of Pharmacy. The student notes that most of his peers see liberal arts courses "as a weight on their shoulders—'Why put extra burdens on yourself,' they say," and as not relevant to their major. But this student found that Faith, Doubt, and Reason, gave him a start toward discovering that liberal education "actually reinforces and enlarges my life experiences." He has been pleased to find that the liberal arts open him "to a wide, wide range of ideas."

The results have shown up in both the academic and the personal realm: "Taking Renaissance literature or a course on faith gives me something more than the value of the class work," the student remarked. "When life is bogged down, you can get started again by stepping back and asking 'Why am I doing this?' or 'What's the larger picture here?' " He notes that to the majority of his Pharmacy classmates, courses are "mostly about getting the skills necessary for the job I'm pursuing." By contrast, this student's position is that, "I'm interested in getting those skills still, but I'm also interested in developing knowledge of other cultures ... I'm finding that I'm more willing to connect with others' beliefs. For instance, my World Religions course has given me an interest in Buddhism, which growing up as Roman Catholic I knew little about."

In fact, Butler is visibly pluralistic in religious possibilities. While Butler severed its ties to the Disciples of Christ in the late 1970s, today it hosts an Episcopal-Lutheran campus ministry staffed by an Episcopal priest, a Catholic priest overseeing a reconstituted Catholic fellowship, a Campus Crusade staff ministering to evangelicals, as well as a flourishing Hillel chapter advised by a local rabbi and an Islamic student group with a faculty advisor. This climate of receptiveness to religious questions and openness to traditions of varying kinds has been strengthened by the PTEV program, but its impetus has come from the leadership of the university's president, Dr. Bobby Fong, through the first decade of the century. Explaining his position, Fong notes that while "rationality may chart cause and effect, it does not exhaust meaning. Epistemologists have suggested that what and how we know are premised on assumptions of what we imagine our world and ourselves to be. There is no value-free inquiry because values necessarily underlie inquiry." Therefore, Fong welcomed the Lilly Endowment's initiative on vocation as a way to make good, in a pluralistic environment, what he believes to be the academy's responsibility to respond to universal longings for a better world. He made raising an endowment for the Center for Faith and Vocation a university priority. This is because Fong thinks that universities need to find "ways to speak authoritatively and constructively to issues of citizenship, service, leadership, and character without imposing a single model of morality ... to provide space to engender not only habits of the mind, but also, in de Tocqueville's famous phrase, habits of the heart which will enable students not only to make a living but also to make lives that are personally fulfilling precisely because they are implicated in the well-being of others."[7]

At Butler, growing support for pursuing questions of meaning is interwoven with the success of the Center for Faith and Vocation. In addition to the small-group student reflection activities already noted, the Center presents an annual series of four lectures on the theme, "Religion and

World Civilization," for which students can receive academic credit if they take an accompanying seminar. It has also sponsored short retreat programs for faculty and staff, as well as a year-long Faculty and Staff Workshop on Faith and Vocation, open to 12 faculty and staff participants. For over half a decade, this seminar, led by a committee of faculty and staff under the direction of Judith Cebula, has enabled nearly 100 participants to explore and reflect together upon their own sense of calling, "to be in this profession ... in this place rather than another, at this time." The workshop has engaged with approaches to fostering dialogues about purpose and values beyond as well as within the university setting, working with the Project on Civic Reflection of Valparaiso University, another PTEV campus. The spillover effects have, according to Cebula, been felt in a variety of campus sectors: in service learning courses, in student advising, in the greater ease faculty and student services staff have developed in working together, above all in making it easier for both faculty and staff to talk with students about issues of their values and their futures. The Center's emphasis upon reflection, then, has spread beyond students into Butler's staff in far-reaching ways.

This larger PTEV-instigated movement toward inclusion of attention to these themes in students' development has provided an opening for courses like Faith, Doubt, and Reason or World Religions to become parts of the core curriculum. Paul Valliere described his course as "about three things: big questions, great books, and basic skills such as critical thinking, good writing, and oral communication abilities." He went on to say that "it's an opportunity for beginning students to think very broadly about large moral, philosophical, and religious questions and how these relate to their lives." Over two semesters, students who elect the course focus first on questions of self and identity and then, in the second semester, on issues of justice and society. The "great books" are drawn from the Graeco-Roman and biblical sources, along with modern works such as those the students found so significant for thinking about their own situations. As Valliere described his pedagogical purpose, "This is something that is good for people to do when they are trying to figure out what they are going to do with their lives."

A typical class might begin with Valliere asking students how that day's reading has affected them, proceeding to the more analytical question of how it is like and unlike other works on that theme that they have read. Listening to student responses and their observations, Valliere moves the class to review analytically how the author has produced the effects they have felt by means of organization of the text, including its genre and rhetorical style, placing these considerations within the work's historical and cultural context. All this, however, culminates in questions designed to provoke students to self-reflection on how the reading might apply in their own lives. These are often questions about personal reception—or resistance: What is the point, the moral of this? What did you enjoy—or dislike—about reading it? Why was that? In these ways, students learn the basic practices of textual analysis and interpretation: the ability to make sense of complex writing; a skill in explicating its meaning; but also practice in learning how the text might apply to actual life situations.[8] To these ends, students are required to produce written analyses of the works, often comparing and contrasting several disparate works, even disparate traditions, such as Plato's compared to the biblical accounts of justice. Students do some of their work in small tutorial groups, supplemented by online communication and discussion. Valliere is unapologetic in hoping that students leave the course with a "love of the classics." But the course is structured to highlight the potential of these works and authors as cultural resources for enabling better comprehension of self and world.

Valliere brought this approach directly from the core program at Columbia University in which he taught as a beginning instructor. There, nearly a century ago, John Erskine developed the first such "great books" course to introduce students to "the masterpieces in literature, poetry, history, philosophy, and in science." His expressed aim was to counter the specialization already dominant in Columbia's curriculum with a vision of intellectual unity and common values. By doing so, Erskine believed he could "moderate students' 'egotism' and broaden their sympathies."[9] The Columbia program was picking up threads that had already been spun at the end of the 19th century by Harvard Professor Charles Eliot Norton, one of the first educators to use the term "humanities" to refer to the disciplines that Erskine would later invite into the great books curriculum.

At Harvard in the 1890s, Norton introduced an enormously popular course that provided the first curricular effort to employ a historical sweep of the evolution of knowledge and culture as a way to orient students' intellectual and moral growth in college. While providing this synthetic picture of what would later be called "Western Civilization," Norton insisted to his fellow instructors that they should keep in the forefront of instruction "the relation to actual life and conduct" of what the course proposed for students' consideration.[10] Butler's renewed curricular experiments with these concerns are thus direct descendants of those earlier efforts to develop a form of liberal learning appropriate for the challenges of modern life. At a time when, in a vastly enlarged higher education sector, the twin threats Norton perceived to liberal education—disciplinary specialization and the trump of immediate marketability—continue to haunt the enterprise, the PTEV's emphasis on the third apprenticeship of identity and purpose has given new life to the first apprenticeship of liberal learning.

They talk at Butler about the "two doors" that the vocation initiative has provided to encourage students to engage with questions about their lives and their futures. One is the "faith door," meaning the greater visibility and legitimacy of religious questions in the formal organization of the university. Before the PTEV, as one staff member put it, there was "this huge elephant in the room that no one wanted to talk about." That unspoken presence was student interest and concerns about religion. It is no longer necessary for students to leave the campus or turn to outside organizations to seriously explore religious concerns. The other door is "the career door." As more integration between academic and students' life concerns has developed, students are increasingly provided the tools, the context, and the encouragement to think deeply about work and career. Through structured experiences of reflection, students are better able to relate these concerns realistically to their developing sense of personal and social identity. In sum, by giving renewed importance to exploring identity and purpose in relation to calling, the PTEV has sparked a renewal of liberal learning as a development of the whole student.

Macalester College: Where Vocational Reflection Intersects Secularity

A selective, liberal arts institution in St. Paul, Minnesota, Macalester College's participation in the PTEV coincided with its internal reevaluation of the place of religion on campus. In this way, it was like Butler University. But the shape of the Macalester program evolved differently, engaging a smaller number of students but in an intensive program of activity and reflection over their undergraduate years. The two themes of the project were "Vocation and Ethical Leadership." Macalester is affiliated with the Presbyterian Church (U.S.A.), but the spirit of its campus is in many respects self-consciously secular, particularly regarding the content of its demanding academic program. While seeking participation in the PTEV, Macalester's president, Michael McPherson, also undertook a reorganization of its chaplaincy. Indeed, a number of important changes concurred with Macalester receiving a sustaining grant. The chapel program became the Center for Religious and Spiritual Life (CRSL) and the college chaplain added Associate Dean of Religious and Spiritual Life to her title. What became known as the "Lilly Project" was placed under the newly formed Institute for Global Citizenship, which houses the Civic Engagement Center (CEC), allowing these organizations to deepen a history of collaboration.

The vocation project began in both the curricular and co-curricular but especially flourished in the co-curricular. That is, it was rooted in the second apprenticeship among those campus agencies also concerned with third apprenticeship themes of purpose and identity: the chaplaincy, the placement of Macalester students through the Center for Religious and Spiritual Life, and, later, the Institute for Global Citizenship. Nevertheless, over time the project had significant effects on the environment of learning at the college, not least in the expansion of communication between academic learning and other aspects of student and faculty lives. With its strong academic programs, Macalester faculty have identified with their disciplines and encouraged students to do so. In most fields, this has meant a concentration upon learning theoretical knowledge and conceptual skills as defined and emphasized by that discipline. Although Macalester students enjoy a reputation for being less competitive, more mutually supportive, and more concerned with service to the world than many of their peers in similar institutions, academic culture at Macalester has also been described as overshadowing concerns about the meaning and purpose of learning. Students talk of a campus culture that tends toward "analysis to the point of paralysis." Certainly, all agree that while the ethical dimension of problems and disciplines receive attention in classes, religious concerns and motivations that cannot be described in wholly secular language have rarely been topics of emphasis.

In this context, the directors of the vocation project focused upon providing a variety of ways in which students could join with staff and peers to reflect upon the significance of their college experience. They chose three key transitional points to build the program around: moving from high school to college; preparing to leave Macalester for career or more study; and the initial year after graduation. These are matters of great importance to students. Administrators at Macalester believe that the project's emphasis upon vocational reflection has made a difference in campus culture. Provost Kathleen Murray notes that the project's injection of opportunities to reflect on life "after Mac" has made it easier for faculty and staff to "think with students about these issues." Along with help in learning how to recover from failure and reset goals, vice president for student affairs Laurie Hamre thinks that the vocation project has given students enlarged capacities for linking long-term goals to their daily affairs.

The project enabled students to take part in a year-long, first-year group experience called "Lives of Commitment." There, freshman explored the issues of meaning and purpose by reflecting with staff on their experience in projects of social service. Sophomore alumni of the program served as group leaders, adding a note of continuity and helping provide freshmen with perspective. As seniors, many of these students, joined by others, elected to take part in the "Lilly Senior Keystone," which is described as offering a year-long, small-group "conversation that can hold your many identities and experiences all in place" while providing "a space that will engage the anxiety of transition [from college to work or professional school] as an opportunity to discover the fullness of self." In addition, students could be a part of a summer program called Lilly Summer Fellows, a group living experience of intensive reflection on vocation. This opportunity is available to rising juniors and seniors.

The focus on transitional moments seems an effective approach. So does allowing students to enter the stream at various points. As one student remarked, while he thought of himself as way too "cool" as a freshman to get involved, after hearing from students who had taken part in "Lives of Commitment" about the insights into themselves and the evident sense of community they continued to enjoy, he eventually signed up for the "Lilly Senior Keystone." He found that it opened up a deeper perspective for reflecting on what to do with his academic skills by providing in the midst of conflicting pressures a "centering" point around which to plot a path toward post-college life that fit with his ethical commitments. As this testimony suggests, much of the emphasis in the program is on helping students confront personal and practical issues of who they want to become, what challenges they face, what capacities they can nurture, and what they find especially compelling. It is noteworthy that one result of the project has been a substantial increase in the number of Macalester graduates who have gone on to study for the professional ministry and other kinds of spiritual leadership. These students took part in a reflective community called Chiasma, from the Greek for crossbeam or connecting point, a term the project borrowed from its use in medicine to describe how the two strands of the optic nerve connect to produce three-dimensional vision.

For some faculty and administrators at Macalester, the biggest effect of the project was what they called "a change in atmosphere." Paula Cooey, professor of Religious Studies, attributes this to the fact that a substantial portion of the academic funds were devoted to academic course development on issues on work and values (as related to vocation in both a religious and secular sense). She judges that the project has "opened more room for everybody to think and speak about values," religious or not, "thawing" an earlier informal prohibition on discussing issues of calling and religious meaning on campus. Paul Schadewald, associate director of the Civic Engagement Center and a former staff leader in the "Lives of Commitment Program," also sees the effects of the project over its decade of activities as opening new possibilities for conversations about values. Many faculty seemed initially suspicious of this kind of talk, he noted, but by "putting people into relationships" in new ways, through connecting students in service projects with recent immigrants to the Twin Cities and refugees, the project has put human faces on global issues. This has been of significant educational value. For example, it has led to greater emphasis upon reflection, Schadewald noted, but not just about student identity or theories of global development and politics, but about how encounters with immigrants and refugees might be speaking to the future purposes and careers of Macalester students.

This increased presence of religious and vocational issues at Macalester brought by the vocation project coincided with another novel project at the college. Supported by the Teagle Foundation between 2006 and 2009, faculty from the college collaborated with faculty participants from three other self-identified secular, liberal arts institutions: Bucknell University, Vassar, and Williams Colleges. They carried out some qualitative research and held a series of discussions on the issue of religious and secular viewpoints in liberal education as experienced by students, staff, and faculty in their institutions. They presented their findings and key argument in a series of workshops at the participating colleges and then published a summary of their conclusions entitled "Reconceiving the Secular and the Practice of the Liberal Arts." In this summary essay the authors described a common, though little-acknowledged problem campuses such as Macalester face: the challenging, unintended consequence of their institutions' embrace of the creed of secularism as a context for liberal education.

They noted that while "our campuses have long valued a notion of the secular that limits and restricts religious expression in order, ostensibly, to promote tolerance, and political engagement," the result has been a "policing of discursive boundaries" that not only protects intellectual freedom from religious dogmatism but by ruling out a whole set of cultural meanings as appropriate for intellectual engagement, also constricts one of liberal education's key purposes: students' pursuit of the "larger questions of meaning and value."[11]

The authors identified the origins of this constriction in the academy's embrace of the Western Enlightenment's confidence that modern science would provide a universally valid theoretical position from which both empirical truth and moral validity could be defined. A major corollary has been the so-called secularization thesis that declared that scientific and technological progress would mean the replacement of tradition-based, especially religious, cultural groundings by a single dominant viewpoint based on the findings of rational inquiry. This conception of one-way historical progress has been enormously influential, of course. It stretches from Auguste Comte in the 19th century, through H. G. Wells's idea of the "World Brain" in the 20th, to Ray Kurzweil's "Singularity" in our own time.

"Secularism" was the ideology that sought to enforce the exclusive truth about history's inevitability. The authors of the SSRC blog argue that secularism is no longer intellectually compelling. More importantly for their purposes, they assert that exclusive secularism has grown educationally counterproductive. Today's learning theory emphasizes the importance of "authentic" learning, that which engages students' enduring concerns, particularly purpose and meaning, as key motivating factors. The exclusion or suppression of such concerns in higher education, the authors argue, is likely to have long-term detrimental effects for liberal learning. This is because liberal education is centrally concerned with students' engagement with questions of meaning, especially in its personal and civic dimensions. If, as they believe their evidence shows, the "policing of cultural boundaries" enjoined by secularism restricts and stultifies this kind of deep personal involvement in learning for many students, especially in regard to issues of major concern for the larger polity and world, then it has outlived its usefulness and needs to be reformed.

In the place of dogmatic secularism the authors propose not regression to other forms of enforced intellectual conformity, but a consciousness that they refer to as "secularity."

By this they mean that exploration of questions of meaning cannot take for granted common agreement on value assumptions, whether religious or secular in origin. These conditions define ours as a "secular age," as Charles Taylor has described it, in which learning the practices of discourse and cooperation with those of different persuasions, rather than enforcing an authoritative set of beliefs, becomes a key aim of liberal education.[12] "The goal of our project," the authors state, "is to develop better models of how citizens of a democracy can engage with their counterparts despite deep and abiding differences." Recovering through this reconceived notion of the secular a new educational focus on learning for citizenship "speaks to the enduring practical value of liberal arts education."[13] It also opens the possibility of critical intellectual engagement with religious traditions and their values rather than their dismissal or suppression. That these ideas were seen as challenging and gave rise to controversy among Macalester's faculty clarifies the wisdom of initially locating the project's reflective practices outside the academic area.

For many of the Macalester students, staff, and faculty who have taken part in vocational reflection, the experience has been one of connecting parts of their college lives that had remained largely in separate zones. Where their academic experience has emphasized the standpoint of the "third person," critical observer (at its extreme producing the "analysis to paralysis" problem), the vocation project asks students to think about what they have received from their families, their community and friends, and the world at large. They are invited, in other words, to think from the "first and second person" point of view, as persons interacting with others and their environment. The project provides the context within which the stance of response to calling can make sense. It is not always an easy process. One student spoke about the new uncertainties that opened up as she began to think more about her future aims. However, this same student reported that the sense of sharing the situation with trusted others also nurtured a new strength: the "ability to sit with uncertainty."

The vocation project students seem to be more intentional about their career choices. They are willing to delve more deeply into how particular careers might fit with their evolving sense of calling. When these students choose a major field of concentration, they also appear more likely than their peers to consciously consider how involvement in that field is likely to align with their exploration of purposes in the world. The Project recently published short biographies of some of their recent graduates who made telling points about the difference the experience has made in their transition beyond college. Luke Calhoun, Class of 2005, has become a high school teacher in the Southwest. Of his Keystone experience, he said: "If I could have understood [better] the relationship between what I feel obliged to do and what I love doing, it would have clarified my path. I suggest to current Macalester students: Focus less on what you might see as necessary and choose instead what you most love. That will best serve everyone."[14] Another member of Luke's class, Rachel Farris, administers a social service program in the Twin Cities for single mothers pursuing education. She noted that "having regular time and a dedicated space to be quiet or thoughtful or reflective or spiritual, or whatever you want to call it, grounded me in a way that almost nothing else did during my four years. It was an amazing counterweight to the academic challenges and the exhilarating, exhausting business of becoming an adult person in college."[15]

Eily Marlow is a Presbyterian minister and program associate who works with colleges to develop the structured reflection component of the vocation project. The experience of project staff has been that as students mature from freshmen to seniors the focus of their reflection broadens: from an initial emphasis upon understanding themselves and finding their "own voices," toward greater awareness of how others can "call" forth a conscious commitment to act in certain ways. For some students this culminates in the ideal of living lives as "global citizens" who intend to weave together their career and personal strivings to identify ways to contribute to the world that are rooted in these evolving values. Above all, it seems to be the experience of learning to trust and share their lives within a community similarly engaged in searching for how best to fulfill their calling that has been the decisive contribution the vocation project has made to their education. And at the heart of this community experience have been practices of reflection.

Eily Marlow points out that the focus on reflection provides a dimension of maturation that is often in short supply. "Some students start in the program asking mostly personal questions—Who am I? What are my gifts and my needs?—and then move toward the larger questions [of purpose] as they become more secure, feel more "heard" by others. For others, the starting point is the big questions. Macalester students often come here motivated by ethical aims and a commitment to social justice. But these concerns can be hard to activate in their academic work. So, for these students it's about seeing themselves, and what they can learn to do, more clearly in relation to these larger issues ... to connect the purpose questions with their own development and responses to what and whom they encounter." This kind of personal development is fed by growth in cultivating empathic imagination.

These things seemed to the students to often be missing in the standard teaching at Macalester, and Marlow believes that students have been drawn to the vocation project by a hunger for connecting the intellectual and the ethical, and spiritual, dimensions of their identities. The kind of reflective practice she teaches is a method inspired by "narrative therapy." Taking inspiration from the work of psychologist Jerome Bruner, the originators of narrative therapy emphasized Bruner's insight that human development occurs largely through absorbing, retelling, and expanding narratives through which experience takes on meaningful form. Narratives "make" the person (or, as some anthropologists would point out, the social group) as much as the person (or group) forms narratives. The positive implication of the approach is that persons can grow toward more vibrant and coherent lives by learning to imagine new stories for themselves and their future, seeking connections with others engaged in a similar quest.[16]

As developed in the Macalester project, the emphasis upon narrative provides a way to bring students' concerns with making sense of their own lives together with the idea of vocation. In the first-year "Lives of Commitment," Eily Marlow presents students with practices of reflection that aim to engage students in expanding their perspective on their own lives and vocational possibilities. For example, during a time in the program when they are working to assist recent immigrants settling into the United States, students spend a several-hour session reflecting on the theme of "Finding a Sense of Belonging in the World." First, they are asked to tell stories about their own experiences of "feeling like you belonged." (Coming to college is often the common reference point.) They are then asked about how they sense that they are achieving "belonging"—again by telling specific stories about themselves or others—how important they think this is for them, and finally how these experiences, now referring to their recent times working with the immigrant families, may help them understand themselves: do they immediately identify with others or situations?, or do they tend to observe cautiously?, etc.

This session is followed by another in which the students listen to a panel of Macalester upper-class students who have themselves immigrated from elsewhere. These students also tell their stories in response to the same questions. The students are then led through an exercise the point of which is for each to see themselves and their struggles from the viewpoint of the other. It is often a highly charged session. It ends with questions about what might be common and what might be particular about desires for "belonging" across different experiences and what might be appropriate responses to the way in which the personal, the local society, and the global context are linked in contemporary life.

Were these things presented as simply knowledge and theories about immigration or globalization, it could have important effects on the students' understanding. It is unlikely, however, that such treatment, in the "third person" alone, could have the formative impact of the self-examination spurred by the reflective encounters in the "first and second person." The religious commitments of the vocation project made this engaged perspective seem the natural complement to the detached criticism practiced in the curriculum. In this way, the vocation project has helped strengthen the links between tenuously connected but essential elements of educating the whole student at Macalester.

Reflection, Relationship, and the Promise of Vocation

The metaphor of call suggests movement, challenge, and response. It invokes an awakened awareness that life is a process of change and development. Call implies a narrative of transformation from a less to a more realized stance toward living. This makes it a logically appealing metaphor to describe education, which has often been understood as a "leading out" toward growth and maturity. The resonance built into the language of call is surely one source of the PTEV's appeal at Butler and Macalester. Invited to discover more about themselves and their potentials within a supportive community, students were able to open outward with less anxiety. In some cases, as we have seen, this process became self-sustaining and led to successful development toward adulthood.

To experience college education as a process of discovering a purpose for life is very different from the more typical instrumental view of higher education as an expensive and time-consuming package while the real excitement and interest of life lie elsewhere. Reflection on vocation, grounded in a community of shared interest and support, shifts the frame. It invites students to understand themselves as protagonists in a collective drama with real import. It provides a space in which students can safely rehearse and evaluate the challenges they must meet and engage new possibilities to be explored. As we have seen, such communities can also encourage the growth of empathy beyond the familiar circle of parents and peers.

Reflective practices make it possible for students to put the elements of their lives together more coherently. The notion of calling provides a narrative structure for students' experiments. Especially in a time when life feels less a flow than a succession of discontinuous bits of experience, there is appeal in the sense that decisions have visible implications on present relationships as well as future possibilities, which the idea of vocational narrative brings. Such narrative framing has long been part of liberal learning, from the *Bildungsroman* of coming of age in the 19th century through Erik Erikson's influential framing of the life course as development through crises of meaning toward integral identity and positive purpose. Like the PTEV's vocation narratives, all these hold out to youth the possibility that life can be more than just "one damned thing after another." Instead, they inspire the idea of life as a worthwhile struggle for coherence. They promise a wisdom that can be won through application and participation in the life of a community similarly awakened.

Recent research on learning underscores the importance of organizing undergraduate experience as this kind of growth process, one that integrates the three apprenticeships of the academic, the social, and the purposive. In a study that argues for a radical reshaping of higher education to promote learning more effectively, Richard Keeling and Richard Hersh provide an overview of the major implications of learning research. "Learning that sticks," they write, "the kind that leads to the kind of changes we expect of college, what we call higher learning, requires rich engagement with new material and that the outcome of this engagement is a concrete and tangible change in the mind—a change in how one thinks and makes sense of the world." Making the critical point that studies show that colleges and universities can demonstrate quite limited success on these measures for large numbers of their students, Keeling and Hersh go on to argue that effective learning requires not only cognitive involvement on the part of learners but also important engagement of emotional energy, imagination, and perseverance.[17]

In sum, college-level learning is demonstrated by greater depth of understanding; the ability to apply new knowledge to the world; the ability to articulate and defend a new perspective; and growth in personal, social, and civic maturity. Keeling and Hersh emphasize that the available knowledge shows that "learning occurs horizontally, across experiences in and out of the classroom, vertically within majors and disciplines," and that real learning is "necessarily cumulative ... the whole is greater than the sum of the parts."[18] They insist that this happens far too rarely, given the amount of resources devoted to higher education. What is usually missing is "mindful, coherent, and integrated design" of curricula and learning experiences to provide appropriate challenges, demanding teaching with constructive feedback, and supportive mentoring. The essential need is for "integrated learning." By this, Keeling and Hersh mean learning that it is "personally meaningful, informs authentic problem-solving, inspires imagination, and enables further learning." Such education has to be holistic and include "identity formation as well as the development of resilience, perseverance, and emotional maturity."[19] To achieve this, student motivation is key. And this is closely related to the quality of faculty-student interaction, the sense of being engaged in a common endeavor of great value for both parties.

The contemporary challenge is that both academic and student culture are often poorly aligned with this developmental trajectory. This and the previous chapter have examined some of the negative effects of current academic culture, particularly the disciplinary pressures on faculty and the dominance of the knowledge expert as faculty self-image. For its part, much of student life also tends to short-circuit efforts at developmental education. In a recent study of college students, Arthur Levine and Diane Dean build on Levine's two earlier studies of student generations of the 1970s and 1990s. Today's generation is more connected to their parents than past generations, while also being more enmeshed in close contacts with peers on and off campus through electronic social media. Levine and Dean describe them as "digital natives" and believe this is the most conspicuous defining trait of today's youth.

The result of the greater involvement with their parents is a generation characterized by "a delayed sense of independence and being a grown up" who are less likely than their predecessors to move from "encounters" with others, including sexual as well as virtual or online, to "relationships." Both parents and students share a belief that higher education functions like any profit-seeking business and cares more about financial success than about providing a good education. So like their parents, students naturally think of themselves as consumers and, notoriously to student life personnel, can be quite demanding.[20] Thanks to today's information technologies, students can be "gatherers" of information rather than "hunters" like their faculty, with access to a huge expanse of possible forms of self-cultivation. In practice, however, they mostly use communication technology to provide stimulation in the form of games and videos and to enter and keep up with the constant talk, texting, and imaging of a self-selected "digital community." So, compared to their predecessors, collegians are both more enmeshed in tight circles of the like-minded and more isolated from others outside those circles.[21] Much of students' social lives revolve around parties, drinking, and carousing in mixed-gendered "packs," facilitated and augmented by digital exchanges. There is perhaps more support from parents and peers than in the past, but there is decidedly more peer pressure to conform as well. And, significantly, both the "packs" and the choice of social media sites are typically stratified by social status, family background, and race.

Whatever one may think of these developments, what these virtual worlds provide students is not trivial. The constant communication gives reminders of personal significance and desirability. The parties and "hook ups" may be casual and "drive-by," lacking deep engagement, but they also give students a sense of being participants together, of sharing energy and excitement in practices that provide their own rewards, however transient. The exchange of images and videos online keep memories current and connections alive. So, there is intensity of experience and a sense of recognition and connection, however uncertain and shifting. While these protean social communities are largely confined to age peers and fail to connect with either other generations or with concerns for a life beyond the present, they are the stuff of life for many college youth. The challenge for educators is how to connect with students through this dauntingly closed social boundary to invite them into wider forms of participation.

In American society, long characterized by a powerful current of individualism (though today's generation seems to prefer a distinctly less "rugged" kind than in the past), it has been the role of all levels of education to inspire and facilitate young adults' development toward becoming contributing members of society. Today's lengthened "emerging adulthood" is still centrally concerned with three tasks Erik Erikson believed essential to this process: the struggle to establish a stable and enduring identity; the development of viable forms of intimate love relationships; and what he called "generativity," the ability to sustain caring concern for others and to contribute to the larger society and the world.[22] The evidence is that this transition is harder and likely to be more prolonged than in the past, but not that it is impossible or any the less desirable.

The PTEV experience suggests that there are three essential conditions for making these connections productive of student growth. The first of these is the establishment of communities that include faculty, students, and staff, and which provide recognition and empathy as they help students consider their gifts within the perspective of a life purpose. The Butler Center for Faith and Vocation has operated as just such a place, providing both face-to-face and virtual connections, one-on-one and group experiences that connect with and go beyond academic and residential life on campus. In a similar way, the Macalester Lilly Program drew students because it offered students a community life to share and an intensity of focus around matters that they felt were largely ignored by their peers and their teachers.

The second essential condition is the dissemination within such communities of practices of reflection that, in a context of mutual trust, can encourage self-examination and the exploration of vocational questions. The third condition is the provision of possibilities for sampling "real life" experiences in company with trusted mentors and peers that open students to the currents of the wider society and world. Each of these conditions employs, builds upon, and completes the others, so that the sense of recognition in community, which is the essential basis for involving students in vocational exploration, gains depth and scope for wider exploration as students come to embrace the struggle for meaning and find part of their significance in assisting others in doing so as well.

The PTEV programs profiled in this chapter stand out for having addressed these two current misalignments in undergraduate education. As we have seen, faculty involved in the PTEV at Butler appealed to students in part because they showed real interest in the students' learning as it might enrich their lives and futures. At Macalester, the students involved in the vocation project especially appreciated a context in which they could relate their lives and college-instigated involvements with the larger society to their classroom learning, and vice versa. The psychology of the process was essentially the same. The communities established around the idea of the exploration of vocation provided the living context in which students learned to expand their attention from absorption in immediate, self-focused concerns toward responding to the needs of others and the attractions of service to a larger cause. They often seemed to find, paradoxically, that it was by devoting more of their energies to such cooperation that they became freer and willing to take responsibility for their learning and future lives.

The following chapter will continue to examine strategies to engage students in vocational exploration by PTEV campuses that were able to draw directly upon distinctive religious traditions of reflection for the discernment of purpose.

4

Renewing Heritage to Meet the Contemporary Challenge

EACH YEAR IN the United States about a million undergraduates receive bachelors' degrees from private, religiously affiliated colleges and universities. Many of these, including the majority of the PTEV campuses, provide an educational atmosphere that, while religiously pluralistic and in many ways like that at secular colleges and universities, is also shaped by living traditions of faith and practice. Such college education has been described as "tradition-enhanced."[1] The enhanced value depends upon these institutions' capacity to draw upon the resources their traditions provide in order to align their practices, and faculty and staff priorities, with educational mission. As the campuses described in the previous chapter illustrate, the vocation initiative has had significant effects on revitalizing these alignments even at institutions that have lost or attenuated their connections to explicitly religious traditions. This is good news for the efforts of all such colleges and universities to make liberal education vital and efficacious for more undergraduates.

At the same time, even on religiously affiliated campuses faculty members often do not find it easy or desirable to talk about religion, either among themselves or with their students. Moreover, the problem is not only talking about religion but about values and life purposes beyond the boundaries of their academic discipline.[2] While almost all professors identify the teaching of critical thinking as a professional obligation, far fewer believe that as educators they have a responsibility to help students make sense of their lives and goals.[3] This is unfortunate for advocates of tradition-enhanced learning. Research shows that contemporary college-age youth are not on the whole natively very interested in religious quests or questions. While few students "lose their faith" today because of their experience of higher education, and some do in fact grow more religiously interested or observant, in the aggregate student cohorts leave college with the same degree of religious involvement with which they entered. It seems that the popular view of today's student generation as earnest spiritual seekers is considerably exaggerated. Religion, as most emerging adults see it, is of value if it helps people "be good." Otherwise, it is of only marginal concern.[4]

It also turns out that most students are not very interested in what are sometimes called the "big questions" of life. While highly tolerant and open to a plurality of values and cultures, only a minority are natively curious about the nature of reality, the clash of worldviews, or issues of human destiny and history. But neither are many students interested in civic or political views or commitments. Emerging adults are optimistic about their own futures while pessimistic about their ability to influence the larger world. As we noted in the previous chapter, today's students typically remain deeply involved with their parents while in college. They spend much of their time in virtual as well as immediate relationships with peers, mediated by digital media. These "digital communities" are the sustaining environment for students and while conformist also provide essential empathy, support, and a sense of participation in common activities that carry their own immediate gratification. But such student social networks are typically inward-turning, stratified by social status, race, and family background, and they do not typically connect with the larger society around them. As the sociologist Christian Smith puts it, from the point of view of civic culture, most are "withdrawn from the public square and instead submerged in interpersonal relationships in their private worlds." For such students, college is about two things: gaining credentials for pursuing a comfortable later life and enjoying present social life with peers in a reasonably safe and undemanding context. Important life questions can be postponed to an indefinite future time of "settling down."[5] This is certainly not encouraging for the cause of liberal education.

In distilling the import of these findings for student learning, Christian Smith has singled out three key implications. First, since most students are not asking the "big questions," they will only do so if they encounter a challenging educational context that can prompt their engagement with broad, intellectual concerns. Relatively few campuses at present provide this. Second, the key to motivation for learning and individual development is personal relationship, especially with faculty and mentoring adults. To provide more of this experience would, in many institutions, require significant realignment of faculty interests and rewards. This finding should give pause to the current vogue for imagining online instruction as a kind of panacea. Third, Smith contends that engaging students in the big questions, especially the normative or religious issues, depends upon removing the barriers that currently separate academic learning from students' life concerns. Addressing this need also demands a fairly sweeping shift in the institutional culture of much of higher education. It means reintegrating the apprenticeships, with the third apprenticeship of identity and purpose providing the lead and inspiration for liberal learning, an education that can enable students to make sense of the world and find their way in it.

This chapter will explore the efforts of two PTEV campuses to address these three challenges by drawing upon and recasting their distinctive religious traditions of education. Earlham College is a Midwestern liberal arts campus affiliated with the Religious Society of Friends. Santa Clara University is a Catholic, Jesuit, comprehensive university located in Northern California. By drawing upon very different religious heritages, one Protestant, the other Catholic, both institutions have innovated in ways that extend and reformulate their distinctive traditions to meet contemporary challenges. Both Quakers and Jesuits have for centuries practiced and taught well-formulated practices of reflection as central features of their paths to practical wisdom. The resources supplied by the vocation initiative enabled both campuses to reflect collectively on these traditions while devising innovative ways to adapt their core practices of practical reasoning to motivate student development toward purposeful lives.

Developing a Reflective Posture at Earlham College

Earlham College enrolls about 1200 students in the liberal arts in the small city of Richmond, Indiana. Founded in the 19th century by the Society of Friends on the original National Road to the West, it now attracts students from all over the United States, with about 16 percent from other nations. The Religious Society of Friends, as the Quakers are officially known, has long been identified with a distinctive moral heritage. Quakers have placed great emphasis upon what they call the Society's Peace Testimony in opposition to war and on efforts to mediate conflict and support human dignity, activities carried on by the American Friends Service Committee today with roots in antislavery Abolition and the Underground Railroad. While the Quakers maintain many schools and established a number of colleges, including Haverford, Swarthmore, and Guilford, Earlham is notable for drawing significant inspiration from its Quaker heritage.

At Earlham, the PTEV provided impetus for the college to rethink that heritage while examining the ways in which its academic program, which Earlham describes as challenging, could be better connected to its other emphases: "global engagement, social concern, and the future direction" of its students and alumni. By the time the PTEV arrived on campus, Earlham had already expanded its focus on both student development and its teaching mission. Career services, for example, were intentionally connected to the college's commitment to social service by being located in the Bonner Center for Service Learning, supported by the Bonner Scholarship program that gives partial scholarships to students to enable them to engage in social service rather than seek part-time employment. But the vocation project gave new impetus for rearticulating how the college could embody a distinctive educational tradition that combines the liberal arts with social mission.

Provost Nelson Bingham believes that the past decade has seen significant progress, thanks in significant part to the vocation project, in the Earlham administration's efforts to "infuse faith and vocation (the name of the PTEV program) throughout the campus." At Earlham, the faith and vocation program connected quite naturally with the networks of social service and action that were already woven into campus life. Bingham noted that the faith and vocation program was deliberately housed in the Newlin Center on campus, a house whose program and staff were dedicated to "the faith development of Quaker students but also with outreach to other students as well."

The import of the PTEV for Earlham was to enable the college to experiment further with new ways to foster student development, creating courses and programs that could link concerns about conscience, career, and purpose, with academic learning. In this, the Quaker tradition's emphasis upon reflection as a communal practice proved a valuable resource. In the academic area, the college developed new courses and styles of teaching that included vocational themes and reflective activity. For example, within the required set of first-year seminar courses, which students take in groups of no more than 15, a number bear direct vocational import, on topics such as "Faith, Reason, and Imagination," "Religion and Psychology: Mapping Selves," "The Science and Meaning of Science Fiction," and "Love, Faith, and Friendship." A number of senior capstone courses continue the vocational theme in the senior year. Participants in this curricular effort include faculty from the natural science departments, which support Earlham's strong premedical program, as well as from the religion and humanities areas. At the same time, the college also invested in efforts to rearticulate the meaning of Quaker tradition and to reimagine some of its spiritual practices as modes of vocational reflection. The two efforts also overlapped and at points enriched each other. Since both remain continuing parts of campus life, understanding how reflection has developed at Earlham requires some grasp of the different ways these themes played out in the curriculum and co-curriculum.

"I am a big proponent of interweaving the personal and the academic," reported Vincent Punzo, a professor in the Psychology Department. A major innovator responsible for several new courses introduced during the PTEV, Punzo also designed part of the evaluation of the grant and led faculty reading groups and a retreat on the theme of vocation. Speaking of what he believes distinguishes his classes from the typical Earlham academic experience, he stressed that "I want students to bring their full selves to the classroom." Bridging the divide students experience between the formally academic learning of the classroom and the informal education absorbed in campus life was a major aim of the faith and vocation initiative. This found expression in the expectation that it was legitimate to ask students to employ the intellectual tools they were acquiring to think about their lives and future possibilities as part of course work. As Punzo put it, "I want students to become fully engaged with their work in my courses, so that they wake up in the middle of the night and say: 'I can't get that paper out of my mind!'"

For Punzo, learning is a social and visible process. He argues that "self-reflection and articulation of one's understanding are important abilities, like mathematics. And, like mathematics, they can be mastered." Assessing student mastery in these matters is complex, Punzo admits, but it is possible and, for student growth in maturity and ability to engage with their lives such mastery is a critical competence. Punzo teaches both a first-year seminar (at Earlham students are "first-year," not freshmen), entitled "Love, Faith, and Friendship," and a senior-level capstone course, "The Search for Self, Meaning, and Goodness."

Punzo intends both of these courses as "transformative" for students, so that they "walk out of such classes feeling they have been challenged in ways that more typical classes do not challenge them" to think harder and more carefully about their lives. For instance, the assignments used in courses like Love, Faith, and Friendship ask students to consider situations related to the big themes of the course from the point of view of the theories and literature read in the course—and then to question the validity of the theory by asking how well it captures, or fails to capture, their own experience. This sort of dialogue between theory and experience or practice is amplified in the senior capstone in which students are challenged to draw upon the whole range of their college learning to respond to the big questions of living they will soon face upon graduation.

Other faculty members have also become involved in bringing vocational reflection into both the beginning and concluding levels of the curriculum. Lori Watson teaches in the Chemistry Department. She has chosen to teach a first-year course on "Faith, Reason, and Imagination" as well as to integrate vocation themes into the department's senior capstone course. The first-year course deliberately challenges students to think about how they implicitly use different frames of understanding in different aspects of their lives, with the intention of leading students to reflect upon how they relate their academic learning to their personal beliefs. The course introduces students to the scholarly literature on "creation stories" found in many cultures and leads students to compare and contrast these with the way contemporary scientists approach questions about the origins of the universe and of life. Finally, students are given assignments that ask them to reflect on how they themselves think about these matters, taking into account what they have been learning in the course.

As Lori Watson noted, "The Quaker tradition does not polarize faith and scientific reason." Accordingly, in the seminar students discuss and write about the different roles their religious faith and questions, as well as their understanding of science, play in how they make sense of the world. These students are learning that Earlham College is a place where such exploration and questioning are valued and supported. In one writing assignment, students are asked to draw on what they've learned in order to compare the modern narrative of the genesis of the universe from the Big Bang with the biblical creation account, and several stories from native peoples. Then, as a thought experiment, the students are asked to construct their own account.

While the differences between the "religious" and the "scientific" creation stories are often obvious to students, they are usually less aware that
even the modern account shares with the traditional stories a trust that
it is possible to connect events into a narrative whole. Science students
in particular, according to Watson, are often surprised to discover that
modern accounts are not just reports on scientific findings but often constructed with a moral intent, such as evoking a sense of human responsibility for the well-being of the biosphere. The class discovers evidence
that, along with skeptical questioning and rigorous standards of evidence,
scientific thinking also makes use of imagination and that it connects at
various points with moral beliefs, even a sense of reverence toward the
natural world.

In this seminar at the beginning of their academic career, first-year
students receive guidance in learning analytical distinctions among the
ways different disciplines approach the world. They are given practice in
moving back and forth among the divergent realms of rigorous scientific
analysis, religious concerns with making sense of the whole of things,
and their personal quests for significance and purpose. Such teaching
brings all three apprenticeships into play in the classroom. Students are
taught to think analytically about how a specific discipline frames its aims
and methods. They are then led to apply this kind of analysis compara-
tively, across several genres of subject matter, noting the ways the several
disciplines frame problems and define key issues. They are also asked to
consider how the academic issues about truth and meaning that surfaced
through their reading, writing, and class discussions might bear on their
lives both as students and in future careers. In her first-year seminar as
well as in her senior capstone course, Watson sees the same basic pedagogical challenge: how to set up learning experiences, appropriate to the
students' level of development, in which they can practice moving "from
the student mind-set of learning in order to fulfill requirements toward
adult concerns with acquiring competence so as to decide what to do with
the knowledge and skills college can provide."

The place "where the [important] learning takes place," according to
Jay Roberts, then associate professor of Education and Environmental
Studies, "is where students engage in dialogue between theoretical framing and their actual practical experience." Roberts, who is also director of
the Center for Environmental Education, was drawing on a good deal of
experience in developing forms of teaching that promote what he terms
"iterative reflection." This occurs when students return to a practice they

are trying to master, or a situation they are trying to understand, after receiving feedback on their previous performance and attempt it again, now explicitly attending to how their efforts match—or modify—their intended aims.

"Learning is a social, visible, practical, and ethical activity," Roberts holds, and students need to become self-aware about themselves, the context, and the process of their learning, as well as its goals. Besides skill and knowledge, approaching learning this way is in the end about "developing students' integrative capacities" as persons. Roberts sees developing these as the real goal of higher education, and he argues this can be most effectively done in "long-term relationships with communities as partners." In environmental education, classroom learning is an important resource for this effort, but it is reflection, understood as something that members of the college community do together, that enables students to integrate their learning toward becoming persons who can participate in the larger life that flows through the college but leads beyond it.

It is not clear that Earlham as a whole has realized this kind of highly interconnecting learning environment. Provost Bingham, for example, worried that the college community still lacks a "general sense of the big picture." But Earlham seems to be trying to learn more about students' understanding of their educational experience and aspirations, comparing those with the views of recent graduates. And Bingham does think that "talk about faith and vocation are now woven into the fabric of who we are." There seems little doubt that the PTEV has fostered more intentional and holistic student development in a number of contexts. The Newlin Center, directed by Michael Birkel of the Religion Department, is a focus for the college's more visible Quaker identity. Birkel directs the Friends Colloquium, a course on Quaker spiritual practices that is open to students of any major or year. "Students have a profound spiritual hunger," according to Michael Birkel, "but they lack any traditional language for reflecting on their own deepest experience—they just don't know the 'menu.'" One purpose of the Quaker Studies program that he directs is to provide some of these "menu" options in the form of spiritual practices and intellectual resources from the tradition of Quaker thinkers.

For example, students talked about the importance to them of experiencing what in Quaker parlance are known as "clearness committees." Originally a practice provided by Meetings for Worship for young Friends contemplating marriage, the practice has been adapted to help students think seriously about themselves, their beliefs, and their possible vocations. Emma Churchman, a staff member at the Newlin Center who leads clearness committees, remarked that "Quakers seem to 'listen' each other into self-discovery." She was referring to the basic practice in which a student may request that she form and lead a small group of other students to meet with the student seeking "clearness" about vocation through a number of meetings. Each time the group meets, the students begin with a period of silence, similar to the basic pattern of the Friends' Meeting for Worship. The student seeking guidance may then explain what he or she wants clarity about, placing this question within a narrative of how that student has come to this 'concern.'" The "committee" members are there not to give advice but to aid the seeker in gaining clarity in discernment about authentic identity and direction. Their role is to serve as "witnesses," and they may ask questions about where, when, and with whom that person has experienced a sense of deepest engagement in life, felt most connected to others, least anxious, and most "centered" in a sense of openness to reality. Sometimes the clearness committees may employ traditional Quaker language about attending to the "leadings" of the "inner light," or searching for "conviction" of the rightness of a direction that seems to be emerging in the consensus of the group. Students report these practices as helping them become more "grounded" and "centered" in responding to the demands of their studies and their relationships.

The newest development of the college's emphasis upon spiritual maturity is the program of Quaker Fellows. These are students who apply for partial scholarships, eight per year, which provide financial support in exchange for their commitment to exploring Quaker values and spirituality. The Fellows meet weekly at the Newlin Center as part of an organized program of involvement in social action and religious reflection, including a yearly retreat. The students come from various traditions of Quaker life, some from "programmed" meetings, typically in the West, which bear a resemblance to many other Protestant denominations in their worship, organization, and theology. Others have been raised in meetings, often in the East, which have continued the early tradition of silent worship without ministers or communal prayers. Others come from Southern meetings that have elements of both styles. Some of the Quaker Fellows consider themselves Christians, read the Bible as the Word of God, and speak easily about the Holy Spirit. Others are more familiar with language that is explicitly universal in its references, preferring "that which is of God in everyone" or more secular terms.

The students seem to value encountering and exploring this diversity within their own religious tradition. They spoke of the thrill of "exploring our own Quakerness, especially seeing the connection between personal religion and community." Student life at Earlham, they pointed out, is very diverse religiously, including students hostile to religion, so they find it valuable to have these times with others who share their desire to deepen their religious quest. The weekly sessions typically begin with a potluck supper that includes adult Friends as well as a variety of students besides Fellows. At these suppers, too, there is communal silence and a short time when each participant reflects upon something that day for which they are grateful or about which they are seeking guidance. As with the clearness committees, the shared sense of mutual concern and support is woven into the practice of quiet awareness. Students reported learning how to ask and answer the question of "where are you spiritually?" As Emma Churchman commented, "Unlike in therapy, the big 'aha' moment for the students here is realizing that the goal or activity they find most fulfilling can provide a thread to guide their choices of courses, community engagements, and ultimately career."

Newlin Center director Michael Birkel believes that these programs of spiritual practice and reflection are important for the college's identity and, in turn, for its educational mission. Because students, even Quaker students, so often lack a religious vocabulary, it is important to adapt a pedagogy that both "respects students' experience" and yet does not acquiesce in the "view of all religion as the media presents it: biased, bigoted, and dysfunctional." Whereas at one time Earlham's Quakers could expect that their values and ethos would be transmitted "by osmosis" through daily campus life, today "we have to articulate the things that are precious to us." The Quaker tradition provides conceptual resources for doing this, since it has included since its 17th-century founding two strands: one religiously particular, as a Christian movement; the other universalist in aspiration, seeking "access to the goodness in the universe." In the 19th century the evangelical revival pushed Quakers to identify with these as polarities. Hence, the division noted among the students between more typically "Protestant" Quakers and those not identifying as Christian. In the early 20th century Earlham turned away from being an evangelical Bible college toward a liberal arts curriculum and identity. That gives it, in Birkel's view, a position from which to mediate these tensions, and the Quaker Studies program is aimed to enable faculty, staff, and students alike to grasp the riches of this tradition that continues to provide eloquent expression, through its myriad social involvements around the world, to its founding values. It is a natural extension to include interfaith conversations. So, Earlham supports a Bodhi Center on campus as a gathering place for Buddhist students and staff. Indeed, Birkel contends, such dialogue with other religious traditions is good for everyone, as it "clarifies one's own faith while also expanding one's stance to learn from others."

Earlham seems dedicated to modeling and inculcating a reflective posture in both the curricular and co-curricular areas. There is interest among the faculty in enabling students to find personal significance in the life of the mind as a way to explore identities and orient their search for a purposeful life. Some of the first-year and senior courses employ teaching practices that explicitly lead students to consider how their academic experiences in the liberal arts bear upon their future identities and careers. The vocational emphasis uses the third apprenticeship to give larger significance to students' experience of both the first and second apprenticeships. At the same time, the college's expanded religious programs offer access to the spiritual practices of the Friends' tradition. These practices seem intended to support and personalize vocational discernment. At the same time, they offer the possibility of exploring a larger realm of meaning embodied in the Quaker way of life.

This added emphasis upon Earlham's religious heritage is a direct impact of the PTEV. It has been important to the life of the college, but it has not gone unopposed. Both Michael Birkel and Vincent Punzo emphasized that the stronger Quaker presence has provoked skepticism among many faculty, as well as some overt hostility. As Birkel put it, "Living out one's principles with integrity gets respect here," yet "tension over the issue of the role of religion at the college seems to be growing." While still in process, Earlham's direction represents an institutional achievement of significance for the future of higher education.

A Mentoring Community for Jesuit Discernment at Santa Clara University

Santa Clara University's experience with the PTEV, like Earlham's, emphasized connecting academic with student and religious life around the themes of faith and vocation. Santa Clara has relied upon and deepened its heritage of Jesuit Catholicism in a strategy of permeating campus life with vocational themes. Santa Clara is a place of "high student–faculty connectivity," according to Provost Dennis Jacobs, where there is also considerable commitment across a religiously diverse faculty and staff to "the Jesuit formative mission." The university called its project DISCOVER. The acronym stood for "Developing and Inspiring Scholarly Communities Oriented toward Vocational Engagement and Reflection." The aim was to extend and deepen the university's efforts to fashion itself as a "mentoring community in which students could discern vocation" while also "reaffirming the vocation of faculty and staff as teachers, scholars, and mentors." Reflective practices have been at the core of this effort, helping to bridge the gap in many students' experience between their lives in college and their future, as well as between curricular and co-curricular life. Faculty and staff have also engaged in a number of activities in which they have been able to explore with their peers their own sense of calling in their work, as well as how they view themselves in relation to the educational mission of the university.

As part of DISCOVER, practices of reflection have been introduced into a revised academic curriculum, especially the interdisciplinary "Pathways" core. The "Personal Renaissance" course described in chapter 1 exemplifies this approach. The pedagogical strategy of the course is to engage students in understanding the inspirations and challenges, setbacks and crises, of Renaissance figures as examples of the search for purpose and meaning. Along with developing the intellectual capacities of critical interpretation and contextual understanding, the course prompts students to view these lives as distant mirrors for probing their own aspirations, struggles, and possibilities. This process of seeking intellectual insight is complemented by a spiritual practice of meditation in class as a way to deepen reflection by keeping the issues encountered personal and vivid.

Santa Clara students are also invited to participate in other kinds of reflective exercises in a variety of campus venues. Residence halls, organized to be "learning communities," hold weekly reflective meetings at which students are invited to drop in. Santa Clara has reshaped its Career Center to expand counseling about career choice to incorporate the bigger question of life purpose. There are vocationally oriented overnight retreats that emphasize reflection upon vocational themes. Perhaps most dramatically, students may elect a number of "immersion" experiences during academic holidays. On these intensive group trips staff mentors lead reflection on the students' experience of life in marginalized communities at home and abroad. Both before leaving campus and after returning, students are asked to consider how issues of global social justice might affect choices in their lives.

Judith Dunbar is a professor in the English Department who teaches courses such as "Women Poets, Spirituality and Justice," in both the "Justice and the Arts" and the "Vocation" Pathway programs. She has also co-facilitated the Ignatian Faculty Forum. This is an ongoing series of meetings among groups of faculty who come together monthly during the academic year to explore the elements of a modern Ignatian—derived from the Jesuit order's founder, St. Ignatius of Loyola—spirituality that would be true to their lived experiences and challenges as faculty members fully engaged in their professional work. Among their shared readings for discussion are topics involving vocation. As they discuss their own sense of calling to the academic profession, they reflect on how to integrate this sense of purpose more fully into their teaching, scholarly research, and service to the university community.

Thinking, in addition, about programs for students that explore vocation, Judith Dunbar believes that the PTEV Discover program has made a real impact on students' classroom experience, breaking down the accustomed barriers between "academic" learning and life concerns. "In courses developed with the support of the Discover program's focus on vocation, students can more deeply experience that reflection about their lives can interweave with what they learn and do in their courses. They also grow more open to issues of spirituality as topics for shared discussion." Asked about the further causes of this growth in student attitudes, Dunbar suggested "the residential programs that came in with the Lilly project." These were the Residential Learning Communities that were established as part of Discover.

This judgment is shared by Zoë Segnitz, now Kranzler, a part-time Resident Minister and member of the campus ministry staff living in one of the student residences. She pointed out that the formation of Residential Learning Communities, with each dormitory organized around a particular theme, including two directly focused on the exploration of calling, was "meant to blur the distinction between formal and informal learning." Each Resident Minister became responsible for holding a weekly "hospitality" open house as well as organizing weekly discussions based on material provided by the resident life office. "In their training for the position, the R.M.'s had to develop their own narratives about how they discern their direction," said Zoë, "and this has helped to make it possible to listen to students with more awareness." Zoë has also served as part of the leadership staff for the annual Discover retreats in which students spend a weekend off-campus thinking through some of these same questions in a more intensive way.

As an undergraduate, Zoë had been a student athlete while majoring in studio arts. She remembers the difficulty of finding an adviser who could help her reflect on her life as a whole. "The coaches were focused on the sport; for them, courses were at best a necessary distraction," Zoë reports, "while my professors were often discouraging about my involvement in sports." By contrast, the DISCOVER program has provided her with training and encouragement for "housing the whole conversation" about college life in her advisory role with freshman students. She describes her own growth through her several years' experience in the program as producing a surprising discovery. "I find myself becoming more Jesuit, more concerned about relating to students as whole persons," she exclaimed. In the Residential Learning Communities program, the theme of connecting the classroom with life has been reinforced by recruiting faculty to take part in activities such as the popular "Café Socrates," in which faculty from various departments hold open discussion sessions with interested students.

One of the most striking ways Santa Clara has tried to deepen students' concern with their own life purposes has been its program of "immersion" experiences. These are organized study trips that take place during university vacations. Organized through the Ignatian Center for Jesuit Education, these trips are led by faculty or staff who serve as teachers and mentors to promote students' reflection on their experience. The Ignatian Center is the result of a consolidation, spurred by the vocation project, to unify the university's several ventures into experiential and civic learning. The theme of these immersion trips derives from the Jesuit sense of educational mission: to provide relatively privileged Santa Clara students with firsthand encounters with some of the injustices that are part of contemporary life at home and abroad, through living and working briefly with people in marginal communities. The Ignatian Center describes immersion trips as intended to serve as "catalysts for solidarity" with the marginalized groups the students meet, as well as vivid incitements to "intellectual inquiry and moral reflection on the gritty reality of our globalizing world."

Michael Nuttall is the staff member of the Ignatian Center in charge of the immersion program. As part of the PTEV initiative, he came to Santa Clara from Boston College, another Jesuit institution, where he worked in their student retreat program called Halftime, which is offered to sophomores. The Boston College program poses three large questions to student retreatants. These are questions about what has given the students enthusiasm and joy in using their capacities to the full; whether their skills match their enthusiasms; and whether they can see ways to employ their skills to follow their enthusiasms to connect with the needs of others in the larger world. Now, in the Santa Clara immersion program, Nuttall engaged in helping students confront similar questions during their encounters with some of the "gritty realities" of the places they visit.

"We're developing a curriculum for immersions," Michael Nuttall explained. "Students don't just go away and come back. They must commit to four sessions together as a group before the trip, plus three more to debrief the experience afterward." These pre- and post-sessions are structured around themes, starting with students' experience of the Santa Clara community, moving toward principles of social justice as understood in the Roman Catholic tradition, and then toward questions of personal meaning and purpose. On the trip, the faculty or staff mentors hold nightly sessions of one to two hours to enable the students to talk and think about what they are experiencing. These sessions are designed to build solidarity within the group as well as well as empathy with those the students are meeting.

This group connection is then continued in the three post-trip meetings of the immersion group. There, students are encouraged to relate their reactions to the experience to their own sense of purpose and value. Some students have indeed taken their immersion experiences to heart in a directly vocational way, developing careers in legal and social service work concerned with new immigrants from the Central American countries visited on immersion trips. Others report considering new career paths or volunteer involvements as a direct result of immersions. Faculty, too, have responded to immersion experiences with innovation. For example, Godfrey Mungal, dean of the School of Engineering, has promoted a shift in faculty research and teaching toward more attention to connecting engineering know-how to problems in developing countries, what he calls "engineering with a mission," leading to the formation of the Frugal Innovation Lab.

All this suggests that these themes resonate well at Santa Clara. Since Santa Clara's population is about 50 percent Roman Catholic in identification, programs like immersion must be carried out within a consciously interreligious context. The Ignatian Center includes interreligious discussions in its program, but the effort of DISCOVER seems to have been mostly to translate many Catholic themes, such as social justice, into language that those outside the Church can affirm, simultaneously emphasizing the distinctively Catholic and Jesuit heritage of the core values around which the programs were constructed. While complementary in principle, there is also tension between the universalism of the values and the particularity of the Christian articulation, which Santa Clara seems to use constructively in order to generate energy for probing the questions more deeply.

The wide reach of the vocational theme and the dissemination of reflective practices such as those employed in the retreats and immersion experiences stems from the synergy between the PTEV and efforts already underway at the university. The initiative coincided with a significant movement within Jesuit higher education to connect more organically a rethinking of its mission with a renewed appreciation of the spiritual ethos and practices of the Jesuit order. The Rev. Paul Locatelli, S.J., who was president during most of the Lilly grant period had already introduced a broad-gauged effort at institutionalizing the university's ideals throughout campus life through the "Three C's:" competence, conscience, and compassion. DISCOVER, in turn, sought to translate these values by providing educational programs that would provide a "mentoring community" that would encourage students to shape their own development around standards and values consonant with this Jesuit ethos of the "faith that does justice."

At the center of this process is the notion of "discernment." As employed at Santa Clara, discernment indicates a process of bringing knowledge and critical intelligence to bear on one's own experience in order to interpret the meaning and bearing of this experience for how to live out the espoused values of faith and justice. The first director of the DISCOVER program was William Spohn, a member of the Religion Department. Spohn emphasized the key role of imagination as way to conceive how the PTEV could contribute to and deepen the university's educational mission. For Spohn, the exercise and cultivation of the imagination is essential to human growth and flourishing and is one of the primary purposes of liberal education. It "places particular realities in a context, an intelligible landscape," a context of relationship. Imagination provides the basis for how we think about ourselves and our relations with others and the world. Spohn argues that this was a basic premise of Ignatius Loyola's conception of spiritual development—and of education. The educational significance of Christian religious practices, Ignatius understood, lies in their ability to shape a "moral imagination," a framework for experiencing and judging that "links questions of living with normative patterns."[6]

In Spohn's conception of Ignatian education, the purpose of classical humanistic learning for the Jesuits has been to shape the moral imagination through the exploration of positive and negative examples of human lives and projects. The specifically religious and Christian contribution to this formation process is to put forward for exploration and emulation the normative patterns derived from the Christian narrative of the life of Jesus as the herald and exemplar of the reign of God. This background cultivates a specific framing of the human situation, developing an imaginative horizon for "an informed reading of the [present] situation to discover a way of acting that is harmonious with the story of Jesus and faithful to the present call of the Spirit."[7] The Jesuit mission to address global social justice can be seen as the vocational application of this normative pattern. What Christian practices, images, and texts provide, then, is a store of memories and models that can serve as suggestive analogies for critical reasoning about how to construe and respond well in life's situations. The development of the capacity to reason well by analogy, to "apply" the images and precedents in new situations in ways that are faithful to the tradition but give it new shape, is training in discernment. The DISCOVER program was intended to expand Santa Clara's ability to foster skills of discernment for a variety of contexts and situations across the life of the university.

Carrying out these intentions, Santa Clara's PTEV, the DISCOVER project, has built new connections within the institution to further these goals. Today's Career Center speaks in a language that is consistent with the university's mission. Students meet the three questions: What gives you joy? What are you good at? Does anybody need you to do these things?—the same questions that structure Ignatian Center retreats and reflection on immersion experiences. Elizabeth Thompson, now Krishnan, joined the Career Center as part of DISCOVER in order to better integrate this office, which helps students with their transition to adult life, with the educational aims of the curriculum and co-curriculum. "Bridging 'career' language, which was what most of the staff had grown up in, and talk of 'calling' was the initial problem," she reported," but increasingly I've found that our career counselors get inspired by the idea of vocational discernment." It seems to give them a way to connect with students on a deeper level, which makes their work more satisfying. This emphasis resonates with and reinforces the curricular attention to the same theme which we saw exemplified in the "Vocation: Your Personal Renaissance" course in chapter 1. As a continuing effect of the initiative,

vocation themes help Santa Clara students bridge their experience of the
first and second apprenticeships through multiple connections.

In addition, as Elizabeth pointed out, having career counselors working in the medium of vocational discernment helps students make better
connections between their present activities and their futures. As freshmen, students are mostly focused on making a life for themselves as
college students. But the Career Center can help students expand their
awareness from the present toward what they might do and become over
their life trajectory. To do this, they must develop "the language and the
concrete resources to explore, articulate, and follow alternative possibilities." And one of Thompson's main roles has been to develop and deliver
to students resources for doing these things.

Elizabeth Thompson, a Santa Clara graduate herself, has developed a
program that brings university alumni to campus on a regular basis. "Let
Your Life Speak" provides a congenial setting in which undergraduates
can meet, listen to, and interact with alumni. The Career Center emphasizes the ways in which these sessions can help students learn "reflection,
trust, exploration, and discernment" about their own lives, personalities,
and possibilities. More recently, Thompson has begun offering "Careers
for the Common Good," a course for which students can earn academic
credit that is recommended for sophomores and juniors embarked on
the vocation Pathway. The course meets 10 times a quarter and includes
speakers as well as student discussion. The three themes of the "Careers
for the Common Good" are posed as questions: What are my interests and
talents? How can I apply my unique gifts to make a difference in my life
and work? What are today's pressing social realities and injustices?

To give some immediacy to the last question, students participate in
a "community-based learning placement" with a variety of community
organizations in Silicon Valley. While learning how to write an atten-
tion-catching résumé, students are also learning more about careers that
address the issues they experience firsthand in their placements and read
about and analyze theoretically in class. What makes this course unusual
is that while it is part of the curriculum, it is offered by the Career Center
as part of the core curriculum. In addition to community placements, students participate on a site visit to a high-tech corporation (e.g., Google,
Symantec) to understand the interconnections in the Valley between corporations and the lives of the marginalized and how corporations address
social responsibility, The intention is that no matter what organization
students pursue after graduation they understand the larger social context

that organization operates in and what role students can have in contributing to the common good within that organization.

Clearly, then, the course bridges the first two apprenticeships, moving from the social apprenticeship toward employing academic knowledge and techniques to inform students' understanding of their social context. They also develop skill in presenting themselves and their learning in the job market, but their knowledge and skill is given its point through the third apprenticeship. It is common for career offices to teach undergraduates how to explore the question of "What are the most likely lucrative career options in today's economy?" At Santa Clara, students are also asked to consider their futures in light of the larger social reality, especially issues of injustice and need. As students practice reflecting on their skills, their context, and their future, it is this normative background that gives perspective to their discernment.

This seems evidently true for one student, a second-quarter sophomore, who credits his participation in the vocation Pathway, and especially Elizabeth Thompson's "Careers for the Common Good," with his movement from majoring in finance to a concentration in Environmental Studies with a goal of further study in sustainable agriculture. This student came to Santa Clara from Catholic schools, with what he called an "already strong spiritual base." His studies and involvements in college have helped him see that "spirituality" needs to be integrated with life and work in the world. Always interested in food and gardening, he described his motivation changing, from self-expression and an interest in the aesthetics of gardening to "the bigger picture, of becoming a steward of the earth instead of just doing what would look good or please me in the moment. I feel that I'm taking all my knowledge and applying myself as much as I can."

The practical expression of this development has been his change of academic major, "taking all the science courses I can to understand how things like fertilizer work and affect the environment," and getting involved in an AmeriCorps community garden program in local schools that uses horticulture as a means of environmental education. All this has been leading him to explore possible careers and advanced degrees that would enable him to keep these concerns as parts of his future possibilities. Asked how he had come to this realization, the student traced it to several academic experiences. "I've taken a philosophy course about self-identity and community. That was interesting and got me thinking about how identity develops through involvements with social purposes and issues." He commented that a course in ethics was useful, as was an accounting course that stressed "that whatever comes from one place has to go somewhere and, finally, be accounted for, which is true for environmental and social matters as well as for economics." But it was the "Careers for the Common Good" that he credits for "redirecting my sense of spiritual purpose" and "how I reflect on myself while I'm working. It made me much more aware of who I am and what I might be able to do and contribute."

As it has evolved, Santa Clara's focus on vocation has given a distinctive quality to the university's participation in a larger movement to rethink and reformulate Jesuit educational institutions. To a significant degree, the university has been able to institutionalize interactions among the three apprenticeships. This has in turn been grounded in its particularly Ignatian form of Christian faith, especially seeking to discern ways of "finding God in all things." The model practice has been the Jesuit daily "examen," a reflective pause to review one's experience as framed explicitly by the values espoused in faith, the commitment to becoming "men and women for others." These efforts resonate with similar developments in the Boston College PTEV program, which produced a document setting out an interpretation of the Ignatian tradition for contemporary higher education.

In *A Journey to Adulthood*, the authors described the key practice of reflection as "paying attention to one's experience; reflecting on its meaning; and making good decisions in the light of what has been learned." They presented reflection as both a social and an individual practice, complementary to the communal effort to enlist "all adults on campus" in an effort to mentor students by engaging them in "expert conversations" toward taking a proactive stance toward their own education and development. Summing up their notion of education for vocation, the Boston College authors seem to speak for Santa Clara's PTEV as well when they assert that it is "through their human gifts and their educated use of them that God's vision for the world will be accomplished." Placing this faith in a universal perspective, they conclude that the fundamental vocation is to achieve full human flourishing and to help others, especially those most in need, to join in flourishing as well.[8]

Ways to Wisdom

Exploring the idea of calling can energize a quest to understand the reality of things and to pursue goals in light of this understanding. In separate ways, Earlham and Santa Clara have shown this. They have each devised educational experiences that engage significant numbers of their students in learning to investigate the big questions of living in very personal ways—discovering what they can be through projects that also deeply fascinate them and which the world needs. Both institutions have addressed the challenge of helping today's students find their way to lives of significance and purpose. By drawing upon their heritage, the Peace Testimony or the "faith that does justice," they have created innovative programs that lead students to expand their sense of possibility as they deepen their understanding of the world and intensify their commitment to it. These institutions further illustrate how a focus on exploring calling can weave new connections between knowledge and the development of life skills. When students are understood as "called" and not simply "driven," the search for these connections becomes the natural progression of personal development rather than an imposed task. Seeking an integrated education becomes "second nature."

At both Santa Clara and Earlham these developments have been forwarded by the spread through curricular and co-curricular venues of practices of reflection, both personal and communal. Through their campus programs, grounded in normative visions of the good person in a good society deriving from their religious traditions, more educators and students are able to employ educated reason to make sense of their experience. The emphasis upon vocation and reflection has made it hard to ignore the question of how they, as persons, might be called to respond to the emerging situations that confront them as individuals and as members of the human community. It has also enhanced the educational atmosphere by increasing the areas of common concern and even common practice between the generations. The barriers between academic learning, campus life, and involvements with the larger society have been reduced, producing deeper student engagement and a subtle encouragement for faculty to experiment with providing more mentorship for students.

These features of the PTEV at Earlham and Santa Clara also display a commitment to organizational learning and collective growth toward more effective education. What this entails has been summarized, as we have seen in the previous chapter, by Richard Keeling and Richard Hersh in their presentation of the current state of knowledge about developmental learning. Positive intellectual and personal growth, they write, "occurs horizontally, across experience in and out of the classroom, vertically within majors and disciplines and in ways that are necessarily cumulative." On this basis, they argue that that too often today's typically fragmented curriculum and diffuse campus life fails to produce learning because it tacitly misses the point. In real education ". . . the whole is greater than the sum of the parts, that higher education is not simply incremental and additive but is in fact synergistic and requires mindful, coherent, and integrated design."[9] At Earlham and Santa Clara it has been the strengthening of the third apprenticeship of identity and purpose that has, under the rubric of vocational exploration, stimulated deeper integration within the educational mission both within the curriculum and across the campus.

The larger implications of these developments for the organization and conduct of higher education are potentially radical and momentous. If successful education for student development requires both horizontal and vertical integration, then the current dissociation among the apprenticeships is a major impediment to effective learning. Because of its broad aim at student development, spurred by commitment to the value-centered aim at human flourishing, the PTEV has sparked experiments with various ways by which the several departments of campus life can be engaged more effectively in the common educational enterprise. For development learning, it takes a campus to educate. The next chapter will explore ways in which various PTEV institutions have taken on the challenge of realizing more "mindful, coherent, and integrated" cooperation across the campus in the service of exploring vocation.

5

How Vocation Integrates

THE VIRTUE OF COMMUNITY

"THERE IS NO longer an invisible line separating the sisters' community from the university." Such was the judgment of a member of the Congregation of Divine Providence, the order of religious women that founded Our Lady of the Lake University in San Antonio, Texas, at the end of the 19th century. The sisters have continued to live on campus in a large convent dating back 100 years, but the order's aging members had become increasingly withdrawn from its life. "The Lilly Grant enabled the congregation to regain connection to the university," said another sister, "because its focus on helping students explore various forms of lay ministry created a critical mass of mutual concern about spirituality and social service that linked us with the students and faculty in new ways." Yet another sister was even more sweeping in her view, asserting that increased involvement with students had "rejuvenated" the sisters in ways that amounted to nearly a "refounding of the Congregation."

Inspired by the PTEV program, known as *La Llamada*, "The Call," the sisters have expanded their practice of hospitality into a program of lay Associates. Now, numbers of students and faculty regularly take meals with the sisters in the convent and meet for times of discussion and reflection. (There are also outings, such as trips to basketball games on which the older sisters and students share camaraderie.) Students are encouraged to apply to join the Providence Leadership Program, which provides retreats and insight into the purposes that animate the sisters' work. One senior majoring in counseling, self-described as having come to Our Lady of the Lake "without much religious interest," found that "the sisters' sense of calling showed me a new outlook on my studies and my career." Alumni are encouraged to maintain these ties, providing support for them as they venture into the worlds of work and family. For her part, Jennifer Bendele, who heads the university's program on service learning and volunteerism, noted that "visiting the sisters' home" has, over time, influenced many of the students who pass through the various service experiences offered through the Providence Leadership Program, extracurricular volunteer projects, and those that are mandated parts of some academic courses. She concluded that "the students have much more comfort in speaking about spiritual matters in relation to discerning their life choices."

Revitalizing an Institution's Collective Sense of Calling

These efforts integrate the concerns of the third apprenticeship of identity and purpose into the academic apprenticeship. There is also direct attention to the social apprenticeship of developing students' personal capacities thanks to the particular form the PTEV has taken at Our Lady of the Lake. *La Llamada* provided small grants to faculty to incorporate into their courses a service experience in the community of San Antonio's West Side. This largely Hispanic neighborhood is home to many immigrant families and, in some cases, the university's students as well. The Religion and Social Work departments in particular began adding service experiences, framed by readings in Catholic Social Teaching with its stress on the moral values of solidarity and social justice.[1] After these course experiences, students could apply to take part in the Providence Retreat Outreach Program, or PROP. For students, this internship program provided financial support in exchange for 50 hours of work per semester. A senior student about to move into a graduate program in theology and youth ministry at Notre Dame emphasized the effects of his participation in youth ministry in Roman Catholic parishes on the West Side. It was this supervised work with youth in parish activities that provided him with the realization that it was this kind of "positive involvement in the lives of youth" that gave him a sense that "at the end of the day, this is where I should be."

The Providence Retreat Outreach Program was the invention of Gloria Urrabazo, vice president of Mission and Ministry at the university. Beginning in the campus ministry office, over the course of the past decade Gloria built the overall PTEV program through weaving ties among a number of campus departments: the academic, Student Life, campus ministry, service learning, and career planning and counseling. But PROP and its connections with the larger community was perhaps Gloria Urrabazo's most seminal contribution to the program and the university. Aimed at promoting "leadership in Hispanic ministry," the program has student interns working together for several hours each week to plan, organize, and finally carry out three short retreats for middle and high school students in local parishes each semester. In these settings, students give talks and conduct discussions with local teenagers on religious and developmental themes. They produce skits and musical segments illustrating the value of education and aspiration to college, as well as key concepts of Catholic belief, including faith, the sacraments, and social justice. Not all the interns have been either ethnically Hispanic or Roman Catholic. One such student, Enjoli Page, found the calling language quite strange, having been raised Baptist. Today, she works with Gloria on the university staff.

These student interns are coached and assessed on their performance by parish staff members who guide them toward understanding the circumstances and struggles of the families of the West Side. As one supervisor put it, interns often become "quite immersed in the fabric of the parish." For some of the students, this provides a kind of renewed connection with their own ethnic roots that going off to college had threatened to sever. By being entrusted with responsible roles in parish life, another supervisor noted, students begin to see themselves in new ways, both as "belonging" to the parish but also "as responsible actors, with contributions to make" to the life of the community. As one student summed up her experience, "most of the ideas [we invented for the retreats] come from putting ourselves in the position of the kids we're working with."

These experiences have clear educational value. A number of internship sites complement the campus work of the PTEV by providing and requiring explicit reflection by the interns. They meet regularly with their supervisors and each other to consider what they are encountering and learning, about the teenagers and families they are serving, and the ways that their academic learning can contribute to this work in the parishes they serve as well as to their own future careers. Some of the on-site supervisors require their interns to present their written reflections on their experience to the parish for feedback and comment. As one student put it, more than other campus involvements, "the Lilly program has put me in touch with real things." In the case of one senior student, as we have seen, these experiences crystallized his sense that he could find his life's calling in such work. Or, as another student said, "It has been a huge learning experience for me, not just spiritually, but in terms of personal self-confidence and my ability to work as a team member. It has helped me develop better as a person ... I've learned to engage with many points of view and people at different levels."

Our Lady of the Lake University is in a unique position to foster such education through cultivating relationships with the Hispanic community of San Antonio. The coeducational institution enrolls about 1500 undergraduates, both resident and commuter and many the first generation in their families to go to college, in a wide variety of major programs, with business, education, and social work predominating. The campus spirit is perhaps best revealed in its strong recovery from a fire which in 2008 devastated one of the most treasured buildings from the early days of the campus. Its reopening in 2011 was greeted by many as visibly reconnecting with a proud history. That history traces a long concern with equipping graduates to engage successfully with the turbulent tides of economic and demographic change that have characterized the American Southwest.

Our Lady of the Lake began the first program in social work in the region, with its Worden School of Social Service. It has long maintained connections with the Roman Catholic diocese of San Antonio, educating students in the liberal arts for careers in teaching, business, and government services. It has thereby participated in the international process of economic development and human migration, providing a base for enriching the material as well as spiritual lives of residents and immigrants alike. In doing so, the Sisters of the Congregation of Divine Providence have been important to the larger story. Like other orders of women religious in the West, they embody a long tradition of strengthening human connection and community, providing human understanding amid often baffling waves of change and conflict.[2]

Providing Positive Connection to the Life of Their Times

Today, Our Lady of the Lake continues to provide its students the opportunity for upward mobility and personal achievement, launching them into productive lives. The university has reason to be proud of its record in providing these opportunities on a slender resource base. But with the PTEV, it has added the conscious task of preparing its students to take a constructive part in one of the marked features of today's globalization. For the first time in human history, the majority of the human race now lives no longer in the countryside but shares increasingly globalized forms of urban life. Each month, five million people begin a great life transformation, as they move from the relative poverty of their villages in the countryside to burgeoning cities in search of a better life.[3] In the process, whole regions around the world are depleted of the young and aspiring. After making the trek, millions more continue to struggle, working to establish new ways of life amid the swirl of metropolitan development, more connected to their societies of origin than migrants in the past yet often unsure of their footing in the new society. For those caught up in this vast process, the new conditions bring freedoms unimaginable in village life and work on the land. Yet, these conditions can often be economically marginal and socially unmoored, making it harder to locate oneself, to make supportive connections in the new context, and to forge a new identity that builds upon and connects with the old.

In the United States, this now universal process has taken specific forms, first with vast immigrations from Europe, then the Great Migration of African-Americans from the South to the North and West, and again today as Asians, Africans, and Hispanic peoples from Latin America make their way across North America. Like Augsburg and Macalester Colleges in Minneapolis, Our Lady of the Lake finds itself at a confluence of these movements, and like them it has found the PTEV's focus on cultivating vocation a source of inspiration in shaping a response. *La Llamada*'s program of connecting students and staff with the work of Catholic parishes on the West Side provides a context within which both students and faculty can develop an understanding of the effects of these processes on their actual neighbors. As we have seen, the university's program supports strong interconnections between OLLU and these communities. At the same time, the themes of the Religion Department courses in which students begin their service work, which are based in contemporary Catholic Social Teaching, with its moral emphasis upon solidarity, human dignity, and the value of human flourishing, provide a lens for grasping the local situation as part of larger social patterns.

In addition to these local connections, a number of faculty and students have also taken part in "immersion" trips to rural Mexico. Here the great currents of change and migration become immediate and concrete. These experiences have been supported by the PTEV and link to the sisters' "Women of Providence" initiative. The sisters at the university maintain strong connections with their sisters in the Mexican province of their order. One result has been these trips in which the Mexican sisters provide hospitality—a major theme in the life of the Congregation of Divine Providence—as both they and the visitors are encouraged to share their life stories as they join with the Mexican sisters in projects the order is carrying out in the villages, supported in part by their North American sisters.

Participants are also taught how to reflect ethically on their experience, drawing from Latin American Theology of Liberation. For example, during the trip, sisters and faculty model for students a process of becoming critically aware of stereotypical responses to the poor and marginal. The first step is for the participants to acknowledge the force of the stereotype as they encounter poor and culturally or racially different people in the countryside. But rather than carrying through on the emotional response, perhaps a feeling of disgust or moral condemnation, the exercise asks participants to imagine responding, in speech or act, from a deliberate effort to extend dignity and a sense of inclusion to the person being encountered. Participants are then asked about how these two different modes of response affect their perception of the other, and then how they affect their sense of themselves. During their time on the trip, these exercises are repeating in varying contexts.

Another example of the reflective exercises these immersion trips entail is a debriefing exercise the students complete at the conclusion of each trip. Students are asked to describe several of the most surprising or moving experiences of their time away. They are then asked to respond to several questions regarding the social position of those they met, compared to that of their faculty and classmates. They are asked to consider the effects of these various social positions on their respective sense of self and possibilities. They are asked, in effect, to use their experience in rural Mexico as a catalyst to think about their own place in the world and to make more conscious their connections with others, both local and distant. Finally, students are asked explicitly to describe how these encounters with poverty, development, migration, and community building are affecting their own sense of purpose and future possibility. Student response has been highly positive, shown by the high level of interest the immersion trips continue to attract.

By conducting these reflections on campus, the organizers of the immersion experiences are hoping the students will learn to carry over something of this critical awareness into the shaping of their future lives. In fact, once students have returned to campus they are invited in a variety of ways to continue their vocational exploration and reflection. A business major reported choosing a nonprofit internship in order to "give back" to the community more directly than a career in business seemed likely to provide. These directions receive support from a number of offices on campus besides *La Llamada*. But it is importantly because of the program that these other offices now also incorporate encouraging students to reflect on their purposes and future vocation. As a staff person with the Career Services office reports, providing stipends for internships in non-profit organizations, spurred by the PTEV success with parish ministry, has materially changed the way students now think about their futures. While students have not typically considered the faith-based dimension when making decisions about jobs and careers, now they do. Increasingly at Our Lady of the Lake, students show a greater level of self-awareness of the potential meaning of their career choices for their lives.

At Our Lady of the Lake the PTEV was a key part of developing learning experiences that could address the whole student so powerfully. The process that Gloria Urrabazo led drew together personnel from both the academic and practical apprenticeships around the exploration of vocation. The key was building relationships, both on campus and between the campus and the larger world, local and more global. Thanks to her exceptionally creative personal leadership, Urrabazo has been able to gather a large number of collaborators, who in turn keep recruiting others. These include the students who reported conversations with Gloria that had recurring themes. "I see something in you ... try this ... keep at it ... what are you going to do next?" Once established, the university has helped sustain these networks of trust by incorporating them into everyday operations. For her part, Gloria talks about the project as "transforming my life" and "finding a deeper sense of vocation, of which God has clearly been a part." To date, the integrative energy stirred up by the Lilly grant has continued to revitalize a collective sense of agency and collective vocation on campus.

These are educational experiences that give globalization a human face while they provide students' personal development a community context. For the participants, both students and staff, the experiences are highly motivating. By prompting students to consider their own lives and relationships within a much wider perspective than most students consider, they introduce students to one of liberal education's most important values, learning to focus their academic knowledge and practical skills toward enriching the life of their times.

Building Community as the Organizational Context for Formative Learning

At the end of chapter 3, we noted three aspects of successful PTEV programs: the ongoing development of a faculty, staff, and student community focused around vocational exploration; ways of carrying the insights achieved in these groups into daily life through practices of self-reflection; plus the motivation to learn provided by encounters with people and situations outside the classroom. The pattern of integration developed at Our Lady of the Lake contains all three of these elements. As with other PTEV campus initiatives, the theme of vocation appealed to many students, as intended by the initiative. But it also caught the enthusiasm of faculty and staff, reshaping campus communities to make the exploration of vocation an organizing center of attention.[4] This in turn enabled these institutions to realize more fully core goals of liberal learning, especially helping students to use their developing academic knowledge to make sense of the world, and employing practical involvements to enable them to find a place from which to engage responsibly with their times. It seems that the exploration of vocation imparted a moral seriousness to their education that enhanced students' morale as well as their resilience in the face of difficulties. Awareness of the sacred likewise has fostered comprehensive concern with the whole of life, adding depth to individual quests for meaning.

In sum, the relationships into which the PTEV invited students, faculty, and staff alike provided a purposeful social nexus that also contributed to positive outcomes for many students, so that it became feasible to sustain programs that address students as whole persons preparing to live whole lives. Yet, colleges and universities share with business organizations and government agencies qualities of what sociologists call formal organizations. They are characterized by division of personnel by function, hierarchical relations of authority, and governed overall by formal rules and procedures. Their performance is monitored and measured to ensure that they achieve specified outcomes. Students experience these

features routinely as they move from the academic realm to student services, negotiating financial commitments, and the like.

As we have seen, however, the PTEV programs on the whole were not
like that. Rather, they were mostly organized to bring people together
because they shared aims and values with others. They were mostly
horizontal in structure, with little formal hierarchy or formal designa-
tion of authority. Instead, individuals were often recruited because they
knew and trusted others already so involved. Once they began to participate, however, these persons frequently spent time and effort cultivating
bonds of trust and mutual support, motivated by their realization that
they gained value from pursuing the exploration of purpose in common.
Social scientists consider these the traits typical of what they call a community type of organization. Indeed, social scientists have long noted that
in modern societies, even as formal organization proliferates to handle
growing social complexity, at the ground level people depend upon community forms of organization to develop dignity and gain a sense of significance for their lives. So, what gave the PTEV, with its communal form
of organization, its staying power amid the formal structure of college and
university organization?

The answer lies in the fact that the initiative was able to connect with
and often give new impetus to certain features of colleges that mark them
as partly organized on a communal basis. Higher educational institutions
are not, apart perhaps from some of the "for-profit" sector, simply formal
organizations. As phenomena like collegiate athletics and active alumni
support testify, they also embody conspicuous features of a community,
real or imagined, missing in many modern organizations. (Who, after all,
contributes to a former employer no matter how much they may recognize having benefited from having been employed there?) Learning and
personal development require strong formative environments. This is an
important reason education at all levels so often works through cohorts,
"small platoons" in which personal connection and shared history can
be expected to generate loyalty and engagement. While these communal
threads of higher educational institutions are tenuous in the contemporary context, the PTEV often gave them new efficacy.

A strength of community as a form of organization is that it provides
effective motivation for learning. Communities educate by mentoring. As
individuals participate in learning activities at the center of the community's concerns, they gain personal recognition, becoming more closely
bonded with the group and committed to its common aims. This is true

of athletic teams as well as high-performing groups in virtually every sector of society. Participation in such organizations brings into play all dimensions of the personality, so that the holistic, integrative aspects of identity formation become salient. This, in turn, promotes perseverance, resilience, and maturity.

A notable example of these features occurs in the preparation of professionals. Professions are defined, and their operations are to a significant degree guided by, shared knowledge, standards of practice, and norms of practice that they enforce on themselves and their members. These community features of professions can be contrasted to the incentives at work in bureaucratic organizations or in the one-off interactions typical of market relationships. While they are necessarily involved in both markets and bureaucratic organizations, professions continue to exhibit a "third logic" emphasizing the specific expertise and intrinsic values around which the profession is organized.[5] Indeed, it is typically in situations of communal mentorship, when novices begin to assume responsibility, under expert direction, for the effects of their actions on patients and clients in the actual world of work, that they develop the dispositions essential for professional identity.

These peculiar strengths of community organization have caught the attention of social scientists. Noting that schools with strong features of community organization outperformed otherwise comparable schools, James Coleman coined the term "social capital" to refer to the networks of connection and reciprocal support enjoyed by the staff and students of such organizations.[6] In a now-famous set of studies of the social bases of democratic government in Europe and the United States, Robert Putnam expanded the applicability of the concept of social capital beyond organizations to whole societies. "Social capital," wrote Putnam, "refers to connections among individuals—social networks and the norms of reciprocity and trustworthiness that arise from them." Putnam produced empirical evidence for the dependence of a host of positive social indicators on high levels of social capital. Societies high in social capital operate with what Putnam called a culture of "civic community." This gives them advantages less civic societies cannot share: they gain in efficiency while they are also more resilient in the face of problems because they can draw upon greater reserves of mutual trust and voluntary cooperation than more atomized and distrustful societies.[7]

There are resonances between these findings and developments in the world of global business, though with an important cautionary message as well. Recent decades of economic turmoil have produced radical restructuring in the business world. Seeking to gain the advantages of faster innovation in delivering goods and services more profitably, firms have experimented with more horizontally organized forms. Such organization has proven highly flexible in its ability to innovate as well as to learn and develop expertise. The key to such firms lies in developing their employees' skills and enlisting their loyalty and dedication. Management, for its part, must reciprocate with comparable loyalty over time in order to cultivate a strong shared commitment to common values and aims. To this extent, these experiments present a further demonstration of the value of relationships of the community-type, or social capital, for the efficiency of formal organizations. However, they also have revealed the fragility of communal organization in the face of intense competitive pressures that set off a "race to the bottom." Some businesses pressed by shareholders for greater profitability and by competitors for survival have simply reverted to cost-cutting and the use of short-term self-interest as alternative strategies. The result has been to undermine the social capital of the firm, weakening employee commitment. Whatever its effects on the company's profitability in the short term, such strategies do not build the capacities of their organizations to learn and innovate over the long run.[8] These experiences ought to serve as an important warning to higher education enterprises looking to emulate the "lean and mean" business organization as a guide to their own futures.

Vocation and Communal Organization: The Link between Form and Content

For effective educational enterprises, however, the fostering of community and social capital is anything but optional. These factors are key to the effectiveness in the core activity of the enterprise. This has been well illustrated by Anthony Bryk and Barbara Schneider in their study of a large-scale school improvement project in Chicago during the 1990s. In searching for factors that distinguished successful from unsuccessful schools, Bryk and Schneider identified a form of social capital as the most critical or "core" resource that made for school improvement. They contrasted the kind of "organic" trust typical of high social capital situations with the sort of "instrumental" trust more often found in short-term transactional relationships such as those between buyers and sellers in a market. For effective education, however, instrumental trust—the kind consumers may have for products they purchase—is insufficient.

This is because in educational organizations the quality of social relations is, as they wrote, "not just a mechanism of production but are a valued outcome in their own right ... [these relations] shape participants' lives ... they provide opportunities for self-identification and affiliation around an enterprise of much social value."[9] Because, Bryk and Schneider argued, "the aims of schooling are multiple and interrelated, the social dynamics of such workplaces are much more important, from a productivity perspective than ... [such social dynamics are in] well-defined and routinized production." Effective schools, they found, depend upon cooperation in pursuit of shared, valued ends, which requires successfully institutionalizing particular kinds of social relationships. These are based on specific role relationships that are governed by conscious reciprocity, in which long-term partnership and shared responsibility are built up over time.[10] In schools, the authors noted, achieving the kind of workplace organization that can produce the effects they document depends upon what they called "interpersonal discernment." By this they meant local leadership that is sensitive to these aims and able to manage complex relationships among staff, pupils, parents, and the larger community. It also requires similar qualities of the teaching staff, including the moral virtues of regard for others and responsibility. For community organization to be effective in particular schools, it also turned out, the school district itself had to actively facilitate and reward the cultivation of this kind of workplace culture of "intentional communities" based on strong organic trust among the participants.

The parallels between these findings about the educational effectiveness of community-type organizations that generate social capital through their functioning, and the record of the PTEV are striking. The successes of the PTEV programs resulted from similar kinds of organization. Significantly, as we have seen, successful programs relied on project leadership with strong capacities of interpersonal discernment. Our Lady of the Lake, profiled in this chapter, is one example. There is also evidence that in higher education, as in schools, results are stronger and more predictable over time when overall administrative leadership thinks and functions in a similar way.[11] Moreover, there is a fit between the way in which community type organizations educate, the focus on the whole student, and the vocational content the initiative was crafted to promote.

When communities are functioning well, the norms of everyday activity, such as teaching, learning, and being a "good citizen" of the organization tend to cohere and reinforce each other. To participate in good standing, members must enact the norms of reciprocity and mutual respect that govern the organization. Therefore, continued participation shapes dispositions to perceive and act that are congruent with those norms. Individuals can initially be engaged in groups for the sake of the expanded sense of self that recognition by others provides. But the norms in question, akin to those Putnam described as constituting a "civic community," add a dimension of concern about one's fellow members and therefore about the "common good" of the organization. The communal dimension of their interaction leads members to extend their concern beyond conformity to individual role or self-interest toward a spontaneous sharing of responsibility for making the whole enterprise go. These are familiar features of the life of successful teams and clubs of all sorts, which is why they provide such powerfully formative educational experiences. Carried out in this context, education necessarily involves each individual in developing habits of mind and a range of skills and competencies, even as community-regarding dispositions are being formed.

The kinds of experiential learning that PTEV programs brought into academic coursework often stimulated students in these directions. Through practices of self-reflection, they were led to consider the relevance of their learning for probing new questions about their social context as well as about their future. By provoking such reflection within the context of shared concern about what their lives might stand for, the programs opened new and personally significant questions for the students. The vocation programs, then, had two important, mutually reinforcing aspects. There was both a specific content—ideals of human community rooted in theological as well as secular cultural resources—and also an experiential basis for imagining how such notions of a common good might actually inflect the students' own futures.

As we have seen in a number of cases, these programs enabled their participants to make sense of their experience of a particular community of vocational quest not only as an individual exploration but as connected to a much broader human horizon. In this important sense, the participatory pedagogies employed by the initiative embody the civic aims of humanistic education. They employ a variety of academic disciplines to do this, but they give a new significance to the disciplines by placing them in dialogue with the concerns of the other apprenticeships.

This kind of educational context seems especially appropriate for today's students. As noted earlier, compared to their predecessors this generation of college students strikes informed observers as showing "reluctance to move from encounters to relationships," even though the vast majority of undergraduates declare that having a good marriage or committed relationship is an essential life goal. Intimacy now seems a scarce, much-sought after good. In practice, however, there is a preference for "dancing alone together," supported by parental involvements and mediated through digital media. These findings go along with reports of a generational delay of independence. That corresponds to a reluctance to become a "grown-up," so that present experiences do not seem to build toward future significance.[12] Reliable, ongoing relationships formed around significant issues in living, such as the vocation programs provided, were positive counterweights to these tendencies. Because they generate social capital, well-functioning vocational communities can deliver on the promise of stronger connectedness, making it possible for undergraduates to experience and judge for themselves the quality of life made possible by more engaged, adult styles of relating to the world and self.

The macro-social basis for undergraduate reluctance to engage and commit, as we saw in chapter 1, is a society in which all social relationships have become drastically more tenuous for everyone, but especially for the current youthful generation. This was the major finding of Robert Putnam's massive, landmark study that traced the significant weakening of American social connections.[13] These trends are tracked by economic changes, especially the hardening of barriers to social mobility and the deepening of the divides created by growing social inequality. Recent epidemiological research has shown this inequality to be correlated with falling levels of health and well-being in the United States, especially among the young.[14] Living as they do among all this, it is not surprising that many students feel uncertain and under stress, seeking more satisfying relations with others, even if they are not always effective at finding them. On the campuses reported in earlier chapters, the PTEV projects have been able to connect with these hungers, often to very good effect for the undergraduates involved. The projects have enabled many students to develop more hopeful outlooks and stronger coping skills as well as inspiration, enabling them to shape their lives in ways that contribute significance and value to the world as well as themselves.

"Being Heard": Recognition and Renewal
of Calling among Educators

While undergraduates were the primary intended beneficiaries of the initiative, however, they have been by no means the only participants to have received positive benefits from the projects. Faculty and staff live in the same larger social world as their students. They confront similarly bewildering challenges, augmented by adult worries about the responsibilities of their professional, family, and personal lives. One of the PTEV's strengths was its striking and positive effects on the faculty and staff who took part in the projects. How, then, did these adult communities of vocational nurture develop?

Because of their value, in hindsight it is striking that most of the successful programs developed spontaneously over time, often as a critical structural element that was not envisioned, or only vaguely imagined, at the beginning of the initiative. The spontaneous discovery was the importance for the larger effort of a community of faculty, usually extended over time to include staff from other areas of the campus. These groups provided a nucleus from which concern with vocational discernment could grow on campus. Establishing and expanding these groups was the key ingredient that enabled the programs to recruit suitable new teachers and mentors and, equally important, to nurture and develop them as professionals with a renewed sense of educational mission.

While each campus had its own nuanced story, a common outline is clear. The specific programs usually grew from the small groups of faculty, staff, and administrators appointed by top administration, often in some haste, in order to plan how to respond to the initiative. Since the focus of the initiative was firmly on students and their development, these groups generally included personnel responsible for all three kinds of apprenticeship. Leadership, as we have seen, was often handed by top administration to campus ministry or religious life. At Our Lady of the Lake, for example, the president appointed Gloria Urrabazo, then assistant director in campus ministry, to gather seven faculty and seven leaders from various campus departments to develop a first grant proposal to the Lilly Endowment. Out of discussions among this disparate planning group there emerged a plan for student internships, experiential course modules, and the many elements that would make *La Llamada* effective as a program. But it was the need to develop a common understanding of the meaning of vocational exploration, as well as to ensure that faculty and staff members could explain and recruit for the program in a consistent way, which led to continued meetings among the planners and, later, participating faculty and staff. Out of these developing conversations came the invitation to sisters of the Congregation of Divine Providence to become formally part of the effort.

Similar stories emerged on the other campuses. The communities of educators frequently came together initially for instrumental reasons. They worked together to support the "real work" of the PTEV, directed at students. Fairly quickly, however, the participants realized that they had almost accidentally created something of intrinsic rather than simply instrumental value for institutionalizing vocational discernment on campus.

These experiences illustrate a paradox that applies to all projects that depend upon strengthening communal forms of organization. While everyone stands to benefit from the positive social effects of higher levels of social capital, few individuals or groups have an immediate self-interest sufficient to motivate them to undertake the hard work of building trust and enforcing norms of reciprocity outside their immediate context. Few people, in other words, are primarily motivated by the desire to "build community" for its own sake. There usually has to be some other goal or good being sought, such as safety or efficiency, to enlist large numbers in developing new relationships based on reciprocity and trust. The idea of enabling students to find their calling in life proved to be one such motivating goal. In the process of pursuing it, the educators in the vocation projects also discovered a synergy between cultivating a community of educators and educating the whole student.

Asked about the value these groups had for them, over and over faculty and staff members spoke of "being heard." By this they meant their deepened realization that what they contributed to the campus was recognized by others, especially high administration, as having value for the greater enterprise. The very existence of the groups was sometimes taken as a refreshing sign that administrators cared about the vocational lives of staff and faculty. In these groups, faculty and staff took part in conversations as peers—something that was often reported as especially important by chaplains, student affairs, counseling, and career office participants. They spoke about themselves and their own struggles to find purpose or, sometimes the difficulties of sustaining a sense of meaning through periods of difficulty or times of disengagement from their careers. The apparently escalating demands of work performance intensified their concerns about balancing work, family, and personal life. Participants reported feeling freer to talk about their own quests for larger meaning and religious understanding with others they had grown to respect and trust. Faculty spoke a lot about the pressures of disciplinary scholarship versus time with students. Staff talked about worries about recognition as educators in their own right. Many reported developing greater ease in speaking about the ups and downs of their lives in terms of purpose and calling, saying that this had been important in enabling them to engage with similar themes with students.

The experience of such faculty–staff vocation groups did not resolve all problems, personal or organizational, but it did expand the bandwidth for conversations and connections. Such groups enhanced the communal qualities of campus life, especially through the spillover effects of these conversations into faculty and staff work with students. In some cases, this raised new questions about how to maintain appropriate distinctions between communication with students about vocational themes and religious and moral freedom. The value added here was that these themes could be surfaced as matters the campus community as a whole could work toward understanding better and responding to more effectively. The revivified bonds of trust and cooperation among educators provided more resilience for engaging in difficult conversations amid conflicting agendas on campus, making the formal organizational structures work better because they could be seen as furthering a common purpose rather than dampening spontaneous energy. Such a record of achievement provokes a reasonable question about how such groups worked. What were the kinds of activities that made them flourish?

A *Faculty Learning Community: The Manresa for Faculty Project at Marquette University*

The idea of learning communities has been part of higher education for some decades. The notion is that liberal learning happens best when students and educators work together over time in communities that are small enough so that everyone knows everyone else's name and yet span a significant breadth of disciplines trained on wide-angle questions. The PTEV at Marquette University in Milwaukee, Wisconsin, adapted this organizational model to an experiment with what they called "a faculty learning community focused on Ignatian pedagogy." Like Santa Clara,

Marquette is a Roman Catholic, Jesuit institution of medium size, offering a wide range of arts and sciences majors as well as professional programs in a number of fields at the undergraduate and graduate levels. Unlike its California cousin, however, Marquette is rooted in the old industrial heartland of the Midwest and draws its students primarily from that region. Of the nearly 2000 first-year students enrolled in 2013 (of 8,365 undergraduates total), 66 percent were Catholic, 20 percent belonged to another Christian religion, and 22 percent represented ethnic minorities.[15]

The organizers of Manresa drew upon their growing experience in the PTEV to add a faculty learning community to enhance the visibility of the vocational theme in students' academic learning. So, while the PTEV at Marquette emphasized student retreats, educational programs, and service projects, this latter development recognized the importance of a strong basis for vocational discernment within the first apprenticeship. A salient aim of constituting a faculty learning community was a common focus on teaching: to enable interested educators to develop vocational emphases in their courses and to explore the rich heritage of vocational discernment laid out in the spiritual tradition of St. Ignatius, the founder of the Jesuits. The approach was to foster this in an authentic way, as a consequence of the faculty members' engagement with the theme in their own professional work. To spread the influence of the PTEV, the team imagined faculty cohorts drawn from across the university, including the professional schools as well as the arts and sciences disciplines.

Susan Mountin, director of Manresa for Faculty and Rebecca Nowacek of the English Department led the effort, supported by Philip Rossi, S. J., interim dean of Arts and Sciences and member of the Theology Department faculty (he and Mountin were coauthors of the PTEV grant). They brought different disciplinary and career perspectives to imagining a faculty learning community. When combined, these proved complementary yet diverse enough to give rise to a novel program. The watchword was reflection, which the program's designers understood as a practice of "stopping and entering a text or a situation with empathy and sensory imagination as well as critical reasoning."

Rebecca Nowacek brought to the design her experience as a scholar in the Carnegie Academy for Scholarship of Teaching and Learning (CASTL), supported by the Carnegie Foundation for the Advancement of Teaching during the past decade. At the CASTL workshops, Nowacek had been impressed by the idea that various fields give rise to distinctive modes of teaching that present to students in compressed form the core concepts of the field, and its view of the world. This notion of "signature pedagogy" had been developed by Lee S. Shulman, former president of the Carnegie Foundation, from research on education in professional fields such as law and medicine.[16] Such signature pedagogies link together habits of head, hand, and heart. For instance, a crucial stage of medical education takes place in the hospital or clinic, where medical students and residents have the responsibility for presenting patients' cases to the supervising physician and are questioned about their understanding of the case in the therapeutic context itself. Other disciplines and professions have developed signature pedagogies of their own. Was there, Rebecca and Susan wondered, a signature pedagogy that embodied the Jesuit emphasis upon vocational discernment?

Using the concept of signature pedagogy as a lens for understanding the Jesuit educational mission produced an important result. The positive answer the team formulated relied on an analysis of contemporary Jesuit education as it has shaped pedagogical practice in Jesuit institutions in recent decades. Philip Rossi summarized this analysis by first noting that since the Second Vatican Council of the 1960s, the Jesuit order has sharpened its own mission around a renewed emphasis upon the larger Christian mission of social justice and service to humanity. In more recent decades, however, this outward-looking emphasis has been increasingly complemented by a renewed appreciation of one the fundamental spiritual practices of the order's founder, Ignatius of Loyola. The team noticed how closely the focus of the educational mission corresponded to the central aim of Jesuit spirituality itself. As articulated by Jesuit leaders in recent decades, this aim has become clearer. It represents a new form of a key practice of the order's founder, Ignatius of Loyola. This is what the Jesuits call the "Examen of Consciousness," which is intended to bring the discernment of vocation into everyday living.

In an earlier chapter, we have seen this practice extended and applied at other Jesuit universities such as Santa Clara and Boston College. At Marquette, thanks to the collaboration of the Manresa team, it was formulated as a signature pedagogy first explored and rehearsed by the participating faculty themselves. In its classic form, as set out in the *Spiritual Exercises* of St. Ignatius, the Examen of Consciousness is a method for discovering what Ignatius called the "movements" of the inner self and through probing these, working to bring to greater clarity one's patterns of response to the world and to others, based upon a faith that divine goodness, which is already present in the self and the world, calls forth a response of cooperation and creation. To discern where, when, and how to make—and sustain—this response is to find one's vocation. Seen in light of this approach, the signature pedagogy emerges as a learning process that is reflective and dialogical in character. Its aim is to discern possible larger significance in present experience and to pursue the positive potentials for action such a meaning might entail.

The Manresa learning community set out, then, to translate this spiritual vision into practices of teaching and learning. As examples of the signature pedagogy, these practices were intended to bring the process of discernment into the particular intellectual inquiries of various disciplines and professions. To make this effective, Susan Mountin developed the idea of adapting the familiar Jesuit format of a retreat in order to involve participating faculty directly in the discernment process. Manresa begins with selecting a cohort of eight faculty members who receive a small stipend. They are religiously pluralistic (the 2010 cohort, for example, consisted of Roman Catholics, Protestants, and Muslims, as well as agnostics) and include tenured senior faculty, tenure-track junior faculty, and contingent faculty, and range across the disciplines, from law and engineering to philosophy and biology.

Participants spend a spring semester meeting monthly for two hours to discuss works selected to open up discussion on issues of Ignatian tradition, on teaching and scholarship as vocation, and texts on contemporary understandings of teaching and learning. Then, in May, they leave the campus for a two-day retreat that includes a day of silent reflection based in Ignatian tradition followed by one devoted to planning for course development. Over the summer, participants develop new course materials and teaching methods, which they try out in the fall semester, while also meeting monthly to discuss their teaching and their developing sense of their academic calling. The experience culminates in public presentations of their experiences.

The three cohorts of the learning community based in Ignatian pedagogy have provided useful feedback as well as impressive examples of the results of their participation. For instance, an economics professor who teaches in the Business School now regularly discusses the tenets of Jesuit education with her students. A theology professor has reshaped a required course to include an opening section in which students investigate the contemporary significance of classic biblical images such as the Good Shepherd, the Prodigal Son, Abraham's Call: what might they reveal about today's world, about what is important? A professor in the law school reported that students were amazed when he asked them to think about future career paths in the law with reference to the value different paths might add to the society. "How are you going to assess us on this?" they asked.

Throughout the diversity of fields, Philip Rossi explained, the participants in the Manresa project have discovered and experimented with a common approach that he contextualized within the Ignatian Pedagogical Paradigm's "Context—Reflection—Evaluation—Action" model. It is a distillation of Jesuit discernment as a signature pedagogy.[17] It also describes the practices of the faculty learning community. The premises of the model come from the religious and cultural traditions that the university embraces. As summarized in the Ignatian tradition, these are ideal aims at human flourishing and reverence for the creator expressed in care for creation. While inspiring, these values are general. But as Rossi pointed out, the point of humanistic education with a focus on vocational discernment is to equip students to resourcefully work out their implications for actual living.

Here, the interpretation of situation, or Context, becomes a major theme. This is where the special expertise of the various disciplines can play a major role. But the second movement, Reflection, involves a kind of dialogue between theory and experience. There is the movement of application of the insights from academic analysis to various kinds of experience, personal, social, or historical. But there is also the testing of the insights offered by this movement against experience itself: Evaluation. This mutual testing leads naturally toward the fourth movement of Action. And it is here, in working out how to bring together the insights of the earlier movements with the values embodied in the religious and cultural traditions that the university embraces, that the major work of discernment takes place. In the faculty learning community, the primary locus of Action is the participants' teaching and scholarship.

While Manresa has given its signature pedagogy a specifically Ignatian inflection, it resonates with many forms of humanistic learning. Humanistic thinking is distinctive in its emphasis upon interpretation, and therefore upon texts and inherited traditions of thought, as a primary way of engaging the world. The humanistic tradition presupposes that as social and historical beings, we are already engaged in making sense of the world and seeking a meaningful way to respond to experience. Inquiry's task is to make explicit and public these implicit efforts at making sense of things as well as to open them to criticism. Cultural traditions can function as repositories of imaginative possibilities for constructing, and criticizing, such responses. The communities of inquiry that universities and colleges are at their best continue to enact these humanistic aims whenever they allow questions of purpose to become objects of exploration. One of the contributions of the Manresa project to its university is that, inspired by the PTEV, it has given new seriousness to this enduring educational aim.

Nurturing a Community of Educators: The Provost's Seminar at Messiah College

"Groups like Amnesty International and the International Justice Mission raise awareness of global injustice, and missionary agencies, charities, and newspapers inform us of the needs of our local and international neighbors. How do you decide when to get involved?"[18] So asks *Gracious Christianity*, authored by former college president Rodney Sawatsky and Douglas Jacobsen, senior member of the Religion Department. The subtitle, *Living the Love We Profess*, underscores that it is a book about vocation. It is required reading by every first-year student at Messiah College in "Created and Called for Community," a course that was developed as part of the PTEV. The same text is also read in the Provost's Seminar. This is required of all new faculty, who receive a course release in order to join during their first semester at the college. In fact, all new employees of a professional grade, including resident directors, some admissions personnel, counselors, and administrators, take part in the seminar. It, too, is a learning community, one centered on their common vocation as educators. The urgency of the quotation above conveys one key aspect of the spirit of Messiah College. The inclusive nature of the Provost Seminar suggests another feature of the institution's tradition. In essence, a new learning community is formed annually that focuses on the meaning of vocation for incoming educators. Members of this learning community cross all parts of campus and often include people who are arriving as full professors (with years of experience) as well as just-out-of-grad-school professors and student life professionals. But typically they bond and they stay connected, often for many years after the formal seminar has concluded.

Messiah College is rooted in the Brethren in Christ tradition. This is a Christian body derived from several strands within Anabaptist and Protestant traditions (e.g., Wesleyan, Pietist, and Evangelical) that have sought to infuse spiritual vitality into contemporary life, especially through the personal sharing of faith and the collective discernment of its social implications. The Provost's Seminar can therefore connect with a deep strand within the college's heritage. The Brethren in Christ tradition shares with the "peace churches" such as the Mennonites and Quakers a greater emphasis on religious authenticity and social action than on doctrinal orthodoxy or scriptural literalism. It interprets the Christian gospel as focused on bearing witness in the world to the values of peace, justice, and compassion for the poor and disenfranchised embodied in Christ's proclamation of the kingdom of God. As one of Messiah College's most distinguished alumni, the educator Ernest L. Boyer, put it: "To be truly human, one must serve."[19] And indeed every April the entire campus suspends classes and spends a day in active service. At the same time, Messiah today explicitly welcomes Christians of quite different traditions, including Evangelicals, Catholics, Lutherans, and Presbyterians in the student body and faculty. Of Messiah's roughly 2700 undergraduates 42 percent come from out of state, and 10 percent come from underrepresented racial, ethnic, and cultural populations. Through the College Ministries office, students are encouraged to take a "spiritual formation survey" to help them discover their "spirituality type."[20]

Messiah is like a number of other church-related institutions for whom the initiative provided means to carry further an already embarked-upon trajectory rather than recalling a partially lost heritage. The college's statement of faith is consciously respectful of all the major Christian traditions, for example, Catholic, Pentecostal, and Orthodox, as well as various mainline Protestants and Evangelicals.

The faculty and staff learning community sustained by the Provost's Seminar has had an important effect in bringing the exploration of vocational purpose into higher relief in both the undergraduate program and in faculty and staff routines. For example, it serves as a seedbed for faculty who teach in the required core course, "Created and Called for Community." As in Marquette's Manresa project, faculty here probe their own vocational narratives together, developing mutual trust and coming to conceive their journeys toward purpose as sharing features with others who have been drawn to various aspects of a common, larger vocation to educate. They also use their own experience to help devise strategies for making the exploration of vocation more accessible for their students.

In the first-year seminar, the readings, discussions, and papers are designed to lead students into an appreciation of the vision of life shaped

by the values of the Brethren in Christ tradition. It is not a dogmatic process but one marked by the humanistic practices of critical reading of
texts and reflective writing. This wide-ranging intellectual exploration
is concretely linked to students' experiences during the course through
service learning. This component, called "Service Day," directed by an
alumnus, Chad Frey, is closely interwoven with the classroom experience
through discussions and written reflections that bring both parts of the
students' educational experience into dialogue. The PTEV has had the
effect of greatly enlarging the number of service-learning courses across
the curriculum and co-curriculum that include components of service,
content, and reflection.

At Messiah this kind of back-and-forth between faith and experience,
relationship and reflection is sometimes called "Incarnational Pedagogy."
By this they mean that, just as Christians believe that God's intentions
and purposes were revealed through the words and actions of Christ,
so disciples also need to learn how to find and embody divine purposes
in their lives. In "Created and Called for Community," the aim is that
ideals and doubts discussed be tested and examined reflectively against
encounters and relationships with others from different backgrounds and
understandings of life. All majors conclude with a senior capstone seminar that reintroduces these themes as a way for students to pull together
their growing competence in their major field with the broad aims of a liberal education at Messiah. This same process is modeled in the Provost's
Seminar, where it can be explored in relation to the other educational roles
its members play at the college, in admissions, student services, financial
aid, and career planning. In the process, the definition of "educator" is
consciously extended to include virtually all those on the staff who work
with students in an educational capacity. This is the first apprenticeship
working in close concert with the second and third.

Since the coming of the PTEV, however, not only has vocation become
more focal in the curriculum and the Provost's Seminar, but it has also
taken on heightened salience for younger faculty through the Christian
Scholarship Seminar. This has become the "second semester" extension
of the Provost's Seminar for tenure-track faculty. These cohorts of faculty
new to campus draw members from all departments. Despite differences
in discipline and academic interests, they share an important stage in
their academic careers. The common focus of the seminar is on how their
intellectual quests and research relate to the educational mission of the
college and its institutional embodiments.

Directed by Douglas Jacobsen of the Religion Department and Rhonda Hustedt Jacobsen who heads the Provost's Seminar as well as faculty development at Messiah, this seminar allows newly arrived faculty to get seriously engaged with the issue of how the traditional values of the academy, in which all the members have been deeply shaped by their graduate study, might be related to the themes of Christian vocation such as explored in the Provost's Seminar.

The Christian Scholarship Seminar was one direct result of the Lilly grant. The intention was to initiate a seminar that built a strong sense of vocation into faculty development programming, and to build something that would continue beyond the grant period. The aim is that participants will come to a deeper understanding of the potential of their future scholarly careers, not only as providing advances in knowledge but as contributing to their own vocational purpose of engaging with their students, their disciplines, and the public. As one former participant, Cynthia A. Wells, assistant professor of higher education and fellow at the Ernest L. Boyer Center (named for the alumnus quoted earlier) emphasized, "the seminar is immensely helpful to new faculty, providing a space to engage theological convictions in concert with scholarly and educational commitments." Not surprisingly, the report has been that cohorts have grown close through their mutual exploration and remained so, adding the social lubricant of better mutual understanding and trust to the interplay among the disparate departments of the college.

These learning communities enable faculty and staff at Messiah to engage in a supportive and leisurely context with one of the most important questions confronting academics who espouse the traditional ideals of liberal learning. Is it possible to live a productive life committed to the values of liberal learning and also participate fully and constructively in today's professional world in which narrow specialization and competitive careerism threaten intellectual breadth and integrity of purpose? The urgency of the question is perhaps even greater for those who believe themselves called to a life of teaching and nurturing college students. At Messiah, where the practical commitments of religious faith receive prominence, this issue is especially evocative. A leading scholar of Church History, Richard P. Hughes, heads its Sider Institute for Anabaptist, Wesleyan, and Pietist Studies, which has made these themes prominent for both faculty and students.

The faculty and staff quests for clarity and conviction about how their own vocations have provided a kind of rehearsal for their scholarship and teaching, bringing these perspectives into a variety of areas of campus life. In a similar way, the vocation program at Messiah has given rise to a new initiative known as Eyas. It carries the institution's service orientation outward, as students are asked to participate in giving financially to support the college's service efforts around the world, and inward, as students are asked to reflect on the implications for themselves of what donors have done for them. The idea that one's life purpose, whatever it may become, is rooted in a great exchange of generosity resonates with the college's founding spirit. It also makes the values of community life and responsibility real, shaping lifelong habits of mind and heart. This is education to enable students to contribute their best to the life of their times.

6

Recovering Liberal Education's Humanistic Aims

THE PTEV IN COMPARATIVE PERSPECTIVE

"EVERY STUDENT SHOULD have an experience like this . . . you learn a lot about yourself . . . it allows you to get really close to a small group of peers, and to learn from each other, and to truly see the value of cross-disciplinary study and understanding." This was a Harvard College student's response to a survey of undergraduates who had spent their three-week winter break on a study and service trip to Uganda. Another student commented, "I honestly learned more from this experience than I think I've learned in any given semester at Harvard . . . This type of experience fosters the sense among each student that they have a personal stake in the experience—the fact that everyone is there to learn . . . makes it a lot more fulfilling."[1] While they emphasized the importance of learning from their similarly motivated peers, students also saw the course as providing new relationships with faculty as co-learners or, in the language of the course, "co-creators" of effective knowledge. One student observed that the course "showed me the potential of tackling a world problem with an interdisciplinary team of students and adults . . . through the lenses of different disciplines."[2]

The catalytic experience the students are commenting upon was a course entitled "Leadership, Service, and Collaborative Learning," offered for academic credit during the January term. It was sponsored jointly by the Business School, the School of Education, and the Center for the Environment based in the School of Arts and Sciences, and conceived as a project to combine educational innovation with support for the Kasiisi

Project, an ongoing collaboration between Harvard and the Mountains of the Moon University in Uganda. During the first of the three weeks, Harvard faculty provided preparatory learning about issues of economics and business, environment and climate, and education and social organization. During the two weeks the group spent in Uganda, the students worked alongside Ugandan university students with faculty from the Mountains of the Moon University providing the expertise. In the Uganda context, their institution is particularly focused on the environmental and human challenges attendant on sustainable economic development and adaptation to climate change. Throughout the experience, a team of Harvard faculty provided continuity and sponsored a continuous process of discussion and reflection on the experience.

The course drew sophomore and junior level students, whose nucleus came from Cabot House, a Harvard residential community that joined in sponsoring the trip.

The project's purpose was to teach pupils in primary school—often the final educational experience of Ugandan subsistence farmers—about the impact of human development on the Kimbale National Park, home to a threatened chimpanzee population. The Harvard students in the course described being moved by "the beauty and majesty" of Uganda and the openness and hospitality of its people. At the same time, they became drawn into the complex economic and educational challenges of developing a future workforce attuned to more sustainable methods of farming and marketing within a rapidly changing environment.

Forming a Learning Community through International Collaboration and Service

In the course, students devoted a good deal of their time to researching and developing an agricultural farm club that could promote sustainable new forms of agriculture to provide alternatives to destructive old ones. Through the interchange with both Ugandan faculty and parents and children at the schools, the visiting students came to understand more of the difficulty and complexity of the issues involved, as well as their need to learn and develop more in order to confront them. As one Harvard student put it, "Being in a situation where you are not extremely comfortable ... that is so vastly different from anything you have experienced before, is an incredible way of practicing being adaptive ... you have to be able to find little joys in trying new things and working in [new] ways."[3] A number of students emphasized that their brief encounter with the concrete issues in Uganda had given a new seriousness and depth to their intention to become responsible leaders.

The experimental course was made possible by the President's Fund for Innovation in Teaching and Learning. It was explicitly aimed at three objectives. One was directly pedagogical, to "engage in a new experimental learning model through co-creation with peers and faculty at Harvard College to determine if such an approach could be developed further and serve as a model for future effort." Second, the course sought to enable its participants to "learn about the challenges of the world through an interdisciplinary approach to study." The third objective sought to provide specific knowledge useful for furthering the Kasiisi project in rural Uganda.

From the results of the survey conducted in spring semester, it became clear the experimental course had achieved its aims to a significant extent. Students responded to the challenge of a new situation and complex "real world" problems that spanned the interconnected environmental, economic, and educational issues. They often did so in innovative ways, using their own disciplinary and service backgrounds to provide perspective. For example, some students focused on the environmental issues directly. Others investigated the educational challenge in considerable depth, developing familiarity with the particular features and situation of Uganda's state schooling system. They concluded that Uganda's university graduates were "the key to the country's future," while urging that curricular models not be simply imported wholesale from developed countries but constructed to suit local needs. Students who focused on the business and economic aspects of the situation emphasized the possible contributions of micro-lending and the ecotourism industry for linking subsistence farmers into networks of economic development.

Perhaps most significantly, many of the students emphasized how, by placing Ugandan development within larger frames of reference even as they were immersed in the particularities of the local context, they came to see new implications in what they were learning, both for those they met in Uganda and for their own futures. One student reported being told by one of her Ugandan student peers that "I've learned to see the beauty and resources of Uganda through your eyes." This made clear to that student how developing relationships and shared understanding with others from different contexts can have mutually important effects in expanding both parties' understanding of themselves and their world.

As another student put it, if the school projects for teaching awareness of sustainability succeed, and Ugandans in large numbers can recognize the value of their environment and develop positive links between "modernization and conservation," then the country will be on a path toward a uniquely balanced and viable form of development.[4] These same students reported a strong intention to continue working with the Kasiisi Project and return to Uganda in the summer. They described their involvement as a form of leadership, one of the values much emphasized in Harvard undergraduate education. Through this course, that vague and general idea had come to take on more specific meaning. For students striving to answer the question, "what do I want to do with my life?," the answer would now be bound up with building good communities, a purpose they now realized could motivate a variety of specific careers and a number of possibilities for future study.

The Educative Power of Community: Reflection with a Shared Purpose

In their reflections on the experience, many students stressed how the course had affected their lives as students and their stance toward their own learning. They appreciated the construction of the course: "The pre-trip seminars by professors from the Business School, the School of Education, and Arts and Sciences ... equipped me with new intellectual frameworks that I used to make sense of various issues we encountered on the trip. It has materially changed the way that I view the world." Others responded strongly to the experience of developing a model of "co-creating" knowledge through student–faculty and peer-to-peer dialogue around engagement with complex situations. For such students, much of the appeal of the experience lay in its capacity to "break down the traditional silos of cutthroat competition that ordinarily inhibit genuine student-to-student cooperation." Similarly, others saw great value in escaping the typical classroom demands for "right answers." In this course, by contrast, "learning to ask good questions" was the valued skill, and it was encouraged by the mix of faculty and students, from both the United States and Uganda, who because of their differing backgrounds "noticed different things and contributed different kinds of questions."[5]

Particularly striking was the repeated reference by students to discovering a stronger sense of agency in their learning and, by extension, in determining the direction of their future lives. One student claimed to have never "felt such a powerful sense of agency in shaping my educational experience." When coupled with the testimony about feeling relief from competitive conformity, this provided a window on the experience of Harvard undergraduates that might surprise some. These students, bright, accomplished, and ambitious, nevertheless felt heavily constrained by their institution's culture to think in conventional ways, not to take risks, and to be wary of cooperation and trust. Released from such competitive constraints, students on the trip felt able and interested in suggesting educational innovation. As one student proposed, why not use the course as a model of how to "tweak the freshman seminar system for upperclassmen? . . . One or two professors would be paired up with 10 students from different backgrounds [who then] could look at a challenge that the world faces. It would be discussion-based with case studies, readings, field trips, guest lectures, and a final product." Such a program, this student thought, would be of greater and more transformative value than "various much-discussed classroom technologies for improving undergraduate education."[6]

Such reflection was encouraged by the pedagogy of the course. In addition to common readings and case-based discussions in seminar settings with faculty, plus lectures from professors in the three disciplines in both Cambridge and Uganda, the students were each assigned a study partner for the course. Every day, these study groups met to discuss their experiences and write entries in a trip journal, which they turned in at the end of the course. In addition, students attended lengthy communal debriefings almost every night of the trip, during which they talked through observations, questions, and problems. An interdisciplinary team of faculty led the debriefings and also read and evaluated the journals and final reflective papers. The discussions continued through follow-up meetings held during the following spring semester. And, although there was no requirement for this, students continued to talk with each other about issues from the course through blogs.

"Leadership, Service, and Collaborative Learning" evolved quickly into a learning community similar to those formed on PTEV campuses. But at Harvard, too, the learning community grew from prepared soil. The course was hosted and anchored by Cabot House, once known as the Radcliffe Quadrangle, which houses over 300 students, along with 20 tutors and staff. Under the leadership of House Masters Rakesh Khurana, a professor at the Business School, and Stephanie Khurana, who also holds postgraduate degrees from the university, Cabot House has moved decidedly toward providing more opportunities for student involvement and shared responsibility. The residential complex, at some remove from the center of campus, has developed its own, student-run Cabot Café. The House sponsors speakers and weekly discussions on a variety of topics. So, it was a natural step for Rakesh Khurana to have supported students' interest in applying for a Presidential Fund grant to fund the trip and then to have led the interdisciplinary faculty team. The purpose throughout, according to Khurana, is "to create the next generation of leaders . . . leaders to solve problems of the community wherever they are. This, I tell them, is what the world will expect from you."

In sum, the organization and pedagogy of the course, as well as the organization of Cabot House, exhibit the educational strengths of what the previous chapter described as the community form of organization. There, several examples drawn from the vocation initiative illustrated how the ties of shared expectations and commitment to common purposes can energize and intensify the activities of learning communities, even within formally structured organizations such as universities. In the PTEV, the effects of these learning communities were amplified by the intentional fostering of reflective skills and practices among participants.

The Harvard experiment reveals similar features and produced similar outcomes: high morale among students and faculty, intensified commitment to learning, development of new skills and capacities, and discovery of new implications for living from the content and relationships created during the experience. While the Harvard experiment did not use the vocabulary of vocation, the experience clearly enabled its participants to deepen their concern for and understanding of how to use their educational experiences to shape significant life paths for themselves, and perhaps others.

The students involved in "Leadership, Service, and Collaborative Learning" clearly intensified their engagement with the first apprenticeship of academic learning, in both disciplinary and interdisciplinary ways. The genesis of the course from the communal context of Cabot House testifies to a heightening of the social apprenticeship of personal development. But the overall trajectory of the students' experience exemplifies the apprenticeship of identity and purpose. The course was not directly focused on questions of student identity or purpose, yet it had the effect of broadening the participants' sense of the world while also engaging them in a specific situation and particular relationships.

As intended, the experience fostered strong and exciting cognitive growth. But it also engaged students in other ways that had dramatic effects. By demanding a variety of practical involvements, it stimulated self-reflective questions that the students found compelling and all too rare in their more conventional courses. The students were in no doubt that this course represented something of extraordinary value in their educational experience.

The Thread of Humanistic Learning

This chapter will examine several experiments that, like the Harvard immersion experience, represent important, and pedagogically potent, innovations that center on integrating the college experience through the third apprenticeship. Like the PTEV initiative, these experiments draw upon contemporary knowledge about effective learning practices. But they are also acts of recovery. They are reclaiming insights and approaches to learning that have been relegated to the margins of higher learning during the past century. Focused on students' relation to the subject matter, their evolving self-understanding, and the formative aim of educating active democratic citizens, these approaches have continued or reinvented practices at the historic core of humanistic learning.

The signature of humanistic learning and inquiry is its cultivation of a double or bifocal vision of knowledge. On the one hand, like the sciences, humanistic inquiry demands rigor in the application of cognitive tools of analysis to study events from the *outside*. However, humanistic learning also seeks to understand the meaning of actions and events from *within*, seeing the whole range of human achievement as aspects of a common process in which all persons can claim a share. Humanistic inquiry, even in its formalized manifestations in rhetoric and interpretive theory, always takes place within the larger framework of human communities of speech and interaction, the "cultures" that arise historically from the basic processes of human development.

All human activity, including knowing and judging, occurs within this common framework of communication and interaction. More specialized modes of cognition, including the objectified, analytical view of the sciences, which has proven so powerful for understanding and controlling the environment, still arise from particular stances within the larger frame of historical, cultural interaction.[7] But humanistic inquiry has evolved to be self-consciously aware of its involvement within, rather than outside, the matrix of cultural life.

For this reason, humanistic learning can never be solely cognitive. It is concerned with making sense of cultural life, including criticisms of existing cultural forms, and so demands a response from those who encounter it. Like the arts, the practice of humanistic inquiry cultivates imagination and empathy, as well as aesthetic and moral awareness. It is rooted in participation in what it seeks to understand. Therefore, it employs critical distance but also engaged participation. These are the two, contrasting foci that define the humanistic approach to knowledge. They represent not opposites but an essential polarity that, when creatively combined, fosters not only sharpness of mind but depth of spirit and ethical sensitivity.

An Expansive Idea of a Classic

The story of humanistic learning in modern American higher education has been problematic. The first apprenticeship has grown progressively more distant from students' practical lives as well as from questions of identity and purpose. Today, however, awareness of living in a more interconnected world reveals some deeply problematic consequences of these separations. The import of this for our global era—which demands greater empathic understanding of others as well greater responsibility than previously—has recently been traced by Wm. Theodore de Bary, a distinguished scholar of East Asian culture who helped introduce East Asian thought to Western audiences.

In *The Great Civilized Conversation: Education for a World Community*, de Bary recounts the genesis of "general education" at Columbia University in the years prior to World War I. The classical tradition of the older liberal arts college was already under threat from growing intellectual specialization and the elective system promoted by Charles Eliot's recasting of Harvard on the new research model. A new way to address the formative intentions of the older curriculum was put forward by a now nearly forgotten figure, John Erskine, whom we met briefly in chapter 3, proposed something he called a "general honors" course. Erskine's innovation was an experiment, at first open only to selected undergraduates, in which faculty would read and discuss a variety of works translated from many literatures, rather than the earlier canon consisting entirely of Greek and Roman works.[8]

The key idea was that the texts would be "classics," a term de Bary finds especially resonant since it is also what the great works of Chinese thought have long been called in East Asia. De Bary notes that to Erskine, "a classic text was a great work of art not only in its literary perfection but in its appeal to the heart, the senses, and the aesthetic imagination." Erskine, according to de Bary, ". . . resisted the enshrinement of 'critical thinking' as the be all and end all of learning, which he judged could only result in the narrowing and impoverishment of the self, unless it included sympathetic appreciation and synthesis as well as critical analysis."[9] It is significant that Erskine not only taught literature, but was a creative artist himself, a composer and an author of poetry, plays, and a novel. From the beginning, then, the notion of a "general education" curriculum was intended to engage the student in intellectual, emotional, and social understanding, and not just cognitive awareness. Over time, the works studied expanded to a very rich set of readings in literature, philosophy, and history, including the history of science and the arts. Erskine understood and implemented the twofold quality of humanistic learning.

The key idea revealed in Erskine's original inspiration for what would later be called "great books" was twofold. First, students were to probe and assess the value of the texts for their own lives. Pedagogy was to take the form of active discussion rather than lecture. The idea was to engage students with each other and with the instructor, reinvigorating inherited wisdom by using it to illuminate the contemporary. Surprisingly, Erskine's innovation, renamed the Colloquium, became a general requirement at Columbia, the first part of the "Core" curriculum.

The second element of the Columbia Core was introduced as a response to America's increasing global involvement in the wake of World War I. Called Contemporary Civilization, this was also a discussion-based class, and like the colloquium typically led by a team of two instructors with about a dozen student participants. However, the course was focused directly on social problems of the moment, most notably war and social injustice. As de Bary notes, the rationale for this requirement was "a civic one . . . Columbia should educate its students to deal in an informed way with the shared problems of contemporary society." Here, "the method of personal engagement with urgent contemporary problems, through active discussion . . . was almost an end in itself . . . the discussion method promoted active civil discourse on the nature of civility—learning by doing."[10]

As it developed at Columbia over several decades, the core represented more than just a menu of disparate courses, taught by faculty from disparate disciplines. It became a collegial effort that involved many of the most distinguished names on the Columbia faculty, who taught not as disciplinary specialists but as contributors toward understanding questions of common concern and moment. Such a core curriculum, together with the ongoing intra-faculty conversation it spurred, was intended as "a continuing parallel to specialized study . . . a core understood as central to all new learning, as an integrative function bringing old and new together."[11] It is a hopeful sign that, despite its evident expense, the core program has continued to flourish and evolve as a defining feature of undergraduate education at Columbia as it has also been adopted in a number of other institutions. As earlier chapters have shown, many of these features have been given new expression on PTEV campuses.

The Importance of Humanistic Inquiry
for the New Global Challenge

When bringing this narrative into the 21st century, de Bary uses his familiarity with contemporary East Asia to make a sobering point. East and West, he argues, the situation is dire for the kind of modern humanistic education John Erskine introduced. Institutions of higher education, the self-announced purveyors of intelligent problem solving, are in both East Asia and the West dominated by highly competitive economic and technological elites. Far from providing needed critique of the values currently pursued, higher education often actually helps to fuel what de Bary calls "a runaway market and technology." This could be considered ironic were it not so evidently tragic. For an emerging yet precarious world civilization riven by dangerous conflicts, the great need is to think deeply about "what values might direct and control" its apparently unstoppable rush toward ecological disaster.

In the face of this situation, de Bary insists that a conservative strategy of merely preserving the heritage of the past is not enough. At the same time, higher education's typical efforts to support the needed cultural rethinking are too superficial to address the depth of the problem. This limitation is revealed in the contraction of what is understood by a "core curriculum." Where the classical core had concerned itself with "ways of living," that is, "what the 'Good Life' could mean in human terms," general education has too often narrowed to "ways of knowing," a purely epistemological, "value-free" substitute. This constriction prevents today's educators from seeing that "ways of knowing was one aspect, but only one part" of grappling with the full range of "central human concerns."

A concern with human survival demands that more intellectual attention be given to sources of moral value and meaning as well as critical thought. For de Bary, this entails once again understanding the classics as explorations of what it means to live. But the range of classics also needs expansion to include Asian religious traditions such as Confucianism and Buddhism, as well as the religious thinking of the West and other parts of the globe. These traditions must be approached from both a critical and an appreciative stance. "Without closing the door on intellectual growth," he concludes, "we will have to prepare people to make qualitative judgments as to what is most conducive in the longer run to 'the good life' and as to what human goods are sustainable."[12]

Humanistic Education as Core Resource for the 21st Century

This recasting of the role of humanistic studies from museums enshrining the past to tools for shaping the present and future highlights new possibilities. As it emerged in the early decades of the last century, the original core took its implicit orientation from a historical narrative of progress, in which the West was destined to play the leading role. Among others, de Bary helped to widen the scope and decenter that perspective. The optimism motivating his work was shared by many of the "great" or "civic" American generation, who came to maturity around World War II. De Bary embraced democracy as a real force in the world as well as a moral and political ideal. His scholarship helped shape an understanding in both East Asia and the United States that the classical traditions of China, Japan, and Korea could help promote international cooperation and the affirmation of human dignity.

In the later 20th century, the pressures of the Cold War and continued international violence as well as economic and social inequality at home made such hopes seem naive. A much harsher, more skeptical stance toward ideal aims and universal values became the norm in much of the academy. The earlier narrative faded and was replaced by a harder-edged "realism" that eschewed talk of universal ends or an ideal state of affairs.[13] Yet, implicit in de Bary's argument is a plausible alternative construction of our situation. We have emerged into a new era of technologically enhanced global interconnection. But unlike the simplistic free-market triumphalism of 1990s globalization, this emerging narrative grows from recognition that our era is marked by a deep tension and duality. While increasing global connectedness contains great positive potential, competition, economic and national, abetted by explosive technological growth, poses an enormous threat to humanity and the planet itself. This new narrative ends not with a triumphant vision of future progress, but with a call for a new level of responsibility. It demands collective self-scrutiny and willingness to change.[14] Rather than a reassuring and complacent picture, it holds up a mirror, demanding self-reflection and response.

The challenge facing humanistic education, then, is to inspire and support deeper engagement with the life of our times, the most distinctive feature of which is the emergence of this interdependent yet fragmented global society. To fulfill its own purposes, higher education must help to foster leaders and citizens for whom the challenge of avoiding catastrophe and forging a new level of global solidarity is a matter of real, daily concern. Making this concern actual, and devising forms of thinking and acting that link everyday life consciously to this larger challenge, has become the pedagogical problem of the age. However, the difficulty is not only that contemporary technological affluence seems to foster an often-deplored bubble-like psychic insulation from these issues. Even with good will, the limitations of human experience make the world as a whole, and especially distant others, only potentially real for most of us much of the time.

The diverse aspects of the world only become real to us when we encounter the world in its full immensity, when we recognize something of ourselves in others, whether we meet them in person, virtually, or in imagination. That is why cultivation of moral empathy and imagination, intrinsic to the practice of humanistic inquiry, are essential for contemporary education.[15] If an ethic of responsibility must become a defining aspect of 21st-century identity, then the cultivation of the knowledge and skills needed to sustain such responsibility has to be a pervasive dimension of higher education. Since identity is mediated through membership in communities, including participation in traditions of thought and culture, then higher education's responsibility is to support learning communities aligned with the cultivation of these larger goals.

Potentially, learning communities can provide a common purpose across disciplines and programs. It was John Dewey who declared the "ethical principle underlying education" to be "interest in the community welfare, an interest that is intellectual and practical as well as emotional—an interest, that is to say, in perceiving whatever makes for social order and progress and for carrying these principles into execution." Dewey called this attitude "the ultimate ethical habit" to which all other aspects of education had to be related.[16] Expanded to the wider scope of today's concerns, yet also concretized in social relationships on campus and between the campus and its many publics, Dewey's "ultimate ethical habit" well describes the aim of a viable 21st-century educational outlook. Certainly it highlights the value, even the urgency, of working to integrate undergraduate experience through the third apprenticeship of identity and purpose.

The PTEV campuses described in previous chapters illustrate core aspects of this integration, organized around the narrative of vocation. This chapter presents other examples, such as the Harvard–Uganda collaboration already discussed, as well as others to follow. Each involves common elements—participation in communities of students, faculty, and staff that mediate awakening to larger, global responsibilities, as well as challenging educational experiences including opportunities for service and connection, including active reflection—developed in specific contexts. Comparing these efforts will make it possible to understand in a more informed way the import and value of this kind of education.

"The Practical Liberal Arts" at Wagner College

Wagner College, atop a hill in Staten Island within sight of Manhattan's towers, is a medium-sized, private, comprehensive institution. In the late 1990s, the college developed the Wagner Plan for the Practical Liberal Arts. This is an undergraduate program centered on integrating liberal arts with not only major programs, especially in the professional disciplines, but with extensive experiential and interdisciplinary learning. One measure of its success has been a dramatic boost in the number of student applications and the academic qualifications of the applicants. Wagner has become a "hot" school. Some part of this success probably stems from the college's ability to leverage desirable placements and internships in New York businesses and institutions. Yet, Wagner has not been content to simply provide attractive career ladders for the enterprising among its graduates. It has also enlisted the entire campus community to create a culture that promotes civic engagement and response to social need as a basic context for career and personal accomplishment.

Wagner is a member of the New American Colleges and Universities (NAC&U). This organization defines its mission as advancing higher education that "integrates the liberal arts with professional studies and civic responsibility." The consortium of affiliated campuses now comprises 25 members spread throughout the United States. Founded in 1995, the NAC&U was inspired by the vision of Ernest L. Boyer, the alumnus of Messiah College met in the previous chapter. As president of the Carnegie Foundation for the Advancement of Teaching, Boyer had called for a distinctly American model of higher education to serve the needs of an expanding democracy. The model Boyer proposed was neither a research university nor a liberal arts college but a "liberal arts comprehensive" campus, a genuinely "integrative institution" that would unite professional training with liberal learning. Today, the consortium convenes the leadership of its member institutions several times a year for events focused on educational issues relevant to their common aims. It also provides a number of common programs open to students and faculty of all the members, and provides various kinds of technical support to its member institutions.

Wagner's interpretation of this integrative spirit is the Wagner Plan for the Practical Liberal Arts. Since 1998, Richard Guarasci, Wagner's president, has spurred and guided this program through its development. It is the institution's liberal arts core in which all students enroll. It continues both the humanistic and civic, learn-by-doing intentions of the original Columbia core, while amplifying the latter through experiential learning and supervised service in community organizations. It also embodies today's insights into how practices of reflection can enhance learning. Unlike many other efforts to impart a unity to the undergraduate curriculum by means of first-year and senior-year "bookend" seminars, the Wagner Plan also links the end to the beginning of student experience by adding a third, "intermediate" integrating experience during either the student's second or third year.

The plan is built around three sets of linked courses called Learning Communities, one in the first year, one intermediate, and one in the senior year. These learning communities consist of 14 students and are each led by two faculty members who teach two courses based in their specific disciplines, linked by a common theme or topic. Students spend about three hours per week in off-campus activities ranging from field trips to New York metropolitan institutions to service learning within community organizations. Learning communities typically involve some service experience, although some, such as "Exploring the Cosmos and Our Place Within It," which links astronomy and philosophy, place a greater emphasis on personal reflection. The third component of the Wagner Learning Community is what is called the Reflective Tutorial. Here students analyze intensively, discuss, and write about the connections between the concepts engaged in their classes and their experiences off-campus. The same structure is repeated at the intermediate and senior levels, with increasingly more challenging and complex topics, experiential involvements, and writing assignments.

The Reflective Tutorial is in many ways the most striking part of the program. It is the key to implementing the Wagner Plan's claim to provide a "practical liberal arts." The reflective exercises in the tutorial promote "practical" learning in two senses. Each is important, though they are not always clearly distinguished from each other. In the basic sense, the program is practical in that by connecting concepts with actual institutions and sites in the city, it teaches students to *externalize* their learning, to effect change in the world. This is the sense in which professional disciplines such as business or engineering are practical. But through reflection on their experiences, measuring their goals and expectations against theoretical accounts and actual outcomes, students also *internalize* their knowledge. In this process, students become conscious of how to learn, thereby acquiring a vital new ability for shaping their future lives. This is formative education in the full humanistic sense.

The pedagogies the Wagner Learning Communities employ also represent a real gain for liberal education. Typically, while the professional fields employ case study, laboratory simulation or design experiments, and actual experience with professional practice, the liberal arts fields stop short at the theoretical elaboration of concepts. By using the Reflective Tutorial to weave together the activities of the learning communities, Wagner is augmenting the arts and sciences tool kit with powerful pedagogical practices borrowed from professional and experiential education. Indeed, it is just this interweaving of the learning, application, and criticism of concepts through reflecting on experiences of practice that deepens student engagement with college learning.

These features of the core program embody the insights of current learning science. Making sense of the world and using knowledge and skills in responsible and engaged ways, long the developmental goals of liberal learning, require coherence in curriculum and ways of teaching. Furthermore, as we have noted in earlier chapters, these experiences need to be iterative in nature, so that students keep practicing their skills as they progress through more complex challenges, becoming more self-aware and self-directing as they spiral upward into broader as well as deeper mastery.

The results of the Wagner program are also striking in ways that reinforce the case for more integrated curricula, especially the link between humanistic modes of learning and relationships with community organizations and practitioners beyond the campus. A recent study of Wagner undergraduates confirmed that completion of the first-year program not only correlated with continuing at the college (retention) but also found high levels of well-being among students. However, students whose learning communities had emphasized placements in service contexts showed significantly higher levels of social, emotional, and psychological well-being compared to students whose experiences had been mostly in field-based learning without a service component.

The research also showed that faculty–student interaction, always a major predictor of both learning and student morale, was stronger in the service-oriented courses. This was due to greater engagement of both faculty and students in service contexts with off-campus communities. This research confirmed some of the benefits to students of the Wagner Plan. Students and faculty find their participation in the learning communities meaningful and motivating. It also illustrates again the educative power of communal organizations that make possible mutually supportive relationships among students, faculty, and off-campus community participants.[17]

Toward a "Culture of Learning": Liberal Education and a New Academy

The research on the efficacy of the Wagner Plan just described was supported by a project called Bringing Theory to Practice. Since 2002, Bringing Theory to Practice has pioneered research to discover what supports a "culture of learning" in undergraduate education. Led by Donald W. Harward, for over a decade president of Bates College in Maine, the organization has advanced a twofold agenda. It has sponsored research to determine the most effective practices of teaching and learning for fostering student engagement with learning and has also formed a network of campuses, including institutions that participated in the PTEV, to implement these evidence-based practices.

Bringing Theory to Practice (BTtoP) is a story of fruitful collaboration between Harward and several partners, including the Association of American Colleges and Universities (AAC&U). Sally Engelhard Pingree of the Charles Engelhard Foundation has been particularly important to this effort, as has Carol Geary Schneider, president of the AAC&U. Harward began with what he calls a "hunch" that academic and psychological disengagement by students, as well as behavioral problems such as substance abuse, could be counteracted through strengthening learning experiences and community involvement.

Over the past decade, this hunch has been borne out through a series of research efforts, including national samples of students, aimed at showing which forms of engaged learning are most effective in promoting the positive outcomes sought by most educators. These evidence-based efforts to demonstrate and refine the efficacy of various pedagogies have been organized around reshaping campus cultures to achieve three interrelated purposes, defined by BTtoP as educational outcomes. These are the *epistemic* purpose, or the concern with knowledge; the *eudemonic* purpose, the development of students as persons; and the *civic* purpose, or development of students as self-aware, responsible citizens of the larger world.[18] By design, then, the project has included within its purview all three apprenticeships.

A campus culture of learning may sound vague, but the early phase of BTtoP's work was concentrated on defining and measuring it empirically. The concept was that a culture of learning exists wherever an undergraduate program can demonstrate student growth toward the three key outcomes: in student knowledge, well-being, and civic engagement. When improvements in these areas could be measured, a campus was said to be providing "transformational liberal education." As the Wagner case illustrates, the findings have supported the idea that increasing student involvement in community service, when complemented by academic treatment of these involvements, increases student interest in learning as well as satisfaction with the campus. Following the intensive research phase, BTtoP has since 2008 emphasized dissemination of those educational practices that produced the sought-for outcomes. The initial group of 55 undergraduate programs involved in this effort has continued to grow.

In broad parallel to the vocation initiative, the Bringing Theory to Practice effort has centered on two foci that are complementary yet distinct. As noted, the first of these is an emphasis on improving students' psychosocial well-being through enhanced engagement in learning, on- and off-campus, and community involvements. Since this focus of attention foregrounds the social apprenticeship, it has drawn student services professionals into the project. Research has long shown that student engagement is very much a function of students' abilities to find both intellectual–cultural and social homes in their college or university.[19] A particular feature of the BTtoP approach, however, has been assertion of the need to *counter* what Harward calls a pattern of "campus influences disproportionately directed toward narrow self-interest and forms of disengaged behavior." So, the learning culture promoted by the project is deliberately intended to "nudge" or "guide" students toward more engaged patterns of living.[20] In effect, the strategy is to use enhanced forms of the first and third apprenticeships to reorient the second into forms more aligned with liberal education's goals. For example, Georgetown University has brought faculty and counseling staff together to create courses that directly "infuse" this alternative perspective into subject area learning, such as a service-learning sociology project in which students compare the incidence of depression among homeless populations to that of campus populations and explore explanations of these phenomena.[21]

The second focus of BTtoP has been a stress on the importance of civic education, both as a means toward student well-being and academic engagement and as a proper end of liberal education. The aim here has been to foreground the third apprenticeship in the form of fostering a sense of active citizenship as a life purpose and essential part of students' identity. (Under Harward's leadership, Bates College greatly increased its involvement with its home city of Lewiston, Maine.) Here, too, BTtoP has drawn on its research base to promote, and continually assess the efficacy of, campus efforts to engage with their surrounding communities and to enlist both faculty and students in this process. In this area, too, there is a tradition of research that shows the value of civic education for enhancing the overall learning and psychosocial growth of students.[22] What the project has done is to link that research tightly to the goal of student cognitive and affective development, on the one hand, and American higher education's tradition of public purpose on the other. In recent years, BTtoP has emphasized the civic focus through a series of publications known as the "Civic Series," which are intended to provide perspectives and to also "nudge" institutions toward taking ever more seriously the "civic mission of higher education."

The thread connecting the two foci to the larger endeavor lies in BTtoP's research and analysis of teaching practices in relation to specific learning goals. This pedagogical research also has an activist edge: nothing less than to reshape the way in which liberal education is typically presented. To facilitate this aim, the project has developed and promoted a vocabulary to distinguish among kinds of learning. Each has been defined as essential and complementary to the others but still requiring specific attention.

The scheme identifies five types of learning. The basic perspective is developmental, meaning that student understanding is first of all seen as changing rather than fixed. Secondly, this development is understood as taking place not in discrete zones such as academic or career preparation, but rather as a larger pattern of psychosocial maturation. Third, students are understood to undergo genuine growth as persons, becoming "different people" through their learning. That is, learning becomes integrative, consciously bringing various powers into relationship with each other. Fourth, this "transformative" growth takes place in context, never in isolation, so learners must be given the opportunity to experience themselves in relationship to others and to institutions. Finally, if—but only if—learning takes place in the four previous forms, students will be able to assess, with full self-awareness, whether their learning has been transformative. This is called learning to learn.

BTtoP's research shows that undergraduates do not in fact often learn in all these ways.[23] The five types of learning scheme is thus intended as a both a diagnostic tool and a challenge. On the positive side, BTtoP's research also concluded that learning communities of the kind illustrated at Wagner College as well as on many of the PTEV campuses are effective in promoting learning along all these dimensions.

The project's research and its dissemination of good practices intersect and have come increasingly to interact with the work of the Association of American Colleges and Universities. A national organization with several hundred institutional members, the AAC&U has pursued new directions for liberal education, an undertaking its president, Carol Geary Schneider, has called the invention of a "New Academy." A set of initiatives begun in the 1990s, the New Academy has advanced a reconstruction of liberal learning designed to move beyond the unraveling postwar model of a college education. The central AAC&U claim is that liberal education is more important now than ever, precisely because it has been shown to develop the very capacities the new century will demand from college graduates—in particular, the ability to handle greater complexity, diversity, and large-scale change.

To meet these new challenges, Schneider has emphasized, higher education must reshape its practices to take advantage of new knowledge about effective teaching and learning. These advances have spawned a whole set of new practices that can be demonstrated to have "high impact" on student learning. As staples of PTEV programs, they will be familiar: new organizational forms such as first-year experiences, senior capstone courses, and learning communities; specific pedagogical practices such as writing-intensive courses, undergraduate involvement in faculty research, and the use of "big questions" to prompt thinking; and reflective service and civic learning. When practiced extensively across the curriculum, these practices can enable students more effectively to achieve a set of "essential learning outcomes." These outcomes include demonstrated knowledge of human cultures and the natural world, development of intellectual and practical skills, and, coupled with active involvement in diverse communities and experience with actual social challenges, growth in personal and social responsibility. Learning to integrate knowledge by applying it in complex situations can also be furthered by these practices.

The AAC&U has proposed that these "essential learning outcomes" become the benchmarks for excellence in higher education. But, as AAC&U research also shows, this kind of intentionally designed learning experience is still the exception rather than the rule in most students' undergraduate experience.[24] To address the discrepancy between the potential of liberal learning for achieving these outcomes and the current state of affairs, the AAC&U is engaged in an innovative initiative to increase public appreciation, especially among employers, of the value of liberal learning. The larger aim is to persuade public opinion that higher education should be reshaped to achieve the outcomes just described. Overall, the aim of its Liberal Education and America's Promise (LEAP) project is to persuade and enlist support for this new vision of liberal education by marshaling research findings and presenting examples of what this New Academy can accomplish.[25] AAC&U has put forward both an "economic case" and a "civic case" for the value of liberal learning for educating a more skilled workforce and more engaged and resourceful citizens.

Connecting Means of Livelihood with the Exploration of Purposes for Living

"You've got to prove the concept and that's what we've been doing." So Vice Provost Andy Chan confidently describes a developing program he heads at Wake Forest University. Since fall 2009, Chan has headed a redesigned Office of Personal and Career Development. This office deliberately foregrounds students' (and parents') concerns about future careers toward a pedagogical end; the strategy is to motivate students to consider their choice of livelihood in relation to life's larger purposes. Wake Forest's president, Nathan Hatch, defines the university's mission as educating the whole student "to find good work for a meaningful life." With President Hatch's support, Chan has raised over $10 million to support his office and its work, chiefly from parents of students and alumni. The office reaches out to students from their first days on campus, providing a four-course sequence of for-credit, "College-to-Career" courses taught by Department of Counseling faculty, while also cultivating relationships with faculty, employers, parents, alumni, and community leaders.

Wake Forest sees itself as a "collegiate university," rooted in the liberal arts, but, like most comprehensive universities, has a range of professional programs. A basic aim of the president in establishing the new office was to "level the career playing field" for arts and sciences majors, while giving students in the professional schools more effective ways to engage with liberal learning, especially around the formation of the dispositions that will define their characters. The key concept guiding the Wake Forest efforts is the notion of personal purpose expressed in vocation or particular career choice. This emphasis upon vocation is a legacy of the university's PTEV grant of the previous decade. However, the present program represents a second sailing. In its new form, Wake Forest has become an important part of the Lilly-sponsored Network for Vocation in Undergraduate Education (NetVUE), a more broadly based successor to the PTEV.

Andy Chan came to Wake Forest from the Stanford University Graduate School of Business, where he directed the MBA Career Management Center. Testing the waters, Chan found that the term "vocation" failed to resonate with undergraduates at Wake Forest:

> Many students, especially those with some experience with religion, and many faculty heard it as directing students towards religious ministry [while] other students were simply unfamiliar with it. So, we chose "career development," which many students expected to be essential to the college experience, and added the "personal" dimension, putting it in first place, ahead of career," while making career planning more about personal exploration and understanding rather than just helping senior students master job

search tactics and securing a good first job a few months prior to graduating.[26]

Chan defines his office as providing not just "information" about careers but "interpretation and transformation" that "enables students to learn about who they are, what kinds of work will lead to fulfilling careers, and equip them to pursue their interests and passions with clarity and confidence." The meaning of this interpretative, transformational role is embodied in the structure of programs the office provides.

Significantly, the first thing the office engages students with is the question of choice of academic major. Wake Forest students typically declare majors in their second year, so there is opportunity for most to explore the question during the first year on campus. For the first time, students engage the four questions that structure the entire program: Who am I? What is in the world of work? Where shall I go and how will I get there? What professional and life skills will ensure success?

In addition to the more typical career planning resources and services, Professor Heidi Robinson designed an innovative series of four half-semester courses called College-to-Career. These are taught by the faculty in the Department of Counseling (CNS) and offer academic credit. There are typically three sections of each course, with 15 to 20 students each, offered each semester. The intimate size is intended to provide the kind of liberal arts experience of discussion and reflection the topics demand.

The first of these, CNS 120, emphasizes self-awareness, giving students the tools to better understand their values, beliefs, interests, personality, and abilities while reading and discussing texts concerned with human development and meaning-making. Here students explicitly consider (or reconsider) their choice of major and overall academic and life goals. The second-year course, CNS 220, expands the perspective to thinking about the larger world and how academic and experiential learning influences that process. The third-year course provides the theory as well as the practice of conducting a strategic job search, organized in light of the themes of the previous two courses. The fourth-year course returns to the issues of the first course with a new focus on the question of what personal and professional knowledge and skills will be important for life after graduation and how to ensure that those get developed. Throughout, students are encouraged to form informal peer groups, known as "posses," to support a culture of active engagement in learning. Student response has been very positive. As measured by their willingness to participate as mentors and networking connections, as well as their contributions to the program, parent and alumni response has been positive as well.

When asked how these compared to their other courses, students emphasized that while the workload was rigorous—requiring serious reading and essay writing—they also found the assignments to be "more personal" and "motivating" because they could see the immediate application of what they were learning to their own lives and choices. As one enthusiastic participant proclaimed, "These courses should be required!" In fact, Andy Chan increased student engagement by experimenting with online offerings.

As the office has become more established on campus, it has also partnered with faculty in experimenting with new courses and modifying existing ones as part of the regular academic program. Professor Evelyn Williams piloted a new entry into the university's First-Year Seminar list. Entitled "Life in the Liberal Arts," it brings the perspectives of career and organizational development to help beginning students integrate the new experiences of college into their developing sense of self and purpose. The course is structured around two small groups of six to eight students ("posses" again) who read, discuss, and write together while being introduced to four "streams of learning" in four modules. The first is perspectives on motivation for learning, similar to the CNS 120 College-to-Career Course. The second involves senior faculty showing how their academic disciplines have informed their professional, intellectual, and personal development. The third stream focuses on what is known about emotional or social intelligence, its importance and its cultivation as an aspect of maturation. Finally, the fourth stream presents the program's theory of intellectual community, what it means to live a "life in the liberal arts."

In order for these programs to work, the office must sustain strong ties with campus groups, especially faculty interested in holistic student development and formation, as well as employers and community groups who embrace the value of this kind of integrative educational effort. It is still in an early stage of development, but the office shows promise of infusing into the experience of more and more students at Wake Forest those questions President Hatch believes define a genuine liberal education: Who am I? What matters to me? To what should I devote my energies? These are the questions of humanistic inquiry. That they can be interwoven with, and even come to guide, the very practical questions of life and career, is being demonstrated at Wake

Forest. Like the other cases surveyed in this chapter, Wake Forest presents evidence that liberal learning, and with it key aspects of the undergraduate experience, can be reshaped in ways that integrate the three fragmented apprenticeships of higher education. The PTEV has already shown us what it means to draw on these resources to construct a sustainable future in the 21st century.

7

The Theological Perspective as Educational Resource

THE LAST CHAPTER has surveyed a number of experiments that give undergraduate education a new focus on developing purpose. Like the PTEV, these programs have proven congenial grounds for reanimating a humanistic education that places intellectual rigor in the service of wise practical deliberation. Also like the PTEV, these experiments demonstrate the value of strengthening the integration of the academic and social apprenticeships to support the large aims of the apprenticeship of identity and purpose. With their explicit attention to the global context, these programs also highlight the new challenges of living in the 21st century. They point toward the demands the coming era will place on everyone's aims and sense of identity. Survival in this century will depend upon women and men who understand and can respond constructively to the imperative of global cooperation in the face of multiple threats to the precarious web of human interdependence.

This is a situation in which the pluralism of values and aims among the world's diverse societies and cultures, often celebrated in the academy, takes on an intimidating aspect. How to prepare students to make their way constructively amid the great pluralism of values, including their sometimes violent clashes, that is so much part of our times? The skeptical reader may at this point wonder how an education that takes its inspiration from a religious conception of life as vocational journey can be anything but a contributor to further cultural conflict. To press the skeptic's point: how can a particular religious tradition enhance rather than close down cooperation by its exclusive claims, thereby exacerbating today's seemingly intractable cultural conflicts, many of which are religious in character? This is a serious question that deserves a direct answer.

This chapter will make the argument that the PTEV was able to successfully confront this challenge through its focus on practices for discerning purpose that explicitly acknowledge today's plurality of religious and secular perspectives. Because the vocation initiative's intellectual starting point was the understanding that religious traditions should be seen as formative cultural resources for living rather than closed, dogmatic systems, the campus programs were able to draw upon their inherited theological understandings in creative ways.

These discernment practices, some of which we have already examined and others to be explored in what follows, interpreted inherited, particular religious understandings as inspiration for engagement with today's concerns. This often led student exploration toward concerns with contemporary issues that cut across rather than reinforcing religious and cultural boundaries. In other words, vocational language, supported by learning communities committed to the reflective exploration of meaning, proved sufficiently inspiring to prompt the "translation" of words and symbols so that they spoke beyond as well as within the confines of a particular religious community. As the present chapter will show, these practices sustained a broad space of dialogue about contemporary life that invited participants to explore without defensiveness the insights provided by tradition. These outcomes underscore the educational value of a humanistic pedagogy that interprets and enlivens inherited meanings by seeking their relevance for responsible engagement, including engagement with today's religious pluralism and cultural diversity.

Religious Heritage as Educational Resource: The PTEV at Gordon College

Located not far from Boston, in Wenham, Massachusetts, Gordon College describes itself as an independent, liberal arts college in the evangelical Christian tradition. It is a largely undergraduate institution, with a student body of about 1500, mostly from evangelical Christian backgrounds. The college sees itself as educating future leaders of evangelical faith who will serve church and world in a variety of vocations. It requires twice-weekly attendance at chapel and emphasizes Christian faith and social service. Some, then, might be surprised to find a class of Gordon students struggling with two essays by the sociologist Max Weber dealing with the topic of vocation. These famous essays propose the great difficulty of combining loyalty to ultimate values with the compromising demands of modern living. The students struggle not so much with the task of understanding Weber—they are part of an upper-class honors seminar—as with the challenge of responding to his arguments.

"The fate of our times," Weber tells them, "is characterized by rationalization and intellectualization, and above all, by 'the disenchantment of the world.'" Religious meaning becomes restricted to "the smallest and most intimate circles, in personal human situations, in *pianissimo*," and no longer commands general assent in the public realm.[1] Weber's pessimism about combining worldly callings with religious ethics was part of his diagnosis of modernity. Famously, Weber claimed that while modern persons are freed from many traditional constraints, the dynamism of modern life fragments social relationships and experience, posing challenges to moral conscience and requiring a strenuous "ethics of responsibility."

Modern Western societies, in Weber's analysis, are split along the seams of the separate spheres of the economy, government, education, religion, and domestic and personal life. Each sphere is governed by different expectations and goals. Moreover, in their various roles as workers, consumers, citizens, family members, etc., individuals must meet these disparate expectations even when they realize that the value spheres often conflict—a situation that not infrequently compromises individuals' ability to be faithful in one part of their lives to what they espouse in another part. For example, economic efficiency often requires us to deal with strangers in ways that would not be tolerated among relatives or friends, while the demands of political success can famously undermine other loyalties. These conflicting value spheres make living an ethical life under modern conditions peculiarly unsettled and uncertain.

How, then, is it possible to live a morally coherent life and still be active and effective in the world? More specifically for most Gordon students, how can one pursue an intellectual vocation or take an active role as a citizen in politics and seriously live out Christian values and faith?

As they read, discuss, and write analytical papers on such topics, struggling with these questions becomes more than a cognitive challenge for the students. It takes on a practical, "existential" dimension directly related to their identity and purposes. At the same time, the students are also absorbing larger lessons. One is that mature purpose and faith can be achieved only through struggling with the complexities of life rather than by fleeing them. But another is that they are not on their own in confronting such problems. Through their participation in the seminar they have joined a larger stream of tradition concerned with asking such questions and debating possible answers. This links them to centuries of serious intellectual life in the traditions of Christian thought. They are discovering a fund of sophisticated cultural experience on which they can draw in shaping their personal response to the challenges of living thoughtfully amid contemporary conditions.

Developing Reflective Integrity: The Critical Loyalty Project

The course in question is one of several that have become a regular part of the honors program at Gordon but were initiated through the vocation initiative, known as the Critical Loyalty Project. The guiding question running through various programs within the project has been how to develop a life of thoughtful personal and moral coherence, centered in Christian values yet engaged with the crosscurrents of modern life. The premise of the project is that students and faculty live in an age in which religious belief and practice have become increasingly seen as an optional rather than a necessary aspect of living a good human life. In such a secular age, religious understandings are perceived as one option among many.

Some Christians in various denominations have reacted to these trends by attempting to remain apart from the secular world. In contrast, the Critical Loyalty Project proposes to its students that contemporary identities, including religious identities, necessarily have a reflexive quality. Religious commitment, like discernment of a purpose in living, is not to be taken for granted. It can become an object of question and such questioning is a necessary aspect of achieving a mature identity. Therefore, an affirmation of faith requires active, personal consent. The intellectual formation the Critical Loyalty Project intends to provide Gordon students is premised on their active, reflexive engagement as persons in a quest of meaning and purpose. Its distinctive feature is that it takes place within a context shaped by the normative traditions of Christian intellectual discourse.

Because its programs were constructed all at once, and in response to the concerns of the vocation initiative, the Critical Loyalty Program provides a particularly clear case of how theological exploration can provide a lens for understanding and supporting the quest for vocation. The project was begun in 2002. It intensified Gordon's existing efforts to provide coherence to student experience by foregrounding the notion of discerning one's purposes, a formative goal that leaders of the project believe they have successfully infused widely through the curriculum and co-curriculum. Gordon has an extensive core curriculum, including mandatory foreign language study, mathematics and the natural sciences, history, and literature, as well as courses in Christian theology. The mandatory interdisciplinary first-year writing course, "The Great Conversation—Foundations in Thinking, Reading, and Writing," further complements the core curriculum. The course includes a service learning component centered in nearby Lynn, Massachusetts. Its focus is the connecting question of what constitutes the good life. While introducing students to various genres and contexts for writing, the theme of the "great conversation" enables the instructors and students to reflect on the course theme through the resources of what Gordon calls the "Christian liberal arts tradition."

Since its beginning, the Critical Loyalty Project has been led by Thomas Albert Howard, a professor of history and director of the Center for Christian Studies at the college. The project consists, in part, of two honors programs, described below; a lecture series entitled, "Faith Seeking Understanding"; the A. J. Gordon Scholars, a scholarship program aimed at fostering leadership that provides individualized coaching; and a peer mentors program that builds in more support for first-year students taking the "Great Conversation" course. The way Tal Howard puts it, "The Lilly grant enabled us to intensify the core experience. It also enabled us to create an honors program. This is a very resource-rich experience we wish we could provide for all our students." He notes that to a significant degree the project has brought some of the principles and features of the honors program to core courses generally, especially the theme of vocational exploration. A major effect, everyone at Gordon agrees, has been a higher level of student engagement and the recruitment of more academically oriented students.

The Jerusalem and Athens Forum

Tal Howard talks about the honors program as intended to "take intellectual life at Gordon to the next level, recognizing and fostering the intrinsic good of intellectual life and learning." His course, in which students read the two essays by Max Weber on vocation, is called the "Jerusalem and Athens Forum." Howard calls it a great books seminar on the Columbia model with "the added *gravitas* of the Christian theological tradition," which is itself "large, complex, and conflicted." He thinks appreciating this tradition is especially important for students "who often chafe at the intellectual narrowness" of their evangelical backgrounds, which have typically emphasized piety combined with activism more than theological reflection or depth. The "Jerusalem and Athens Forum" aims to counter that by providing a way to experience the "fascination of ideas, culture, and the arts" in a context also responsive to evangelical Christian values and testimony. Its very concrete purpose is to foster "intellectual vocations" among Gordon students, sending them on to graduate and professional schools to pursue careers in academe, law, medicine, journalism, and a variety of what are often described as "creative class" occupations. The several occasions each year when students can meet returning graduates on an informal basis forms an important part of the course.

The experience provided by the seminar can enhance students' sense of competence as well as develop their ability to grapple with contemporary issues. As an example, Tal Howard talked about a student in one of his classes who, in the immediate aftermath of Hurricane Katrina, expressed misgivings about the value of sitting in a classroom when others were suffering so acutely elsewhere. She was considering leaving school to volunteer in New Orleans. "That was a typical, and admirable, Evangelical impulse: an immediate response to those in need," Howard pointed out. While he honored that impulse, Howard also wanted to help the student understand the call in the context of her own educational and vocational needs, as well as her long-term ability to be of greatest service to others. He discussed with her and other students the complexity of the situation in New Orleans, and that the people there needed not just "first aid," but expertise. Whether in biology, civil engineering, flood control, economics, or the culture of the region, expertise would require education, and, as Howard put it, "slowing down." As one student expressed it at the time, their discussions with Howard helped them discover the value of "expanding our field of vision." Thanks to Gordon's honors program, they had at their disposal the intellectual and cultural resources which could enable them to do just that.

The name "Jerusalem and Athens" is a reference to the Western church father, Tertullian. In the third century, he had famously posed the rhetorical question: "What has Athens to do with Jerusalem? What has the Academy to do with the Church?" With these provocative questions, Tertullian set off a continuing debate about the relationship between what the course description calls "faith and intellect, piety and thought." Whatever Tertullian's own opinion, the larger tradition has mostly affirmed a both/and rather than an either/or in regard to the questions he posed. As a former Stoic philosopher, Tertullian was no stranger to "Athens." As a Christian bishop, he had to interpret "Jerusalem" in ways his North African congregation could understand. Tertullian might stand as a type for a modern as well as ancient identity, aware of spanning cultural difference and concerned to make the best use in the present of the wisdom of the past. Similarly, the program has derived the term "forum" as a metaphor borrowed from the classical humanism of antiquity. In the Roman sense, a forum meant "a place of interaction in the cities of antiquity, where townspeople often discussed political and religious ideas with great vigor. In continuity with this practice," the description goes on, ". . . the program finds its center of gravity in student discussions and debate."

To fill in this broad "open space of interaction," the course divides the academic year into halves. The first semester is concerned with "Tradition." It extends chronologically from readings in ancient Greek literature and thought through the Middle Ages, the Renaissance, and the Protestant Reformation. The spring semester is entitled "Modernity" and includes readings from the Scientific Revolution and the Enlightenment to the present. The course enrolls 14 students each year. This makes it possible to place heavy emphasis upon active discussion and critical reading of the texts assigned. In these ways, it is quite faithful to the ideas, which, as we saw in the previous chapter, were first developed a century ago by John Erskine at Columbia University.

The Jerusalem and Athens Forum has several distinctive features. The most obvious is its emphasis upon the relationship of faith and intellect, so that, for example, the implications of the modern scientific worldview for contemporary understandings of humanity are given salience. A second distinctive aspect is considerable emphasis upon experiences and activities outside the classroom, which extend from cultural events to attending various forms of Christian worship outside the evangelical tradition, activities discussed and reflected upon in writing along with texts. Then there are special events. Once each semester, the course features an evening program, called a Roundtable Discussion. These are centered on a key text and question the students are pursuing, which several faculty members from outside the program are invited to join as participants. These sessions provide a chance for students to interact with professors in a focused yet informal way. In the spring semester, the roundtable takes as its texts Weber's "Politics as a Vocation" and "Science as a Vocation." Then, each spring semester, students prepare and present a full-scale "Oxford Union-style" debate on a major topic of the day. As Tal Howard notes with pleasure, these debates have become major events in the Gordon calendar, drawing audiences of over 300 students and faculty.

Both semesters of the course are taught by Tal Howard, with the assistance of program coordinator Ryan Groff, an honors program alumnus. The design of the program reflects Howard's intellectual approach to liberal arts education. This was, as he put it, "reframed" by two years as a participant in the Lilly Fellows Program in the Humanities and the Arts at Christ College, the honors college of Valparaiso University in Indiana. While it significantly predated the PTEV, the Lilly Fellows Program anticipated many features of the campus learning communities that PTEV faculty have discovered. Significantly, the Lilly Fellows Program also provides mentored experience in learning to teach in a Christian liberal arts context. That has been the work of Mark Schwehn, formerly dean of Christ College and then provost at Valparaiso, and co-author of an anthology on vocation widely used in PTEV programs.[2]

Howard sums up the pedagogical strategy of the Jerusalem and Athens Forum in three principles. First, the course develops an interdisciplinary context woven out of history, literature, philosophy, theology, social and natural sciences, and the fine arts. Second, it focuses throughout on "life questions" rather than disciplinary issues, particularly the questions of purpose and vocation. Finally, the readings, discussions, and assignments all "press the normative," asking students again and again to "make a case for their position," to consider whether an author's arguments "ring true" as compared to others. The aim is to expand students' field of vision while also providing mentored experience with taking a responsible position on matters of significant personal and public moment. We might call this reflective integrity.

The Elijah Project

The Elijah Project was introduced alongside the Jerusalem and Athens Forum as a complementary honors experience. Its focus is less intellectual tradition and more the meaning of work considered as a theological question and as a matter of personal discernment. Occasionally Gordon students take both seminars. The Elijah Project selects 14 students through an application process. It runs over two semesters, with a summer experience of internship and common residence connecting the spring with the fall semester seminars, and also involves an experience of intentional community, as program participants live together for the academic year following the summer internship. The orienting questions are direct, if challenging: "What are you going to do after college? How will your life impact the world?" To these the course adds, in the spirit of Evangelical Christianity, a distinctly theological question: "How will you make decisions about choosing a career and answering a call to use your gifts—how will you use your gifts for the creative and restorative work of the Kingdom?" Like other PTEV courses on vocation, the Elijah Project also emphasizes developing self-knowledge and employs a number of practices of reflection toward discerning vocational purpose. Beginning in the spring semester enables the course to proceed from frameworks of interpretation and normative theories through an experience of practice over the summer to a more contextualized fall semester in which the coursework, in conjunction with community living, can bring theory and practice together in lived experience as well as practical reasoning, or discernment, about decisions concerning career.

In the first (spring) semester, titled "Foundations of Work and Vocation," the seminar emphasizes intense engagement around a set of common readings. These range from theological interpretations of the meaning of calling throughout Christian history and in different theological traditions, to philosophical conceptions of ethical responsibility to cognitive theories of how moral judgments are formed. Students write research reports on their reading as well as a series of reflective essays designed to help them make sense of the several theoretical strands under discussion. Students also spend 12 hours throughout the semester volunteering at nonprofit organizations in the Gordon area in order to practice reading social situations and institutions through the lenses gained through course readings. During spring break, the cohort travels to Manhattan, where they visit with multiple organizations and individuals that are creatively seeking to align their work with their understanding of the mission and purposes of God.

In the summer following the first semester, students are placed in 6- to 10-week internships in their field of interest. These internships are set up for each student with the intent of providing an experience in which each student can gain practical experience "trying on" the type of work to which they feel called. (Examples range from a traditional business internship at Raytheon to language documentation in the Solomon Islands to video or theater production to interning with one of many U.S. and overseas nonprofits.)

In the second (fall) semester course, the three main topics under consideration are the following: Who am I (what are my particular interests, strengths, personality styles, history and passions)? What are the challenges and opportunities extant in the world right now? And how ought I make decisions, both now and in the future, about how to match who I am with the creative and restorative work that God seems to be doing in the world? During this semester students use a number of assessment tools to help them understand who they are. They also do a major research project on one particular challenge or opportunity related to their field of study, focusing on current efforts to address it and suggesting new ways forward. This research is shared with the rest of the cohort in a 40-minute presentation and an extensive paper. The culminating project of the program is a final integrative paper "exploring the relation of topics from reading, class discussion and your summer experience to your current vocational leanings." This essay is also to include a "synthetic and creative investigation of the interface between your strengths, interests, and concerns and a specified problem or opportunity."

During the final semester of the program, and extending on throughout that academic year, students live together in an intentional community. They share an old farmhouse just off-campus that features a large kitchen and living room for community meals, meetings, and life together. Participants cook for each other and eat four meals per week together. They are also required to attend a weekly house fellowship in which they spend time in worship, sharing, prayer, and play, and a weekly business meeting during which they discuss and maintain the practical structures of their life together (chores, cooking, excursions, etc.) and talk about any issues that have arisen in the community during the week. The program directors spend a four-day retreat with the students as they are moving into the house at the end of the summer to facilitate the development of a covenant that will direct the students' life together over the coming year and formulate specific structures that will encourage the realization of the values and commitments expressed in the covenant. This year of intentional community greatly enhances the process of self-discovery and identity formation and allows for extended processing of the course material and an arena for the students to deepen and apply what they are learning about themselves and the world.

For student graduates of the Elijah Project, the highly personal quality of their interaction with their peers during the summer experience in Elijah House stood out. One student used the image of a mirror to emphasize the importance of that experience, observing, "your peers help you see yourself, and your gifts." Another student emphasized how the experience had shifted his attention from "general notions of calling, of what is the good life" discussed during the first semester toward the practical issue of "what in my life is responsive to these values now, and what should become responsive in my future?" Others felt that the internships with social agencies that were "doing redemptive work" in the Boston area had given a concreteness and seriousness to the big questions about meaning and purpose.

It was striking to students who came into the Elijah Project after a year in the Jerusalem and Athens Forum that while there they had learned to appreciate the importance of "the life of thought and contemplation," here they found they needed to conjoin that to "a concept of self-awareness and world-awareness, an opening of self to the world." Indeed, a student who had been impressed by reading St. Augustine's *City of God* reported discovering that he was called upon to be both a "pilgrim on earth passing through, and yet in part responsible for the concrete unfolding of history." Another added, "The important thing is to decide to take a stance, to determine what I am willing to go to bat for."

The Elijah Project is jointly led by Greg Carmer, dean of the chapel and director of the Christian Vocation Institute, and Laura Carmer, a counselor who also directs the College's Mission and Service Learning program. Greg Carmer holds a PhD in Theology, which enables him to combine an academic with a pastoral role. His approach, like the pedagogical strategy of the Elijah Project, provides a contrasting complement to the intellectual history emphasis of the other seminar. Carmer centers his pedagogy on self-understanding and response to the world, within "the broad issues of human identity, the direction of human history, and responsibility." He presents issues of faith within this large horizon, "suggesting that the history, the symbols, the sacraments, and the moral understandings of Christianity have a lot of resources to offer." For example, the record of Evangelical Christianity in leading the movement for abolition in the person of William Wilberforce can become a model of taking responsibility for institutional reform.

"In my taxonomy of thinking," Dean Carmer explains, "there is a general human vocation to responsible care for and development of creation and community with each other, there is a Christian call to grow into the life of Christ under the rule of God, and then there is the specific call of an individual to advance those larger purposes in a particular life and with specific others, and in specific situations. We talk explicitly about that [framework] in the Elijah Project." For many Christian students in this generation, that "middle vocation of being a Christian has lost meaning and needs deepening, and I usually try to enable them to see the tradition as providing resources for fulfilling the human call in ways that I find better than any other." He adds that in this framework the Christian call makes sense as "a way of funding the project of growing as a human." At the same time, Carmer also concedes that there can be "a tension, a kind of back-and-forth" in one's experience of faith between the openness to different notions of worthy ways of life, and continuing loyalty to the Christian expressions of faith and interpretations of life. "Critical Loyalty" as an idea helps mediate and sustain this tension. Such tension seems inevitable in the global era, as cultural and religious pluralism has become an everyday reality for increasing numbers of Americans.[3] Carmer sees one of his tasks as enabling students to find their way in what is for most of them a new and uncertain situation.

As an example of how students at Gordon experience this tension and how the frame of the Elijah Project tries to help them respond, Carmer related the experience of a student he called "Jennifer." Evangelical churches, despite many differences, typically emphasize that faith demands not only personal assent, but a willingness to share that faith with others. Many Gordon students share such views, including Jennifer. Through study abroad in a Muslim country, Jennifer became close friends with a student there named Assad. Jennifer was impressed by Assad's faith in God as well as his evident integrity as a person. She felt that she was also learning from Assad aspects of goodness missing in her life. And despite their serious exchange of views about belief, Assad was unpersuaded to convert to Christianity. So, was this a failing on Jennifer's part? How could she maintain her own sense of integrity without successfully "converting" Assad? The key, according to Greg Carmer, was "enabling Jennifer to recognize that she was not responsible for her friend's decision and that she was not abandoning her own convictions in the process." She could "be faithful in her following of Christ and also remain in a hospitable, friendly relationship with her friend," despite their difference in understanding how best to live a human life.

For students, the Critical Loyalty Project, especially the two honors seminars, often provided the most important intellectual experiences of their careers at Gordon. "So much of intellectual activity in the disciplines, even or especially in fields dealing with religious and ethical matters, is deconstructive," reported Ryan Groff on his student experience, "but the Jerusalem and Athens Forum allows space for your mind to work at integrating." For other students, it was that their experience "created a deep need to talk and think about these texts and the questions they raise," with the honors program serving as a community in which such discussion could go on and be taken seriously in forming one's life.

Finally, it seemed that for many the program really did enable them to integrate their intellectual pursuits with their spiritual and moral concerns. In reflecting on her experience, student Sarah Seibert said, "The Elijah Project was by far the most formative experience of my Gordon career. Dialoguing with a wide variety of authors on the meaning of work and vocation in class, embarking on an internship overseas, and living with 13 people so incredibly different from myself and yet simultaneously committed to learning and growing together stretched me in ways I didn't know I could be stretched and taught me lessons I didn't know I needed to learn. My world was opened to new cares and concerns through the sharing of everyday life with others. I now see myself as a small—but significant—part of a much larger whole and have come to realize that the Christian life is more than just an assent to a set of beliefs but is also the practical outworking of those beliefs in everyday life. As another student put it, "I trust that what I will do in my vocation will be used by Providence for the advancement of God's purposes, but what we do in this program, trying to know ourselves and the world and how to think, is itself a part of glorifying God."

An Architecture of the Imagination: Vocation in Liberal Education

In academic programs like Gordon College's Critical Loyalty Project, Christian intellectual life is framed as a living tradition that provides a set of resources of value for "funding growth of the human." For students in this program, the complexities of that tradition provide a variety of partners for conversation about meaning and purpose. This resonates with Theodore de Bary's portrayal of the need to strengthen the humanistic tradition both East and West in order to shape 21st-century citizens able to steer our civilization toward a sustainable future. De Bary's story points us toward a common educational purpose: to comprehend the human meaning of the contradictory tendencies of a global modernity that offers both unprecedented positive potentials and looming threats of catastrophe. Recall that John Erskine, the originator of the first liberal arts core program, resisted the reduction of humanistic education to "critical thinking." As noted in the previous chapter, humanistic understanding requires a back-and-forth between critical detachment and imaginative participation in the forms of human culture. In our time, there is even greater danger in not attending to the roots of our forms of cognition in practical understandings of self and value. The curricular expression of the impoverishment Erskine feared has been the split between the first apprenticeship and the other two.

The educational value of the vocation narrative that structured the programs of the initiative lies in its ability to overcome this problematic split within liberal education. The PTEV demonstrates that the quest to find and then work out life purposes can provide a powerful motive for learning. The vocation narrative also mimes an architecture of the imagination, a meaningful narrative that makes it possible for students to conceive mature identities. As we have encountered it on various campuses, the discernment of personal vocation opened a variety of imaginative paths for integrating the three apprenticeships on the thread of purpose. And students and faculty alike responded to these features of the PTEV programs, enhancing their engagement with learning, teaching, and the larger educational enterprise.

The vocation narrative presents a particular but broad vision of a meaningful life. Rooted in biblical symbols of the divine call, to discern a vocation means seeking to find one's purpose in contributing in a unique way toward human flourishing and the well-being of the world. The PTEV programs taught practices and supported communities that made it possible for students to share in tradition and enact a significant and authentic way of living. The ideas and practices also traveled well, enlisting those of many and no religious affiliation. While clearly successful for many, the religious origin of the vocation language poses for some the ongoing question of whether or not there can be genuine dialogue between religious and secular humanists about this larger agenda of forming 21st-century citizens.[4]

While this remains a contentious issue for secularists in the academy, there are today hopeful signs of expanding attitudes. As we saw in chapter 3, the "Reconceiving the Secular in the Liberal Arts" project, in which Macalester College joined with several other secular liberal arts institutions, has reopened the question in a provocative way that holds new possibilities. Recall that the project's participants concluded that while it has played the valuable historic role of protecting intellectual freedom from religious dogmatism, the secularist consensus on campus has itself become, unintentionally, a constricting dogmatism. Specifically, the project participants argued that as a norm of intellectual discourse, secular*ism* constricts one of liberal education's key purposes: students' pursuit of the "larger questions of meaning and value" by "ruling out a whole set of cultural meanings as inappropriate for intellectual engagement."[5]

The report defined secularism as "the ideology that sought to enforce an exclusive truth about history's inevitability," meaning the belief that religion was historically determined to wither away as an element in human culture. This view is no longer intellectually compelling. History, as so often happens, did not turn out as expected. More significantly perhaps, ideological secularism is counterproductive educationally. As we have seen, today's learning theory emphasizes as a key motivating factor the importance of "authentic" learning, which engages a student's enduring concerns. Therefore, the exclusion or suppression of such concerns in higher education is likely to have long-term detrimental effects for liberal learning. In place of dogmatic secularism, the project's authors proposed a reshaped educational horizon characterized by "secularity," meaning an acknowledgment of the educational validity of diverse traditions of meaning.

Making Sense of the "Secular Age": Narratives in Conflict

The acknowledgment of secularity, as opposed to secularism, provides a context for liberal learning that means intellectual exploration must be conscious of operating in a context that lacks common agreement on value assumptions. It describes the condition of living culturally in what the philosopher Charles Taylor has termed the "secular age." He defines this as "a new context in which all search and questioning about the moral and spiritual must proceed . . . [and] a global context in which . . . all are very aware of the options favored by the others, and cannot just dismiss

them as inexplicable exotic error."[6] The importance of this new context is
that everywhere people have become more aware of themselves as inhabiting specific cultural spaces, different from others in various ways. For
this reason, modern persons can be said to have a more reflexive sense of
identity. This is the context for the rise of fundamentalism of all stripes,
including the secularist versions. Today's militant advocates must assert
the unique correctness of their views in full awareness that others are
vehemently defending opposing claims.

Ultimately, therefore, the imaginative architecture of the vocation
narrative raises questions about why it represents a plausible life-option.
Under the pluralist conditions of the secular age, a key aim of liberal learning must be developing capacities for communicating, deliberating, and
cooperating with those of different persuasions, rather than enforcing an
authoritative set of beliefs.[7] But to achieve this aim, it is important for
participants to have a way to make sense of their situation, which entails
being able to grasp the import of perspectives on reality that assume secular or religious starting points.

In Charles Taylor's dramatic reframing of the issue, the way contemporary people understand themselves is tied to a sense of living in a modern
and secular era, an understanding inseparable from an implied story of
how they have arrived at their present situation. (Postmodernists share
this reflexive stance, though they draw more skeptical conclusions than
most.) That is, we inhabit narratives, consciously or not, that separate
us as moderns from the past. We now think of ourselves as inhabiting a
world more "advanced" and different in fundamental ways from that of
our ancestors.

The more familiar type of such narratives, which support what has
become the default understanding of who and where we are, Taylor calls
"subtraction stories." In these narratives, becoming modern means "having lost, or sloughed off, or liberated themselves from certain earlier,
confining horizons, or illusions, or limitations of knowledge." This has
allowed certain features of human nature to emerge which, though there
all along, "had been impeded by what is now set aside."[8] Taylor's alternative to this view is what he calls the narrative of "disembedding." It
challenges the dominant story both by criticizing its coherence and by
providing the basis for an alternative, more complex stance toward the
modern situation.

For subtraction stories, human beings are primarily free individuals
able to think and act for themselves. The basic moral characteristic of

individuals is their freedom, understood as their ability to make choices by thinking for themselves, responsible only to their own reason. In philosophical terminology this is called autonomy. The purpose of society and its institutions, then, is to support this inherent autonomy of individuals, creating organized patterns of living in order to make individual growth and fulfillment possible. This anthropology or theory of human nature foregrounds the individual as the basic reality. Social institutions and culture are seen as creations and ultimately tools for individual use. This is a view in harmony with much of contemporary common sense.

Support for this view comes from an equally widespread epistemology positing a permanent gap between the mind and the world. For this epistemological account, the mind exists within individual persons and makes contact with the outside world through sensory perception. Knowledge is then built up through constructing inner representations supplied by the mind but checked against experience. In modern science, this process has been refined into powerful techniques of precise measurement, producing reliable accounts of experience, which then can be put together in chains of cause and effect to explain the workings of the world. The modern sciences of nature, constructed in this way, reveal nature itself as a system of causal relationships. Enlightenment thinkers such as Descartes and Bacon began to conceive perceptual experience as made up of simple units that carry no value or meaning in themselves. Instead, value judgments and significance are thought to reside solely in the mind.

Since nature is a neutral causal system, human individuals are free to impose their choice of "values" to shape natural processes at will. The default anthropology guiding the subtraction stories thereby assumes an instrumental stance toward the world, one embodied in technological control of nature. Superiority to the surrounding world is often conceived as an opposition between human freedom and brute nature. It is used to support claims for human dignity. However, while the dignity of autonomous individuals is assumed to be intrinsic to human nature, this assumption has only become fully apparent in modernity as humanity has come more and more to stand apart from and above the rest of the natural order.

The subtraction stories typically provide various accounts of how humanity has emerged into the modern condition. Some emphasize the overcoming of superstition by rational investigation, while others highlight a narrative of the moral self-assertion of individuals against various authorities such as kings, priests, and other elites, culminating in the great democratic revolutions of modern times. However, Taylor argues that they converge in asserting the priority of autonomy or choice as the proper understanding of humanity's moral nature and, with that, humanity's stance of superiority to the natural order.

The Problem with the "Subtraction" Story of Modernity

There is an internal problem, however, with the subtraction stories. The ideal of autonomy as presented in the subtraction story remains incomplete in that it cannot give an account of its own value. This becomes clear once the question arises as to why autonomy, what Taylor calls self-choosing, is a moral good. If the significance of an individual's life derives from the fact that the individual exercises choice, as was famously argued by John Stuart Mill, then the good of such choosing remains unexplained. Why not, Taylor points out, simply "go with the flow?" Why all the effort to live an "authentic," self-chosen life? Taylor's answer is that to support autonomy as a moral good, it must makes sense in a context shaped by some prior understanding, a background assumption that allows us to make sense of the claim that a self-chosen life is intrinsically worthy. Taylor calls the contextual backgrounds that make certain kinds of life and consciousness possible "horizons of significance."[9]

But where do these horizons of meaning, which provide norms and bestow value on our choices, including the moral significance of choosing itself, come from? Not, surely, individual choice since, as we see, a certain horizon of significance is the logical precondition for the very significance of choosing. As such, horizons of significance have to be trans-individual, shared contexts of cultural meaning that develop over time. If this is so, then the central moral value of secular modernity, autonomy itself, depends upon a historically contingent horizon of significance that grounds it as a moral ideal, a horizon which Taylor will argue has a lot to do with the influence of Greek philosophy and the Reformation on the Enlightenment and the 18th-century revolutions.

The notion of "subtracting" illusory or impeding connections to reveal individual autonomy as the true human nature became plausible under the influence of the moral appeal of freedom. Once developed as a core element of modern culture, however, autonomy has proven an unstable ideal, subject to degenerating into amoral self-assertion, individual or collective. When it becomes detached from significant cultural horizons and the social institutions that support them, this reveals the shadow side of the subtraction stories. The consequences of this detachment have been highlighted by many social analysts, including Max Weber, whose account of the nihilistic effects of the "rationalization" of society and the "disenchantment" of nature we encountered earlier in this chapter.

The most important implication of this critique of the subtraction stories is that the notion of the human self at work in those narratives is incoherent or at least incomplete. At the core, it presents a picture of the human self as fundamentally atomic, alone, and disengaged from larger patterns of cultural meaning and yet in need of invoking specific moral assumptions in order to ground its own significance. So, the ability to choose cannot be, as the default view proclaims, a self-sufficient basis for the moral worth of the individual.

If autonomy, as opposed to mere self-assertion, actually requires a shared moral context for its moral importance, then the modern project must be understood differently. Criticizing authoritarian institutions on the basis of principles and asserting the dignity of autonomy remain sacred modern values. But their support depends not upon subtracting connections of meaning but on recognizing that the very ideals of autonomy and authentic selfhood require connecting to a wider sense of the whole of things. While such connection remains problematic in the individualist account, it offers grounds for asking critical questions about the adequacy of that account.

The vocation initiative has proven educationally powerful precisely because it did not presume the adequacy of the individualist account. By connecting individuals to the horizon of significance supplied by the narrative of vocation, the PTEV helped "fund growth of the human."

Recovering the Engaged Stance and the Place of Religious Discourse

This conclusion returns to the question of religious traditions and their significance to modern discourse about identity, a discussion hobbled by confusion over the nature and place of religious discourse. Current understandings of religion have been importantly shaped by the assumptions of the subtraction account of modernity. Specifically, the great power of the scientific model of explanation has introduced a profound cleavage into modern culture that often sets the context for discussion of religion, especially its role in higher education. The model of taking the disengaged stance of "outside" observation in regard to modern biological science and medical technology has yielded extraordinary gains both in reliable knowledge of nature and in the technological ability to control it. Enthusiasts for that model of thinking have for a long time been eagerly extending their reach into all areas of human experience. However, in the cultural and moral realms, explanatory successes of the kind achieved through study of natural processes have been few.

There seems to be a real difference in kind between the requirements for natural scientific investigation and what is needed in social or cultural inquiry. One basis for this distinction is the observation that in the human realm, theoretical concepts do not simply describe phenomena, as physical laws describe and predict the behavior of atoms and molecules. In the human realm, the descriptions themselves can become part of the horizon of meaning, shaping future understanding. For example, today large numbers of people think, talk, and act as inhabitants of "the economy" or "the financial system," entities generated from social and historical theory. When a person perceives herself to be struggling in a tough economy, she is granting this abstraction considerable power to shape her imagination and experience. This suggests something of the way theory functions in the human sciences and the role it has come to exercise in modern culture.

Theories of human or cultural phenomena are not simply the morally neutral result of detached observation, though they may use such techniques and incorporate findings from the scientific investigation of natural processes. In the human sciences, theories are ultimately narratives or portraits of human experience. These portraits can be "implemented" in ways that change how individuals, institutions, and societies think of themselves and how they enact their identities. So, theory enters the human world not just instrumentally, in the form of technologies, but very importantly from the "inside," as part of the architecture of the worlds of meaning humans inhabit. Ironically, the disengaged stance of theoretical observation finds its significance in the engaged stance of those who attempt to "live" the theory.

Theory's power to define reality is important for understanding the place of religious discourse in contemporary life. The great prestige of the detached theoretical perspective in modern culture has meant that religion, like many other forms of cultural life, has come to be seen primarily as a body of theories. Certainly, much contemporary public discourse treats religious discourse that way, as a set of explanatory claims about nature, humanity, and reality itself. Or, as we have seen, in discussions of religion in liberal education, the emphasis is upon religious discourse as modes of thinking, again analogous to scientific theories. This is not entirely wrong: religious traditions have always made claims about how the world is and what human nature is like, as well as how life should be lived. However, judged by the criterion of the sciences of nature, religious discourse must fail to measure up, just as the vast expanse of social and cultural investigation fails that test.

But treating religion as a science ignores a fundamental fact about religion's presence in the world. Robert Bellah has shown that understanding religions requires seeing them not only as modes of thought but as whole ways of living. For Bellah, the great cultural importance of religious traditions stems from their historic and continuing role in shaping human behavior. By doing that, religions profoundly influence the way any society understands the world.[10] Ultimately, religious discourse, like that of other cultural forms and the arts, is rooted in communities of shared practice. Because of this, its pedagogy, for it performs pedagogical functions, is profound. Religious pedagogy draws upon some of the oldest and deepest features of humanity. It operates on several channels at once, not only providing argumentative accounts of reality and ethical principles, but also embedding these accounts in powerful visions conveyed through rich stories and symbols. As a system of ritual practice, religion has adherents enact those meanings in ways that weave them deeply into group and personal identity.[11]

As Bellah points out, religion operates on a very broad bandwidth. In similar manner, Clifford Geertz defined religion as a "cultural system ... formulating conceptions of a general order of existence" enacted in common so as to "establish powerful, pervasive, and long-lasting moods and motivations."[12] Religious discourse, then, not only talks about the world; it drives an understanding of the world. It is speech for the sake of action. It is primarily concerned with interpreting experience within a world of meaning that also guides action toward purposes exemplified in shared practices. While religious discourse is concerned to interpret those meanings, the significance of religious symbols and practices are not exhausted by linguistic or conceptual formulations.

On the other hand, part of religious discourse in most traditions is concerned with articulating the wider significance of these understandings. In the Christian tradition that kind of religious discourse has been called theology. This is especially relevant for considering the relation of religious traditions to higher education. Theology's task has always had an element of paradox. It employs philosophical argument, attempting to speak in the most general way possible, depending as little as possible on particular cultural understandings—precisely to articulate the significance of the experience of a particular cultural community. Theology's use of philosophical generalization has also been important for the religious community engaged in this kind of discourse. By introducing criticism and standards of rational argument into the practices of religious discourse, theology brings reflexive criticism into the heart of religious discourse. It is vital for keeping open the important dialogue between the particular religious community and participants in the wider cultural world, including adherents of other religions and of none.

Theology is therefore necessarily in tension—or better, in dialogue— with the insider and outsider points of view. But, as we have seen, this is also the situation of humanistic thinking of all kinds. To be part of the academy, such discourse must be willing to employ the distanced viewpoint of critical analysis. But to speak about its subject it must, like literary criticism, also strive to enable learners to enter and understand the world of religious living from within. It is a difficult balance, but not different in kind from that required in all areas of human and social inquiry.

The Relevance of the Engaged Stance: Educating for the Ecological Challenge

The human relation to nature has emerged as a central topic for 21st-century education. How humanity should relate to nature has now become a decisive question for defining what it means to be human in the contemporary world. Perhaps more clearly than any other, this issue reveals the unintended consequences of enacting in policies, institutions, and technologies key assumptions of the subtraction stories we have examined. On the plus side, modernity has brought the developed world liberation from many of the old evils of life, such as high infant mortality and many chronic diseases. Technologies such as electricity have opened up new forms of fulfillment for far greater numbers of people than ever before. But we have now begun to grasp the deeply problematic aspects of some of those advances and the ambiguity lurking in the understanding of the world from which they derive. Modern industrial technology has made it possible for humans to benefit from shaping the processes of nature. Unexpectedly, the consequences of that shaping have also revealed how deeply we are embedded within those natural processes.

As many have noted, there is both irony and pathos in the fact that our technological capacities now threaten the sustainability of human life. The past century has witnessed the fulfillment of René Descartes's great hopes for the new science of nature he championed, predicting it would make us "masters and possessors of nature."[13] Yet our greatest triumphs as a species seem to be recoiling on us without our fully grasping what is happening to us and why. Still dreaming of becoming somehow independent of natural constraints, we are being forced in uncomfortable ways to acknowledge that our well-being is interdependent with that of a complex planetary system of which we are only a part.

Changing course may be possible on the basis of enlightened self-interest. Simply to keep going, human society will need to pay attention to the consequences of its modes of production and consumption of natural resources. However, to date, progress in that direction has been fitful. The very idea of limiting growth remains deeply divisive, giving rise to international stalemate on environmental agreements when these threaten seriously to curtail economic expansion. Here the apparently simple prudential calculus runs up against both issues of justice on a global scale as well as the reality that for the relative have-not societies there is less to preserve through slowing environmental degradation, and much to gain in the short term from pressing ahead with ecologically destructive growth. The vast gap in global development makes consensus on the basis of self-interest difficult and, at times, elusive.

What is missing in current attitudes toward environmental stewardship is a larger shared purpose, a vision of possibility that could elicit sufficient compromises to stave off the worst outcomes and still move toward a more just global order. Such a vision will require taking seriously the reality of interdependence among societies and with the enveloping natural world. Such an understanding could provide the necessary context for motivating effective progress in slowing ecological degradation. But achieving this amounts to a change of perception, a coming to understand the world as a home for humanity, treated as a responsibility rather than as a trove of resources to be used at will. In essence, the needed change demands an openness and responsiveness to the world beyond the human, allowing it to assume intrinsic rather than merely instrumental value.

The uncomfortable fact is that the exploitative attitude toward nature, which has until now tacitly directed much technological development, also embodies many of the chief values of modernity. Ralph Heintzman has provided a useful way to characterize what he calls the "virtues of self-assertion," stressing that these are real virtues that express real human goods, however insufficient for guiding human life into the future. "Reflecting the fundamental impulse from which it proceeds," Heintzman notes, "the language of self-assertion is the language of liberation, of freedom, autonomy, separation, independence, individualism, empowerment . . . and self-realization."[14]

By contrast, what the current environmental situation requires, Heintzman continues, is another set of values and virtues. These have always been part of human life but have been decidedly overshadowed in modern Western culture. These are the values associated with "the natural human impulse to attachment, to union with others and with the surrounding environment." When lived out, they are enacted in a disposition Heintzman calls "reverence," meaning a stance of engagement that is both a value in itself and the necessary starting place for self-assertion. Religious traditions in all societies, according to Heintzman, are best seen as "deepened and more focused expressions of the permanent and universal human instinct of reverence . . . the natural human impulse to attachment, to union with others, and the surrounding environment, a larger whole.[15] This position echoes Robert Bellah's argument in *Religion and Human Evolution* about the formative significance of religious traditions in every culture, including our own. As Bellah notes, these traditions are not unproblematic in many ways, but they provide powerful sources of moral meaning and sense of responsibility.

If this argument is correct, the disposition toward reverence holds a logical priority over the self-assertive virtues. All actions are self-assertions, and can include disengagement and critique, but reverence redefines or rather resituates such acts as responses by the self to those connections on which it depends. Without continuing dialogue with others—that is, without a society and a cultural sphere—there would be no context within which the self could develop or assert its aims, no matter how generous or selfish. The great historic mistake of the individualist account of human nature has been to miss this interdependency of self-assertion and reverence. When understood as an engaged stance responsive to the good of the whole in which the individual participates, reverence completes or fulfills autonomy by allowing self-assertion to become self-affirmation through participation. This shift in perspective has major implications not only for environmental stewardship, but also for democratic education and the cultivation of civic life. It grounds a concern for the common welfare described by John Dewey as the "ultimate ethical habit" that should guide educational formation.[16] This kind of education requires as its premise the understanding of how the self-assertive and reverent impulses need each other and, more, how self-assertion can become self-affirmation in the very act of contributing to sustaining the larger world on which the self depends. As we have seen in previous chapters, students in the PTEV were encouraged to explore their individual abilities, academic learning, and occupational possibilities as ways to participate in, and contribute to, the welfare of the larger reality.

The Alternative Story: Recognizing the Ambiguity of the "Great Disembedding"

The deficiencies of the subtraction stories, and their dangerous consequences for ecological survival, point to the need for a better understanding of the historical genesis of both modern ideals and modern pathologies. To orient such efforts, Charles Taylor proposes an alternative narrative he calls the Great Disembedding. It proposes that modern autonomy emerged from an earlier period in which the individual was more fully immersed, or embedded, within society—a condition mirrored by the embedding of society itself within a cosmos pervaded by higher, spiritual forces. From this earlier condition, not by historical necessity but rather through a series of contingent processes, the modern self has gradually become "disembedded," with the ambiguous outcomes just observed.[17] This account also provides a basis for reconnecting with wider and deeper sources of meaning needed to reorient our precarious global civilization.

Compared to the subtraction accounts, this alternative is premised upon a more socially and historically conditioned understanding of human nature. This, in turn, is supported by an approach to knowledge that locates human understanding within an ongoing process of coping with the environment upon which human life depends. Taylor challenges the common modern epistemology that begins with the alleged problem of how minds can come to hold inner representations of an external reality. Instead, he argues that human beings are always engaged in the world prior to any questions about how they can know it.

Engagement, for this account, is the primordial human situation. Humans are engaged both as biological entities who live through continual interchange with an enveloping environment of air, light, plants, animals, microbes, etc., and also as active social participants who must seek their well-being through continuing receptivity as well as agency in their relations with others. In these fundamental, continuous patterns of interaction, things and persons have significance as features of a practical whole in which the individual is immersed. This is the origin of what becomes more fully developed in the realm of language and symbol as a horizon of significance. That is why value and meaning must come from the contexts constituted by these relationships to significant others and the relationships of interaction on which human life depends. The world, that is, first emerges not as a realm of "neutral" isolated facts "out there" somewhere, but as a whole replete with meaning.

It follows, then, that our representations of the world, even those tested by empirical measurement, derive from these ongoing activities of engaged agents seeking to cope with a world that has physical, social, and cultural significance, before it becomes an object of disinterested observation and study. But "this coping can never be accounted for in terms of representations [ultimately derived from it], but provides the background against which our representations have the sense they do."[18] Prior engagement, physical and social coping with the world, is therefore the necessary platform for developing the disengaged, reflexive stance. This does not deny the value or validity of taking up a disengaged, "outside" point of view. But it does argue that disengagement holds alienating potentials and that criticism needs connection with the modes of engagement that sustain meaning in order to avoid turning destructive. This is the educational logic at work in the PTEV's vocational narrative.

Nor is this the solitary, Robinson Crusoe-like experience conjured by the subtraction stories. "This coping activity and the understanding which inhabits it" is something into which all individuals must be inducted, so that the self emerges within social action.[19] As the Great Disembedding has proceeded, various social practices have arisen which "do indeed call upon us to assume a stance as individuals." Taylor continues:

However, it remains true that human selves, even those with a highly individualistic orientation, only develop, just as they only learn language, through the intimate, conversation-like experiences of reciprocal interaction called primary socialization ... our most primordial identity is as a new player being inducted into an old game.[20]

It is from these ongoing, socially embedded patterns of dialogue that individuals gain orientation for their efforts. Just as significance, including the moral significance of human dignity as well as the reflexivity of scientific and critical inquiry, depends upon practices of engagement with cultural substance, so does an education that seeks to foster these capacities.

Reframing Liberal Education: The Relevance of Vocational Discernment

Effective higher education for the 21st century needs to provide a context for forming meaning and purpose as well as acquiring knowledge and developing skills. Under the fragmented conditions of contemporary culture this has become more important than ever. Educators must attend consciously to the roots of learning in practical understandings of self and value. Liberal education in particular, promising as it does to enable students to make sense of the world and their place in it, needs to cultivate an engaged disposition—a desire to see life steadily and to see it whole—in order to motivate positive intellectual growth. That is the intent of integrating the disparate apprenticeships of undergraduate experience through cultivation of identity and purpose.

As we have seen in an earlier chapter, this can take place within a number of cultural frames, such as education for student well-being, for citizenship, or for service to humanity across national borders. The vocation programs provide impressive proof of the effectiveness of an intentionally integrated approach to undergraduate education. The experience shows that many students and faculty will respond to efforts of this kind with enthusiasm, supporting their growth in maturity and resilience. The vocational narrative, when embodied in a community of learning gathered around its goals, can promote both Socratic engagement with self-reflection and self-development and an ethic of responsibility toward the larger world.

The theological perspective, as this chapter has tried to show, emerged in these programs as a vital horizon of significance that, in various forms, made these achievements possible. As also noted, by emphasizing the discernment of vocation, the programs came to understand theology expansively and practically. Rather than simply as doctrine, theology became important as a resource for sustaining ongoing exploration of identity and purpose with an orientation toward reverence for the sacred and openness toward life and its possibilities.

The focus of such education is the practice of what the PTEV called vocational discernment. That is the most distinctive, and perhaps the most important contribution the vocation initiative has made toward reinventing liberal learning. It holds considerable value for higher education as a whole. Discernment is a reflective practice designed to foster in students, faculty, and staff connections between the liberal arts disciplines, experiential and civic learning, career exploration, and emergent self-understanding. As a discipline of consciously shaping day-to-day responses to their experience, vocational discernment enables individuals to join other learners to explore and test the commitments defining their lives and identities.

Especially today, when life often feels like a succession of discontinuous bits of experience, there is appeal in the notion that education can mean the beginning of a trajectory toward integrity and positive purpose even through uncertainty, crisis, and struggle. Vocation adds the important dimension of a context, lending significance to the call of sacred values as well as the impulse to live with and for others. The PTEV's emphasis upon vocation as a narrative quest, rooted in supportive, reciprocal learning communities, provided students with experiential proof that learning has deep value in shaping a life worth living.

Conclusion

THIS BOOK HAS presented a series of portraits drawn from visits to campus programs that were parts of the Lilly Endowment's Program for the Theological Exploration of Vocation. The book has also placed these within a larger debate about the aims and future direction of higher education. The context of this conversation is being shaped by massive changes affecting America's student population and the larger society in which they live. The thesis of this study is that the initiative points the way toward a reconfiguration of the college experience that, by linking learning to the exploration of meaning and life purpose, can engage the whole student more effectively than is typically the case today. This chapter will provide a summation of the argument for this claim and then draw out its implications for the enterprise of higher education as a whole.

The Good News

Perhaps the most noteworthy aspect of the initiative's programs is that at a time of widespread concern about student disengagement from academic activity, the PTEV campuses succeeded in engaging students in learning. They did this not by limiting their educational aims to workforce preparation or purely academic achievement but by enabling students to connect these aims to exploration of their purposes for living. The ability and willingness of these programs to draw upon theological traditions of vocation produced a galvanizing effect for many participants. However, far from being dogmatically closed, their employment of the religious meaning of vocation resonated widely with humanistic educational ideals among faculty and staff. In the process, the PTEV programs intensified the professional commitment of both faculty and staff to the educational enterprise. As the programs evolved, they often revitalized a sense of common purpose, that often-elusive goal sought by administrative leaders and governing boards of educational institutions.

To achieve the extraordinary outcomes noted in earlier chapters, the PTEV campuses developed programs that deliberately connected the three, often-fragmented aspects of the undergraduate experience. The programs spurred innovative developments in the Academic Apprenticeship of teaching and learning, by linking intellectual disciplines with contemporary challenges and to students' own development. They generated new forms of campus community life, renewing and increasing the potential for learning in the Social Apprenticeship of students' social life and their interaction with faculty and staff. Building on the evidence that personal relationships with faculty and other adult mentors are key to both learning and personal formation, the programs combined the academic and the social through supporting learning communities that involved students, faculty, and staff.

The campus programs did these things with an intention to provide spaces for cultivating meaning and purpose through the language of calling. In these ways, the vocation programs wove the undergraduate experience together around the guiding thread of the Third Apprenticeship of meaning and purpose. As expressed in intensified involvements with community and civic projects, the PTEV's theologically derived orientation toward responsiveness and service proved an effective educational resource. It sustained a supportive climate in which students could work out their own quests for meaning and purpose, in the present as well as for the future.

All the programs shared three structural characteristics: the theme of vocational exploration, the fostering of communities of learning, and the practice of reflection. The exploration of vocation or calling stood at the center of all the programs. Exploring vocation through academic and co-curricular activities provided a coherent conceptual frame within which students could make sense of their activities in and out of the classroom. The distinctive inflection the PTEV gave to this search for purpose centered on the notion that learning entails a responsibility to employ knowledge in serving ends wider than self-advancement. This orientation toward service provided students with a sense of participating in aims larger than the individual that at the same time also enhanced the learners' dignity through being recognized as valuable members who each had something to contribute.

By making this perspective concrete in a variety of educational experiences, the PTEV offered expanded motives for learning and self-development. It also enlarged students' sense of what could matter in life, while extending time horizons to enable participants to think of their college experience as a resource for shaping identity and commitment as they grew into adult life. The positive developmental effects of participation in the programs, as already noted, showed that exploring life purposes directly enhanced students' perseverance, the "grit" typical of resilient people and communities.

The second key feature, the building of learning communities, provided the social nexus within which exploration of the needs of society and the world could factor in students' personal decisions about their future. Such an enlargement of mind and growth in responsibility are traditional aims of liberal education. But the secret of the PTEV's success lay in understanding that larger horizons become real only when such concerns are actively shared among those with whom we live and interact. This is why taking part in these learning communities of shared questions enabled students to find lasting significance in their experiences both in and outside the classroom and campus.

The third common element was the use in all the campus learning communities of practices of group and individual reflection. These practices included Socratic efforts at self-understanding as well as probing the assumptions underlying varying and conflicting views of the good life. Reflection made it possible for students to construct over time an understanding of life as a whole, encompassing connections between interests, immediate goals, and longer life trajectories. Practiced in multiple settings, orally and in writing, both within and outside the formal curriculum, these activities provided ways for students to integrate academic learning and practical experience with important dimensions of meaning in their lives. That made it more likely that they would be able to maintain a sense of direction through the sometimes difficult and disturbing times of their undergraduate lives. Organized reflection also laid a basis for continuing use of these practices for thinking beyond graduation.

The three elements of the PTEV programs—vocational narrative as basic structure, the grounding of this in learning communities, and the cultivation of reflective practices—invited students to engage their college education not as passive consumers but as protagonists in a serious enterprise with lifelong consequences. These programs demonstrated that it is possible to recover the formative power of liberal learning, even in a time when fixation upon its merely instrumental value threatens to overwhelm the deeper and more public ends of higher education. These features have continued to characterize the PTEV's successor program, NetVUE (Network for Vocation in Undergraduate Education) of the Council of Independent Colleges.)

The Argument in Brief

Through the profiles of campus programs and discussion of current literature and arguments about the state of learning in higher education, this book has presented a larger argument for the value and importance of the PTEV initiative for renewing liberal education.

One. The major goal of college education is, as traditionally asserted, supporting students' cognitive growth through academic learning. This is the dimension of undergraduate life that the metaphor of the First Apprenticeship tries to capture. Recent research emphasizes that learning deepens and lasts longer when students use new concepts by applying them to experience. The efficacy of various "high impact" practices that involve students actively in their learning is supported by research. Chapters 1 and 2 reported on some of these used in the programs.

Two. Because learning occurs in informal as well as formal settings, the undergraduate experience needs to be organized as a process of development that is cumulative. To achieve the goals of liberal learning—the ability to make sense of the world and one's place in it so as to use one's abilities to make contributions of value—cognitive growth must be accompanied by enhanced personal and social maturity. College education therefore needs to be holistic in character in ways that involve and connect personal and social development, the substance of the Social Apprenticeship, with the First Apprenticeship of knowledge. By taking as their overarching purpose the enhancement of students' sense of personal meaning and purpose, the Third Apprenticeship, the programs were able to foster a climate supportive of the development of perseverance, emotional maturity, and resilience.

Three. Since learning in all these dimensions depends heavily on student motivation, effective education must evoke and sustain student engagement. The PTEV's grounding in the Third Apprenticeship proved decisive here. While the evidence suggests that deep involvement with learning is exceptional among emerging adults as a whole, the attention the PTEV gave to faculty–student interaction resulted in the growth of a shared and highly motivating sense of common educational purpose.

This made for high-quality learning and, importantly, provided the context for the exploration and maturation of life purpose.

Four. The key to the PTEV's success in this regard came from sustaining communities of learning. As chapter 5 emphasized, these took many forms. On some campuses, it was the integration of civic service with academic pursuit that served as a focus. On others, residence halls became sites for learning that brought together personal development and social relationships within a climate that took both ideas and meaning seriously. High-intensity experiences such as service-study trips acted as strong catalysts. By rooting academic learning in networks of cooperation that linked students vertically across the generations as well as horizontally with peers, the programs were able to stimulate engagement in reflection on personal identity and purpose, typically inflected by the resources offered by the campus's theological tradition. In that way, as chapters 3 and 4 illustrated, the theme of vocation provided students with grounding as they pursued experiences and reflected upon them.

Five. These experiences articulated well with the academic tradition of humanistic culture long associated with liberal learning. On some campuses, it lent these traditions a new vitality. As argued in chapter 6, the signature of humanistic inquiry is its cultivation of a double-stranded, bifocal vision of knowledge. Humanistic education—like humanistic inquiry—demands rigor in applying cognitive tools of analysis. But it also complements this distanced stance with the probing of the meaning of events and ideas for participants who must judge and act as well as observe. This perspective is wider, therefore, than criticism or detached measurement alone. Like the arts, humanistic inquiry cultivates imagination and empathy as well as aesthetic and moral awareness. For many PTEV programs such as those profiled, that meant the deliberate effort to promote practical wisdom through experiment and reflection upon the meaning of values in experience.

Six. The idea of vocation gave content for promoting this kind of humanistic inquiry. As noted in chapter 7, the language of vocation conveyed a narrative pattern that enabled participants to understand the perspective of responsible participation. It also promoted ongoing self-discovery that led participants to take a proactive stance toward their education, their college experience, and future lives and careers. The use of the Christian language of calling provided, through the various forms that were given it by the specific theological tradition of particular campuses, a climate that supported exploration of questions of value and purposes beyond the self.

This proved resonant for students and educators, both across Christian traditions and beyond Christianity, including purely secular forms of humanism. As reported in chapter 3, in some cases it gave rise to new and constructive campus conversations about religion and secularity in undergraduate life and learning. Throughout the programs visited, these reflective activities led participants to cultivate a stance of engaged reflection. It was the focus on meaning, as interpreted through the lens of vocation, which brought reflection into prominence, and so conferred new vitality on a central theme of liberal learning.

In sum, the initiative encouraged students to do the following:

1. Explore their individual talents and interests, now reframed as "gifts" to develop and employ, typically within a learning community concerned with vocational themes.
2. Explore the world of knowledge through various intellectual disciplines and perspectives. Students often did this in relation to either possibilities for careers related to students' interests and concerns or to needs and hopes for the larger world.
3. Frame these explorations as a process of finding oneself through personally chosen participation with a larger purpose. In theological terms, that purpose was seeking the kingdom of God. This moral logic was also articulated in secular terms as participation in citizenship and shared responsibility for the welfare of humanity and its environment.
4. Expand their imaginations and develop empathy for others, with the intent to shift self-concern toward seeking fulfillment in service to others, a process typically supported by the campus learning community.
5. Consider a variety of examples of lives committed to purposes, secular as well as religious, that could provide plausible possibilities for probing and debate, including encounters with mistakes, failure, and suffering.

This educational agenda gave the PTEV programs their distinctive form and spirit, across the range of specific programs with their different emphases. Chapter 5 surveyed a number of kindred efforts that are also attempting to reshape the contemporary undergraduate experience in ways that share a number of the vocation initiative's concerns. A noteworthy common theme among such efforts is the rediscovery of the value of public purposes and connections with the larger world for energizing students' quests for individual significance. Like the PTEV, these projects have also been experimenting with pedagogies of active engagement to give the college experience a more integrated and purposeful character.

The Relevance of the PTEV

These achievements are especially remarkable within the present unsettled situation of American higher education. Undergraduate education in the United States today faces formidable challenges and some large uncertainties. There is the serious problem of rising costs amid lessening public investment. This is compounded by ominous and persisting inequities in access and completion rates for different sectors of the population. In addition, the rapid advances in information technology have unsettled earlier patterns of instruction, faculty careers, and the economics of the enterprise. As earlier chapters have documented, these changes have largely increased rather than reduced the problems of coherence resulting from the misalignments noted earlier among the aims of students, faculty, and academic administrators.

Less noticed is the way these unsettling trends pace and to some degree mirror the rapid, deeply ambiguous, evolution of the larger worlds of work and consumption with which colleges and universities, as well as students and parents, must cope. Yet, it is against this background that the educational vision worked out in the initiative shows their greatest relevance. Chapters 1 and 2 described these trends in some detail. But at this point, it is useful to highlight the most salient features of this background. The rapid expansion of Internet-based information technology provides a useful vantage point because the information technology (IT) revolution is at the center of so many of the important emerging trends, or to use the currently fashionable phrase, disruptions. But the outcomes have so far proven ambiguous. This is because the web can be experienced in two different but deeply interconnected ways: for convenience these might be called the web's Expressive Mode and its Instrumental Mode.

On the one hand, there is the web in the Expressive Mode. Internet-based marketing and shopping have radically expanded choice for everyone, along with the ability to get best value through comparison and demand management programming. Individual self-interest has been empowered mightily through the World Wide Web. It has become a cliché that anyone with resources can get exactly what they want, from anywhere, at the least cost, and, more and more, exactly when they want it—which is

usually "right now." More recent advances in data collection and processing make it increasingly common to shop in virtual marketplaces organized entirely around each individual's preferences. Years of this have
pedagogical effects, so that the same attitudes are naturally applied to
other areas of life, including education and learning. These, too, can be
imagined as no different in kind from other sorts of purchases, as simply
tools to get more of what one wants and on one's own terms. Consumers
formed by these shopping practices are likely to find it obvious that college is about getting a credential for a job in order to increase one's future
access to satisfaction.

In addition to this enormous expansion of the consumer's reach and
the consequent ability to gratify a wider range of desires, the rise of social
media, the so-called Web 2.0, has added vast new possibilities for self-
expression and constant communication with a self-selected network of
partners. And the attitudes of shopping and marketing learned in the
milieu of choosing products and services easily blends into a parallel marketing of the "curated self" in social media. For many, the new opportunities for self-expression have also opened alluring possibilities for being
admired, even "followed" by others eager to know the smallest details of
one's lifestyle. The web holds out the heady allure of celebrity democra-
tized, and appreciation universalized! In this more social and interactive
use of the web, there is also an unmistakable tendency toward closure of
the horizon around the apparently spontaneous desires of the self and
those like oneself.

Ambiguous Freedom: Between Consumer
Wonderland and Darwinian Jungle

The exhilaration of enhanced freedom to fulfill desires and to express
oneself in expanding ways is only one side of the IT revolution. There
is also a more darkly coercive side. It is actually in what we might call
its Instrumental Mode that the web is having its biggest impact. This is
because, as every student of Economics 101 knows, consumption depends
upon production and stimulates it. That is, the other side of the consumer
market is the labor market. And here the experience has been quite different. For a generation, Americans have been told that they must become
more "flexible," able to "reinvent" themselves, upgrade their skills and
aggressively market themselves—precisely because of the fickle demands

placed on producers by the expanding possibilities for consumption. Indeed, the most recent applications of IT to production have proven much more problematic than the effects of the web in its Expressive Mode. This is because the new technologies have made it possible to connect the iridescent webs of consumption ever more tightly to the iron chains of finance and production.

As participants in the labor market, Americans' lives have become more divergent, more stratified into winners and losers: fortunate owners of capital and highly negotiable credentials and skills, on the one hand, and the far more numerous insecure and pressured who must sell their labor with fewer advantages. For several decades, advancing IT has speeded up and consolidated financial activity while also making it possible to realize greater efficiency by rationalizing the management of production and logistics through supply chains now gone global. And developments in robotics continue to turn all routine processes, from auto maintenance to many functions of lawyers and physicians, into computer controlled or guided processes.

While it is enabled by the new technologies, this global drive for increased efficiency in the application of capital is finally being pushed by intensified competitive pressures. The global economy is not only a consumers' wonderland. It is also a scene of Darwinian struggle to best the competition in attracting and retaining investment. It has become quite clear that the chief beneficiaries of the gains in efficiency produced by the emerging technologies have been the global investor class. Since labor is almost always the most expensive factor in any process of production, under conditions of global market competition reducing the cost of labor is a universal imperative.

Today, these trends are on the threshold of a nearly quantum acceleration due to the coming of the so-called Internet of Things, or Web 3.0. This is an emerging global system that uses the Internet to link myriads of sensors to monitor and analyze every activity by processing through networks of computers the data recovered and then feeding it back to guide and anticipate interactions. The potential is already apparent in novel inventions such as driverless automobiles, robotic factories, and self-monitoring surveillance and weapons systems.

This ought to be mostly good news. The potential of the Internet of Things for freeing humanity from burdensome labor and raising many millions from grinding poverty is truly awesome. It is opening up opportunities for a whole generation of technological innovators. But driven by the competitive compulsions of the contemporary global market, its growth is likely to increase the already severe entropic tendencies undermining the social ecology upon which Americans depend, leaving only the shifting trends of consumption and casual connection in its place. Disruption, while it may spur rapid innovation in a market context, is rarely good for organic life forms. The current impact of human expansion on other species shows that the usual effect of rapid disruption of habitat is extinction. Why, then, would one expect that unbuffered economic disruption would be good for humans—unless they are imagined to live, not in societies, but solely in IT-mediated markets of consumption and production?

A Culture of Acquiescence

These are the background conditions that make intelligible the findings of recent studies of emerging adults, surveyed earlier, that have pointed up evidence of widespread disengagement from learning, either drift or narrow achievement orientation, caution about commitment, and a constriction of imagination. Like rising levels of depression and anxiety among the young, they may be taken as symptoms, or more precisely responses, to a society that divides its winners sharply from its losers. By the time they reach college, many already have adopted a strategy of getting by, emphasizing social life, and deferring as long as possible the burdensome business of entering the adult worlds of career and responsibility. Others, more fortunate perhaps, aim directly at the main prizes. These have streamlined their lives for constant achievement, always looking to meet requirements of the next rung in the ladder, and being careful to please those thought to have influence.

In 2014, for instance, William Deresiewicz indicted the nation's most selective, "elite" institutions such as the Ivy League, for, in effect, promoting an education in which the most ambitious and capable students are busy running so hard for competitive distinction that they rarely have either the time or interest to ask questions of purpose or direction beyond the next rung of "success." However hyperbolic, Deresiewicz's claims created a stir. In a contrasting study, Richard Arum and Josipa Roksa followed up—with largely similar results—their much-discussed previous findings about more typical undergraduates "adrift," neither focused on academic achievement nor adequately prepared for making their way in either careers or life. The titles of their respective works describe an ominous bifurcation: Arum and Roksa titled theirs *Aspiring Adults Adrift: Tentative Transitions of College Graduates*, while Deresiewicz called his *Excellent Sheep: The Miseducation of the American Elite and the Way to a Meaningful Life*.[1] Together, these books identify a pervasive and disturbing situation that any realistic reform of higher education must reckon with.

What these otherwise opposed attitudes share is a willingness to accept current conditions as inevitable and, consequently, to adopt a wary strategy of limiting trust and loyalties. These are manifestations of a widespread attitude: a Culture of Acquiescence. These responses are not irrational. Contemporary American life, while it enables individuals to focus on themselves to an unprecedented degree, also inculcates in schools and workplaces a "hidden curriculum." It teaches—and reinforces with brutal sanctions—the dispiriting notion that there is no alternative to the ferocious, Darwinian competition into which today's youth are being inducted. In business, in politics, in personal and social life, they are often warned, both subtly and sometimes directly, they have no option but to relentlessly promote themselves, subordinating attachments whenever necessary in order to be free to grasp the main chance. The evidence, as we have seen, is that this acquiescence comes at a high price in well-being.

The Breakout: Educating for Purpose and the New Relevance of Reverence

In their widespread acquiescence, today's youth are only imitating their elders, most of whom seem to have given up some time ago any hope of collectively changing, or even influencing, the shape of the nation's future. Yet, without a conception of better society, or a more humane and satisfying way of living, acquiescence in the face of what its boosters promote as inevitable "change"—if not "progress"—can appear as grim necessity. From a longer historical perspective, this Culture of Acquiescence can only seem like a kind of failure of nerve for a people that has prided itself on its "can-do" spirit. But the collapse of optimism is not so much about the "me" as about the "we." This reveals a striking erosion of a sense of participating in larger and longer-term values than private satisfactions. This is a genuine "spiritual" struggle over the possibility of meaning for the future.

By both argument and example, this book has tried to make the case that education for individual freedom, or autonomy in its philosophical articulation, logically depends upon and draws its practical strength from connections within a larger community or social ecology. The term for recognizing and actively cultivating awareness of this mutual dependency between self and others can be called citizenship. The disposition that supports it we have seen described as reverence. By attending to our ties with others, by adopting an attitude of reciprocal respect and assistance toward them, we receive back enhanced confidence and dignity.

But in addition to its benefits for the self, reverence corresponds to a human tendency that is as natural as self-assertion: our desire for connection to others, to our past, and to the larger world in which we share. Reverence has long been associated with and cultivated by many religious traditions. And one of the most important contributions of the vocation initiative to contemporary higher education has been its explicit invocation of reverence as an attitude, a virtue, that is worth exploring. It is in relation to this critical dimension of contemporary life that the initiative and its kindred projects become most significant and their achievements most valuable.

The sad irony of the present is that, despite all the hyperbole about the dazzling future betokened by the new technologies of connectivity, the American sense of future possibilities has constricted. The growing insistence that individuals must invest only in and for themselves, shadowed by the demand that individuals must also compete more intensely for survival and depend only on themselves in the face of the blows of fortune, is held out as human progress. As Tom Wolfe described the inevitable moral lesson, the objective is to insulate oneself from these threats, a strategy that starves the self by making the trust and support individuals need ever harder to come by. What is missing is the strength that comes from membership in a polity able and willing to shape emerging technologies to promote norms of fairness, equity, and mutual concern. Absent hope for genuine civic membership, a Culture of Acquiescence does perhaps become inevitable.

This fragmentation of an effective public into warring congeries of self-interested individuals is a recurring threat that has haunted many modern and modernizing societies. This threat—that the nihilism of self-assertion will undercut the moral bonds on which individual agency depends—fuels authoritarianism and fundamentalisms of all stripes. But it is not an inevitable destiny, particularly in a nation as rich in civic experience as the United States. What is necessary, however, is "experiential learning" on the part of citizens of what it is like to be part of a community governed by norms of fairness, mutual respect, and responsibility—a community where individuals' gifts and contributions are seen and valued. The deepest source of strength in the educational programs examined in this book has derived from that kind of participation. In the case of the vocation programs, it was their adaptation of the Christian call to serve and nurture that provided the staying power, and the considerable resources both intellectual and practical, that sustained their enterprise through its difficulties as well as successes. They demonstrated how religiously based education can take part, not dogmatically but still with a life-enhancing integrity, as a participant in the cultural conversation of a secular age.

Higher education in a democratic polity needs to be an institutional pillar supporting these public ends. Providing an integrated apprenticeship to adult living, including intellectual cultivation, personal and social maturation, and the opportunity to explore a life of contributory purpose and significance is the educational challenge of our time. In particular, this is the inherited mission of liberal education. As this book has tried to illustrate, some American colleges and universities are today seedbeds for a number of promising efforts to realign their structures and practices to achieve these aims for a new student generation. They have broken out of the paralyzing Culture of Acquiescence.

The needed development of engagement with purposes beyond the self can take place within a number of cultural frames. We have seen examples of such frames as civic engagement, student well-being, career readiness as responsible service, and service to humanity across borders. Among these, the vocation programs stand out for their proven capacity to engage students in developing self-awareness within a framework of commitment to the welfare of others that also promises integrity and growth in understanding and engagement with the world. The idea of vocational discernment, of reflection cultivated for the sake of responsiveness to the good of the world, is likely to prove of enduring value in reviving the full potential of liberal learning to meet what is sure to be a difficult but very important enterprise.

Notes

INTRODUCTION

1. Craig Dykstra, *Growth in the Life of Faith*, 2nd. Edition (Louisville, KY: Westminster John Knox Press, 2005) [1st edition, 1999], pp. 121ff.
2. Tim Clydesdale, *The Purposeful Graduate: Why Colleges Must Talk to Students about Vocation* (Chicago: University of Chicago Press, 2015), pp. 89–90.
3. Clydesdale, *The Purposeful Graduate*, p. 108.
4. Clydesdale, *The Purposeful Graduate*, pp. 124–125.
5. William Damon, *Path to Purpose: How Young People Find Their Calling in Life* (New York: The Free Press, 2008), p. 33.
6. For example, Harvard University, Stanford University, and others have introduced voluntary discussion programs for their first-year undergraduates called "Reflecting on Your Life," developed by Richard Light, Howard Gardner, and other Harvard faculty members. See Richard J. Light, "How to Live Wisely: Five exercises that tackle the big questions. Try these at home," *The New York Times*, *Sunday Review*, August 2, 2015, p. 3.
7. Clydesdale, *The Purposeful Graduate*, pp. 216–217. Clydesdale also notes that this resonance of the vocational language may be aided by the preponderance of about two out of every three of American undergraduates who identify as in some sense Christian.
8. The Preparation for the Professions Program at the Carnegie Foundation for the Advancement of Teaching produced a series of studies of education for law, engineering, the clergy, nursing, and medicine, as well as a study of liberal education for business undergraduates, which dealt with themes close to those of the present volume. See, for example: Charles R. Foster, Lisa E. Dahill, Lawrence A. Goleman, and Barbara Wang Tolentino, *Educating Clergy: Teaching Practices and Pastoral Imagination* (San Francisco, CA: Jossey-Bass/Wiley, 2006); William M. Sullivan, Anne Colby, Judith Welch Wegner, Lloyd Bond, and Lee S. Shulman, *Educating Lawyers: Preparation for the Profession of Law* (San Francisco, CA: Jossey-Bass/Wiley, 2007); Anne Colby, Thomas Ehrlich, William M. Sullivan, and

Jonathan R. Dolle, *Rethinking Undergraduate Business Education: Liberal Learning for the Profession* (San Francisco, CA: Jossey-Bass/Wiley, 2011).

9. Anne Colby, Thomas Ehrlich, and William M. Sullivan with Jonathan R. Dolle, *Rethinking Undergraduate Business Education: Liberal Learning for the Profession* (San Francisco, CA: Jossey-Bass/Wiley, 2011).

10. Bobby Fong, "The Place of Religion and Spirituality in Twenty-First Century Education," speech at NETVUE conference on "Vocation in Undergraduate Education," Indianapolis, IN, March 11, 2011.

CHAPTER 1

1. Diane Dreher, *Your Personal Renaissance: 12 Steps to Finding Your Life's True Calling* (Philadelphia: DeCapo Press, 2008), p. 3.

2. Syllabus: English 189: "Vocation: Your Personal Renaissance," p. 1

3. Dreher, *Renaissance*, p 5.

4. William Damon, *The Path to Purpose* (New York: Free Press, 2008), p. 33.

5. Martin E. P. Seligman, *Flourish: A Visionary New Understanding of Happiness and Well-Being* (New York: Free Press, 2011). Also see Corey L. M. Keyes, Jonathan Haidt, and Martin E. P. Seligman, *Flourishing: Positive Psychology and the Life Well-Lived* (New York: Free Press, 2002).

6. Damon, *Path to Purpose*, p. 31.

7. Diane Ravitch, "Schools We Can Envy," *New York Review of Books*, March 8, 2012; and "How, and How Not, to Improve the Schools," *New York Review of Books*, March 22, 2012.

8. For a sample of these trends and the underlying data, see Lawrence Mishel, Jared Bernstein, and Heidi Shierholz, *The State of Working America 2008/2009* (Ithaca, NY: Cornell University Press, 2008).

9. John Immerwahr and Jean Johnson, "Squeeze Play 2010: Continued Public Anxiety on Cost, Harsher Judgments on How Colleges Are Run," *Public Agenda* (Washington, DC: February 2010).

10. Joseph Picketty, *Capital in the Twenty-First Century* (Cambridge, MA: The Belknap Press of Harvard University Press, 2014).

11. Robert D. Putnam, *Bowling Alone: The Collapse and Revival of American Community* (New York: Simon and Schuster Publishers, 2001).

12. For an attempt to make sense of these developments, see Sherry Turkle, *Alone Together: Why We Expect More From Technology and Less From Each Other* (New York: Basic Books, 2011).

13. See Jean Johnson and Christopher DiStasi, *Divided We Fail: Why It's Time for a Broader, More Inclusive Conversation on the Future of Higher Education* (Dayton, OH: The Kettering Foundation, 2014).

14. See Richard Wilkinson and Kate Pickett, *The Spirit Level: Why Greater Equality Makes Societies Stronger* (New York: Bloomsbury Press, 2010).

15. Wilkinson, *Spirit Level*, pp. 36–45. See also Richard Kadison and Theresa Foy DiGeronimo, *College of the Overwhelmed: The Campus Mental Health Crisis and What to Do About It* (San Francisco, CA: Jossey-Bass, 2004).

16. Mitchell Stevens, *Creating a Class: College Admission and the Education of Elites* (Cambridge, MA: Harvard University Press, 2007), pp. 13–17.

17. This phenomenon was famously described by David Brooks in "The Organization Kid," *Atlantic Magazine*, April 2001.

18. See Barbara Schneider and David Stevenson, *The Ambitious Generation: America's Teenagers, Motivated but Directionless* (New Haven, CT: Yale University Press, 1999).

19. The contrast was noted in the early 1990s by philosopher Albert Borgmann in *Crossing the Postmodern Divide* (Chicago: University of Chicago Press, 1992), pp. 6–19.

20. There is a considerable body of research literature documenting these trends. For sources, see, among others, Mary Grigsby, *College Life through the Eyes of Students* (Albany: State University of New York Press, 2009); and Richard Arum and Josipa Roksa, *Academically Adrift: Limited Learning on College Campuses* (Chicago: University of Chicago Press, 2011).

21. This was documented in the late 1980s by Michael Moffatt in *Coming of Age in New Jersey: College and American Culture* (New Brunswick, NJ: Rutgers University Press, 1989).

22. For the longer-term view, also documenting some recent turnabout, see John Pryor, Silvia Hurtado, Jaime Saenz, Jaime Santos, and William Korn, *The American Freshman: Forty Year Trends: 1966–2006* (Los Angeles: Higher Education Research Institute, Graduate School of Education and Information Studies, University of California, 2007).

23. See John Pryor, Linda DeAngelo, Laura Blake, Silvia Hurtado, and Serge Tran, *The American Freshman: National Norms Fall 2011* (Los Angeles: Higher Education Research Institute, Graduate School of Education and Information Studies, University of California, 2012).

24. See Larry Braskamp, Lois Calian Trautvetter, and Kelly Ward, *Putting Students First: How Colleges Develop Students Purposefully* (Boston: Anker Publishers, 2006).

25. See Alexander W. Astin, Helen S. Astin, Jennifer A. Lindolm, Alyssa N. Bryant, Shannon Caleron, and Katalin Szelenyi, *The Spiritual Life of College Students: A National Survey of College Students' Search for Meaning and Purpose* (Los Angeles: Higher Education Research Institute, 2005).

26. Christian Smith with Patricia Snell, *Souls in Transition: The Religious and Spiritual Lives of Emerging Adults* (New York: Oxford University Press, 2009), pp. 295–298.

27. In particular, see Derek Bok, *Our Underachieving Colleges: A Candid Look at How Much Students are Learning and Why They Should Be Learning More* (New

Edition) (Princeton, NJ: Princeton University Press, 2008 [1st edition 2006]); Anthony Kronman, *Education's End: Why Our Colleges and Universities Have Given Up on the Meaning of Life* (New Haven, CT: Yale University Press, 2007); and Andrew Delbanco, *College What It Was, Is, and Should Be* (Princeton, NJ: Princeton University Press, 2012).

28. For example, George Kuh, "What We Are Learning About Student Engagement from the National Survey of Student Engagement (NSE)," *Change* (2003), no. 35, pp. 24–32.

29. Arum and Roksa, *Academically Adrift*, p. 69.

30. For the most comprehensive study of these issues to date, see Charles Blaich and Kathleen Wise, "Overview of Findings from the First Year of the Wabash National Study of Liberal Arts Education, http://www.liberalarts.wabash.edu/storage/Overview_of_Findings_from_the_First_Year_web_07.17.09.pdf

31. These were among the most disturbing findings of the study. See Arum and Roksa, *Academically Adrift*, pp. 34–56.

32. The Association of American Colleges and Universities (AAC&U) has emphasized the importance of cultivating the ability to frame and solve "unstructured problems" as one of the signature strengths of liberal learning. See *Greater Expectations: The Commitment to Quality as a Nation Goes to College,* (Washington, DC: Association of American Colleges and Universities, 2002).

33. This is a major conclusion of the study by Daniel F. Chambliss and Christopher G. Takacs, *How College Works* (Cambridge, MA: Harvard University Press, 2014), esp. pp. 3–6.

34. George Kuh, *Student Success in College* (San Francisco, CA: Jossey-Bass, 2007).

35. Tim Clydesdale, *The Purposeful Graduate: Why Colleges Must Talk to Students About Vocation* (Chicago: University of Chicago Press, 2015).

36. Bruce A. Kimball, *The "True Professional Ideal" in America: A History* (Oxford: Basil Blackwell Publishers, 1992), pp. 301–303.

37. This conflict over ideals of freedom has a long history and continuing relevance for today's controversies about the aims and means of higher education. For example, see Robert N. Bellah, Richard Madsen, Ann Swidler, William M. Sullivan, and Steven M. Tipton, *Habits of the Heart: Individualism and Commitment in American Life* (Berkeley and Los Angeles: University of California Press, 2008 [first published 1985]).

38. Alan Ryan, *Liberal Anxieties and Liberal Education* (New York: Hill and Wang, 1998), pp. 54–55 and 71. Quotation from p. 78.

39. The literature on the topic is large. For a historical overview, see John Schmalzbauer and Kathleen Mahoney, "American Scholars Return to Studying Religion," *Contexts*, Winter 2008, pp. 16–21. The contemporary debate was given impetus by George Marsden, *The Soul of the American University: From Protestant Establishment to Established Non-Belief* (New York: Oxford University Press, 1994). For a sense of the current situation in higher education, see

Douglas Jacobsen and Rhonda Hustedt Jacobsen, *No Longer Invisible: Religion in Higher Education* (New York: Oxford University Press, 2012). The larger American context has been exhaustively analyzed by Robert D. Putnam and David E. Campbell in *American Grace: How Religion Divides and Unites Us* (New York: Simon and Schuster, 2010). The current state of the debate about religion, secularism, and secularity in contemporary global perspective is presented in Craig Calhoun, Mark Juergensmeyer, and Jonathan Van Antwerpen (eds.), *Rethinking Secularism* (New York: Oxford University Press, 2011).

40. Clydesdale, *The Purposeful Graduate*, pp. 121–129.
41. See William V. Frame, *The American College Presidency as Vocation: Easing the Burden, Enhancing the Joy* (Abilene, TX: Abilene Christian University Press, 2012).
42. Clydesdale, *The Purposeful Graduate*, p.128.

CHAPTER 2

1. For historical background, see Bruce Kimball, *Orators and Philosophers: A History of the Idea of Liberal Education* (New York: College Board, 1995).
2. See Richard P. Keeling and Richard H. Hersh, *We're Losing Our Minds: Rethinking American Higher Education* (New York: Palgrave Macmillan, 2011).
3. See Christopher Jenks and David Riesman, *The Academic Revolution* (New York: Doubleday, 1968).
4. Tim Clydesdale, *The First Year Out: Understanding American Teens After High School* (Chicago: University of Chicago Press, 2007), p. ix.
5. For another example, see *College Learning for the New Global Century: A Report from the National Leadership Council for Liberal Education and America's Promise* (Washington, DC: The Association of American Colleges and Universities, 2007).
6. See Thomas Bender and Carl Schorske (eds.), *American Academic Culture in Transformation: Fifty Years, Four Disciplines* (Princeton, NJ: Princeton University Press, 1997).
7. See Steven Brint (ed.), *The Future of the City of Intellect: The Changing American University* (Stanford, CA: Stanford University Press, 2002).
8. This aspect of professional education is developed in some detail in William M. Sullivan, *Work and Integrity: The Crisis and Promise of Professionalism in America*, 2nd Edition (San Francisco, CA: Jossey-Bass/Wiley, 2005), pp. 205–226.
9. For an analysis of experiments in this direction, involving educators from both the arts and sciences and professional fields, see William M. Sullivan and Matthew S. Rosin, *A New Agenda for Higher Education: Shaping a Life of the Mind for Practice* (San Francisco, CA: Jossey-Bass/Wiley, 2008). Barry Schwartz and Kenneth Sharpe provide an insightful perspective based in philosophy, neuroscience, and studies of professional practice in: *Practical Wisdom: The Right Way to do the Right Thing* (New York: Riverhead Books [Penguin Group], 2011).

10. See Richard Arum and Josipa Roksa, *Academically Adrift: Limited Learning on College Campuses* (Chicago: University of Chicago Press, 2011).

11. See Diane Ravitch, "Schools We Can Envy," *New York Review of Books*, March 8, 2012.

12. Frances King Stage and Jillian Kinzie, "Reform in Undergraduate Science, Technology, Engineering, and Mathematics: The Classroom Context," *Journal of General Education* 58(2), 2009, pp. 85–105.

13. Stage and Kinzie, 2009.

14. W. B. Carnochan, *The Battleground of the Curriculum* (Stanford, CA: Stanford University Press, 1993), p. 14.

15. Alan Ryan, *Liberal Anxieties and Liberal Education* (New York: Hill and Wang, 1998), pp. 112 and 99.

16. John Dewey, *A Common Faith* (New Haven, CT: Yale University Press, 1908 [1934]), p. 85.

17. For further elaboration of these ideas, see Katharine Brooks, *You Majored in What?: Mapping Your Path from Chaos to Career* (New York: Plume, 2010).

18. http://www.augsburg.edu/about/facts/ downloaded December 19, 2012.

19. http://www.augsburg.edu/academics/core-curriculum/ downloaded December 19, 2012.

20. Jack Fortin, *The Centered Life: Awakened, Called, Set Free, Nurtured* (Minneapolis: Augsburg Fortress Press, 2006), p. 21.

21. William Damon, *Path to Purpose* (New York: Free Press, 2008), p. 33.

22. Damon, *Path to Purpose*, pp. 31 and 29.

CHAPTER 3

1. George Lakoff and Mark Johnson, *Metaphors We Live By* (Chicago: University of Chicago Press, 1980), pp. 10ff. See also Lakoff and Johnson, *The Body in the Mind: The Bodily Basis of Meaning, Imagination, and Reason* (Chicago: University of Chicago Press, 1987).

2. The current findings from psychological studies on reflection's role in learning are summarized by Susan A. Ambrose et al., *How Learning Works: Seven Research-Based Principles for Smart Teaching* (San Francisco, CA: Jossey-Bass/Wiley, 2010), pp. 192–200.

3. Philosopher Paul Ricoeur has famously characterized this family of theories, with origins in the thought of Nietzsche, Marx, and Freud (and later developed in post-structuralism) as constituting a "hermeneutics of suspicion." While affirming the value of such deconstructive techniques for the critique of ideology, Ricoeur argued that meaningful direction in modern environments also requires that suspicion be supplemented by a "hermeneutics of the recovery of meaning." For a summary presentation, see Paul Ricoeur, *The Symbolism of Evil* (Boston: Beacon Press, 1985). Anthony T. Kronman has mounted a

similar argument about what he sees as the self-destructive effects of recent postmodernist efforts to revivify the humanities. See: *Education's End: Why Our Colleges and Universities Have Given Up on the Meaning of Life* (New Haven, CT: Yale University Press, 2007), esp. pp. 184–195.

4. For example, Martha C. Nussbaum, *Cultivating Humanity: A Classical Defense of Reform in Liberal Education* (Cambridge, MA: Harvard University Press, 1998). See also the analysis of practical wisdom as the aim of education in: Barry Schwartz and Kenneth Sharpe, *Practical Wisdom: The Right Way to Do the Right Thing* (New York: Riverhead Books [Penguin Group], 2010), pp. 27–45.

5. Elaine Scarry, *On Beauty and Being Just* (Princeton, NJ: Princeton University Press, 1999), p. 109.

6. Tim Clydesdale, *The Purposeful Graduate: Why Colleges Must Talk to Students About Vocation* (Chicago: University of Chicago Press, 2015), pp. 49–57.

7. Bobby Fong, "The Place of Religion and Spirituality in the Twenty-first Century University," NetVUE Conference, "Vocation in Undergraduate Education," Indianapolis, IN, March 11, 2011.

8. These are the three classic skills of hermeneutical thinking as set out by Hans-Georg Gadamer. See *Truth and Method* 2nd, Revised Edition, Joel Weinsheimer and Donald G. Marshall transl. (New York: Continuum Press, 1993), pp. 307 ff.

9. Quotations in Julie A. Reuben, *The Making of the Modern University: Intellectual Transformation and the Marginalization of Morality* (Chicago: University of Chicago Press, 1996), pp. 228–229.

10. James Turner, *The Liberal Education of Charles Eliot Norton,* (Baltimore: Johns Hopkins University Press, 1999), p. 377.

11. Jonathan Kahn with Paul MacDonald, Ian Oliver, and Sam Speers, "Reconceiving the Secular and the Practices of the Liberal Arts," SSRC (Social Science Research Council) Blog, *The Immanent Frame*, November 24, 2010, pp. 1 and 2.

12. Kahn, "Reconceiving the Secular and the Practices of the Liberal Arts," p. 3. See also Charles Taylor, *A Secular Age* (Cambridge, MA: The Belknap Press of Harvard University Press, 2007), pp. 20–22.

13. Jonathan Kahn et al., "Reconceiving the Secular," p. 5.

14. "A Decade of Reflection on Vocation," *Lilly Project for Vocation and Ethical Leadership* (Macalester College: macalester.edu/lilly), p. 9.

15. "A Decade of Reflection on Vocation," p. 19.

16. For an application of the concept to student development, see Robert J. Nash and Michele C. Murray, *Helping College Students Find Purpose: The Campus Guide to Meaning-Making* (San Francisco, CA: Jossey-Bass/Wiley, 2010), pp. 248–255.

17. Richard P. Keeling and Richard H. Hersh, *We're Losing Our Minds: Rethinking American Higher Education* (New York: Palgrave Macmillan, 2011), p. 7.

18. Keeling and Hersh, *We're Losing Our Minds*, p. 21.

19. Keeling and Hersh, *We're Losing Our Minds*, p. 133.

20. Arthur Levine and Diane R. Dean, *Generation on a Tightrope: A Portrait of Today's College Students* (New York: John Wiley and Sons, 2012), pp. 89–91.
21. Levine and Dean, *Generation on a Tightrope*, p. 68.
22. For a short overview of Erikson's mature thoughts on the life cycle, see Erik H. Erikson, "Reflections on Dr. Borg's Life Cycle," in Erik H. Erikson (ed.), *Adulthood* (New York: W.W. Norton & Co., 1978), pp. 1–32.

CHAPTER 4

1. Douglas Jacobsen and Rhonda Hustedt Jacobsen, "The Ideals and Diversity of Church-Related Higher Education," in Jacobsen and Jacobsen (eds.), *The American University in a Postsecular Age* (Oxford: Oxford University Press, 2008), pp. 64 and 77.
2. Mark U. Edwards Jr., *Religion on Our Campuses: A Professor's Guide to Communities, Conflicts, and Promising Conversations* (New York: Palgrave Macmillan, 2006), pp. 135–164.
3. The percentages are nearly 100 percent for critical thinking, and between 50 percent and 70 percent, depending on the wording of the survey, for formative concerns with meaning and ethics. There may be modest grounds for hope in redressing this imbalance, however. See the careful discussion by Mark William Roche in *Why Choose the Liberal Arts* (Notre Dame, IN: Notre Dame University Press, 2010), pp. 101–103.
4. Christian Smith, with Patricia Snell, *Souls in Transition: The Religious and Spiritual Lives of Emerging Adults* (Oxford: Oxford University Press, 2009), pp. 294–297.
5. Smith, *Souls in Transition*, pp. 45–54.
6. William C. Spohn, *Go and Do Likewise: Jesus and Ethics* (New York: Continuum Books, 2007), pp. 56, 51, and 61.
7. Spohn, *Go and Do Likewise*, p. 51.
8. Boston College, Office of Marketing and Communications, *The Journey into Adulthood; Understanding Student Formation* (2007), pp. 1 and 10. Retrieved from: http://bc.edu/content/dam/files/offices/mission/pdf1/umm1.pdf
9. Richard P. Keeling and Richard H. Hersh, *We're Losing Our Minds: Rethinking American Higher Education* (New York: Palgrave Macmillan, 2011), p. 21.

CHAPTER 5

1. Kenneth Himes (ed.), *Catholic Social Teaching: Communities and Interpretations* (Washington, DC: Georgetown University Press, 2005).
2. Anne Butler, *Across God's Frontier: American Sisters in the American West* (Chapel Hill: University of North Carolina Press, 2013).
3. Edward L. Glaeser, *The Triumph of the City: How Our Greatest Invention Makes Us Richer, Smarter, Greener, Healthier, and Happier* (New York: Penguin Books, 2011), p. 1.

4. Tim Clydesdale, *The Purposeful Graduate: Why Colleges Must Talk to Students about Vocation* (Chicago: University of Chicago Press, 2015), pp. 85–130.
5. Eliot Freidson, *Professionalism: The Third Logic* (Chicago: University of Chicago Press, 2001).
6. James S. Coleman, *Foundations of Social Theory* (Cambridge, MA: Harvard University Press, 1990), pp. 300–321.
7. Robert D. Putnam, *Bowling Alone: The Collapse and Revival of American Community* (New York: Simon and Schuster, 2000), pp. 19 and 21.
8. John Hendry, *Between Enterprise and Ethics: Business and Management in a Bimoral Society* (Oxford: Oxford University Press, 2004), pp. 109–111.
9. Anthony S. Bryk and Barbara Schneider, *Trust in Schools: A Core Resource for Improvement* (New York: Russell Sage, 2002), p.19.
10. Bryk and Schneider, *Trust*, pp. 20–22.
11. William V. Frame, *The American College Presidency as Vocation: Easing the Burden, Enhancing the Joy* (Abilene, TX: Abilene Christian University Press, 2013).
12. Arthur Levine and Diane R. Dean, *Generation on a Tightrope: A Portrait of Today's College Students* (New York: Wiley and Sons, 2012), pp. 68 and 89.
13. Putnam, *Bowling Alone* (note 7 above).
14. Richard Wilkinson and Kate Pickett, *The Spirit Level: Why Greater Equality Makes Societies Stronger* (New York: Bloomsbury Press, 2010). See also the 2013 Institute of Medicine—National Academy of Medicine study, "U.S. Health in International Perspective: Shorter Lives, Poorer Health," January 9, 2013.
15. Retrieved from http://marquette.edu/oira/documents/f_fre_prof_web.pdf
16. Lee S. Shulman, "Searching for Signature Pedagogies; Teaching and Learning in the Professions," *Daedalus* 2005, 134(3): pp. 52–59.
17. This is a connection Susan Mountin and Rebecca Nowacek have further explored in "Reflection in Action: A Signature Ignatian Pedagogy for the 21st Century" in Nancy L. Chick, Aeron Maynie, and Regan A.R. Gurung (eds.) *Exploring More Signature Pedagogies: Approaches to Teaching Disciplinary Habits of Mind* (Sterling, VA: Stylus Publishers, 2012).
18. Douglas Jacobsen and Rodney J. Sawatsky, *Gracious Christianity: Living the Love We Profess* (Grand Rapids, MI: Baker Academic Publishing, 2006), p. 46.
19. Jacobsen and Sawatsky, *Gracious Christianity*, p. 45.
20. Retrieved from http://www.messiah.edu/info/20053/opportunities

CHAPTER 6

1. Harvard Project for "Leadership, Service, and Collaborative Learning" (Winter break, January 2–21, 2013), p. 5.
2. Harvard Project for "Leadership, Service, and Collaborative Learning," p. 6.
3. Harvard Project for "Leadership, Service, and Collaborative Learning," p. 6.
4. Harvard Project for "Leadership, Service, and Collaborative Learning," p. 11.
5. Harvard Project for "Leadership, Service, and Collaborative Learning," p. 7.

6. Harvard Project for "Leadership, Service, and Collaborative Learning," p. 7.

7. Hans-Georg Gadamer, "Rhetoric and Hermeneutics," in Walter Jost and Michael J. Hyde (eds.), *Rhetoric and Hermeneutics in Our Time* (New Haven, CT: Yale University Press, 1997), pp. 57–58.

8. Wm. Theodore de Bary, *The Great Civilized Conversation: Education for a World Community* (New York: Columbia University Press, 2013).

9. de Bary, *The Great Civilized Conversation*, p. 27.

10. de Bary, *The Great Civilized Conversation*, p. 46.

11. de Bary, *The Great Civilized Conversation*, p. 30.

12. de Bary, *The Great Civilized Conversation*, p. 39

13. The Historian Mark Mazower has provided an overview of these complex developments during the period since World War II in: *Governing the World: The History of an Idea* (New York: Penguin Press, 2012).

14. The philosopher Peter Sloterdijk has given this perspective a provocative formulation, taken from the poet Rilke, in the title of his book, *You Must Change Your Life* (Cambridge and Malden, MA: Polity Press, 2013).

15. Paul Tillich sharply articulated the core issue a half-century ago: "The world as a whole is potential, not actual. Those sections are actual with which one partially identifies. The section of reality in which one participates immediately is the community to which one belongs. Through it and only through it participation in the world as a whole and in all its parts is mediated." Paul Tillich, *The Courage to Be* (New Haven, CT: Yale University Press, 1952), pp. 90–91.

16. John Dewey, "Ethical Principles Underlying Education," (1897), in JoAnn Boyelston (ed.), *The Early Works of John Dewey* (Carbondale: Southern Illinois University Press, 1969), vol.5, pp. 54–83, 63.

17. Anne Goodsell Love, "Wagner College: Establishing Positive Links between Civic Engagement and Student Well-Being," *Bringing Theory to Practice Newsletter*, Spring 2013 (Washington, DC: Association of American Colleges and Universities).

18. Both the history of the project and an exposition of its core principles have been provided by Donald Harward in an introductory essay to his edited volume, *Transforming Undergraduate Education: Theory That Compels and Practices That Succeed* (Lanham, MD: Rowan and Littlefield Publishers, 2012), pp. 1–28.

19. See: Vincent Tinto, *Leaving College: Rethinking the Causes and Cures of Student Attrition* (Chicago: University of Chicago Press, 1987).

20. Harward (ed.), *Transforming Undergraduate Education*, p. 24.

21. Joan B. Riley and Mindy McWilliams, "Curriculum Infusion: Educating the Whole Student and Creating Campus Change," in Harward (ed.), *Transforming Undergraduate Education*, pp. 319–324.

22. For example, see Anne Colby, Thomas Ehrlich, Elizabeth Beaumont, Jason Stephens, *Educating Citizens: Preparing America's Undergraduates for Lives of Moral and Civic Responsibility* (San Francisco, CA: Jossey-Bass/Wiley, 2003).

23. Lynn D. Swaner, "The Theories, Contexts, and Multiple Pedagogies of Engaged Learning: What Succeeds and Why?," in Harward (ed.), *Transforming Undergraduate Education*, pp. 73–90.

24. The current state of knowledge is analyzed in Ashley Finley, *Making Progress? What We Know About the Achievement of Liberal Education Outcomes* (Washington, DC: Association of American Colleges and Universities, 2012).

25. "Big Questions, Urgent Challenges; Liberal Education and America's Global Future: Strategic Plan, 2013–17. (Washington, DC: Association of American Colleges and Universities, 2012).

26. This and subsequent quotations are taken from a campus interview of Dr. Chan by the author.

CHAPTER 7

1. Max Weber, "Science as a Vocation," in Hans Gerth and C. Wright Mills (eds.), *From Max Weber: Essays in Sociology* (New York: Oxford University Press, 1946), p. 155.

2. Mark R. Schwehn and Dorothy C. Bass (eds.), *Leading Lives that Matter: What We Should Do and Who We Should Be* (Grand Rapids, MI: Wm. B. Eerdmans Publishing Co., 2006).

3. The pervasive experience of this pluralism in recent decades, and its effects on all groups in the United States, is one of the central findings of the largest study of contemporary attitudes toward religion: Robert D. Putnam and David E. Campbell, *American Grace: How Religion Divides and Unites Us* (New York: Simon and Schuster, 2010).

4. This issue remains a contentious one. For example, in his otherwise careful and valuable history of the discussion of these themes in U.S. higher education, Anthony T. Kronman claims, citing Max Weber, that because religious traditions involve other modes of engagement besides analytical reason, they cannot be admitted as equal partners within an inquiry governed by his ideal of "secular humanism." See Kronman, *Education's End: Why Our Colleges and Universities Have Given Up on the Meaning of Life* (New Haven, CT: Yale University Press, 2007), pp. 198–203.

5. Jonathan Kahn with Paul MacDonald, Ian Oliver, and Sam Speers, "Reconceiving the Secular and the Practices of the Liberal Arts," SSRC (Social Science Research Council) Blog, *The Immanent Frame*, November 24, 2010, pp. 1 and 2.

6. Charles Taylor, *A Secular Age* (Cambridge, MA: The Belknap Press of Harvard University Press, 2007), p. 21.

7. "Reconceiving the Secular," p. 3. See also Taylor, *Secular Age*, pp. 20–22.

8. Taylor, *Secular Age*, p. 22.

9. Taylor, *The Ethics of Authenticity* (Cambridge, MA: Harvard University Press, 1991, pp. 37–39.

10. Robert N. Bellah, *Religion in Human Evolution: From the Paleolithic to the Axial Age* (Cambridge, MA: The Belknap Press of Harvard University Press, 2011), esp. pp. 97–99, and 114–116.

11. Bellah, *Religion in Human Evolution*, pp. 118–138.

12. Clifford Geertz, "Religion as a Cultural System," in *The Interpretation of Cultures* (New York: Basic Books, 1973 [1966]), p. 90.

13. René Descartes, *Discourse on Method* in Elizabeth S. Haldane and G.R.T. Ross, (eds.), *The Philosophical Works of René Descartes*, vol. I (Cambridge: Cambridge University Press, 1969), p. 119.

14. Ralph Heintzman, *Rediscovering Reverence: The Meaning of Faith in a Secular World* (Montreal Que: McGill—Queen's University Press, 2011.), p. 13.

15. Heintzman, *Rediscovering Reverence*, p. 44.

16. John Dewey, "Ethical Principles Underlying Education" (1897), in JoAnn Boylston, (ed.), *The Early Works of John Dewey* (Carbondale: University of Southern Illinois University Press, 1969, vol. 5, pp. 54–83, 63.

17. Taylor, *Secular Age*, pp. 146–158.

18. Taylor, *Secular Age*, pp. 358–359.

19. Taylor, *Secular Age*, p. 559.

20. Taylor, *Secular Age*, p. 559.

CHAPTER 8

1. William Deresiewicz, *Excellent Sheep: The Miseducation of the American Elite and the Way to a Meaningful Life* (Cambridge, MA: Harvard University Press, 2014). Richard Arum and Josipa Roksa, *Aspiring Adults Adrift: Tentative Transitions of College Graduates* (Chicago: University of Chicago Press, 2014).

Index

AAC&U. *See* Association of American Colleges and Universities
academic leadership
   increasing complexity of task faced by, 44
   increasing isolation of, 35
academic study. *See* apprenticeship, academic
administration and staff, importance of interpersonal discernment in, 124
administration and staff in PTEV. *See also* communities of PTEV faculty and staff
   and development of PTEV programs, 127–28
   engagement with PTEV goals, 39
   and gratification of recognized contributions, 128
   renewed educational purpose in, 2
   renewed sense of educational purpose, 191–92
   seminars for, 39
   student interaction with, 89
adulthood, responsible
   expanding students' horizons to include, 15, 16
   necessity of education toward, 203
   as PTEV goal, 5
   PTEV success in creating, 8

three tasks for development of, 88
adversity, learning to cope with. *See* resilience
aesthetic awareness, humanistic learning and, 146, 195
anxiety of students
   career uncertainty as source of, 28–29, 29–30, 126, 200
   PTEV success in lowering, 4, 7, 16
apprenticeship
   contemporary learning theory on, 42
   integrating three types of, *See* integrated education
   liberal education and, 42–43
   and reform efforts, 45–49
   separation of three types in typical programs, 43–44, 87, 112, 176
   three types of, 9–11, 44–46
apprenticeship, academic, 10, 44–45
   controversy over goals of, 49–51
   critical thinking as focus of, 46, 47
   debate on liberal-free *vs. artes liberales* ideals in, 49–52
   as disconnected from student's daily experience, 46
   and efforts to educate whole person, 47–49, 55
   exposure to liberal arts through required courses, 48, 51